First World War
and Army of Occupation
War Diary
France, Belgium and Germany

3 CAVALRY DIVISION
Divisional Troops
Royal Army Service Corps
Headquarters Divisional Army Service Corps (81 Company A.S.C.)
4 September 1914 - 30 June 1919

WO95/1150/1

The Naval & Military Press Ltd
www.nmarchive.com
Published in association with The National Archives

Published by

The Naval & Military Press Ltd

Unit 10 Ridgewood Industrial Park,

Uckfield, East Sussex,

TN22 5QE England

Tel: +44 (0) 1825 749494

www.naval-military-press.com

www.nmarchive.com

This diary has been reprinted in facsimile from the original. Any imperfections are inevitably reproduced and the quality may fall short of modern type and cartographic standards.

© Crown Copyright
Images reproduced by permission of The National Archives, London, England, 2015.

Contents

Document type	Place/Title	Date From	Date To
Heading	WO95/1150/1		
Miscellaneous	B.E.F. France & Flanders.		
Heading	1914-1919 3rd Cavalry Division H.Q 3rd Cavalry Divl A.S.C. Sep 1914 Jun 1919 (81 Coy ASC)		
Heading	Historical Account of Headquarter 3rd Cavalry Divl A.S.C. (81 H.Y. Coy ASC)		
Heading	War Diary Of O.C. 3rd Cavalry Supper Column From 3rd October 1914 To 31st December 1914 June 1919 (Volume I)		
Miscellaneous	Early Records Of 81 Coy. A.S.C.		
Miscellaneous	Early Records Of 81 Coy Reg No 865	04/08/1917	04/08/1917
Miscellaneous			
Miscellaneous	O.C., A.S.C. 3rd Cavalry Division.	30/09/1917	30/09/1917
Miscellaneous	1914		
Miscellaneous	1915		
Miscellaneous	1916		
Miscellaneous	1917		
Miscellaneous	OC Asc 3rd Cav Divn Reg Your 2379 D/26/9/17	05/10/1917	05/10/1917
Miscellaneous	O.C. A.S.C., 1st Cavalry Divn.	23/07/1917	23/07/1917
Miscellaneous	D.D.S.T First Army.	19/07/1917	19/07/1917
Miscellaneous	O.C. A.S.C. 3rd Cav Divn	26/07/1917	26/07/1917
Miscellaneous	A.D.S.T.O.C. No 1512 D of T. G.H.A.	19/07/1917	19/07/1917
Miscellaneous	O.C. A.S.C 3rd Cav Divn	26/07/1917	26/07/1917
Miscellaneous	A.D.S.T Cavalry Corps	19/07/1917	19/07/1917
Miscellaneous			
Miscellaneous	S.O. 6th Cav Bde. B.J.O. 3rd Cas Bde.	26/09/1917	26/09/1917
Miscellaneous	OC A.S.C 3rd Cav Divn	06/08/1915	06/08/1915
Miscellaneous	3rd Cavalry Division.	15/09/1916	15/09/1916
Miscellaneous	14th Corps Q.	22/08/1916	22/08/1916
Miscellaneous	O.C. A.S.C 3rd Cav Div	11/07/1917	11/07/1917
Miscellaneous		26/07/1917	26/07/1917
Heading	War Diary Of Headquarters 3rd Cavalry Divisional A.S.C. From 4th September 1914 To 31st December 1914 Volume 1		
War Diary	London	04/09/1914	30/09/1914
War Diary	Windmill Hill Camp	01/10/1914	06/10/1914
War Diary	Southampton	07/10/1914	07/10/1914
War Diary	Ostende	08/10/1914	08/10/1914
War Diary	Belgium	09/10/1914	09/10/1914
War Diary	Bruges	09/10/1914	11/10/1914
War Diary	Thourout	12/10/1914	12/10/1914
War Diary	Roulers	13/10/1914	13/10/1914
War Diary	Iseghem	14/10/1914	14/10/1914
War Diary	Wythochaete	15/10/1914	16/10/1914
War Diary	Zonnebeke	17/10/1914	20/10/1914
War Diary	St Joan	21/10/1914	21/10/1914
War Diary	Voormezeele	22/10/1914	22/10/1914
War Diary	Zillebeke	23/10/1914	30/10/1914
War Diary	Chateau Beau Sejour	31/10/1914	01/11/1914
War Diary	Chateau Beau Sejour Ypres.	01/11/1914	01/11/1914

War Diary	Frezenberg Ypres	03/11/1914	06/11/1914
War Diary	Ypres	06/11/1914	20/11/1914
War Diary	Hazebrouck	21/11/1914	14/12/1914
War Diary	St Jans Cappel	15/12/1914	16/12/1914
War Diary	Hazebrouck	17/12/1914	31/12/1914
Heading	War Diaries Of Divisional ASC 3rd Cavalry Division January 1915 To December 1915		
Heading	Hd Qrs ASC. 3rd Cavalry Division Vol II 1-31.1.15 June 1915		
War Diary	Hazebrouck	01/01/1915	31/01/1915
Heading	Hd Qrs. ASC 3rd Cavalry Division Vol III 1-28.2.15		
War Diary	Hazebrouck	01/02/1915	03/02/1915
War Diary	Poperinghe	03/02/1915	07/02/1915
War Diary	Hazebrouck Poperinghe	08/02/1915	11/02/1915
War Diary	Hazebrouck	12/02/1915	28/02/1915
Heading	Hd Qrs. ASC. 3rd Cavalry Division Vol IV 1-31.3.15 March 1915		
War Diary	Hazebrouck	01/03/1915	31/03/1915
Heading	Hd Qrs A.S.C. 3rd Cavalry Division Vol V 1-30.4.15 April 1915		
War Diary	Hazebrouck	01/04/1915	24/04/1915
War Diary	Hazebrouck & Steenvoorde	25/04/1915	30/04/1915
Heading	Hd Qrs A.S.C. 3rd Cavalry Division Vol VI 1-31.5.15 May 1915		
War Diary	Hazebrouck & Steenvoorde.	01/05/1915	07/05/1915
War Diary	Hazebrouck	08/05/1915	09/05/1915
War Diary	Hazebrouck Steenvoore	10/05/1915	23/05/1915
War Diary	Hazebrouck	24/05/1915	26/05/1915
War Diary	Renescure	27/05/1915	28/05/1915
War Diary	Steenvoorde	29/05/1915	31/05/1915
Heading	3rd Cavalry Division Hd Qrs A.S.C. 3rd Cavy Division Vol VII June 1915		
War Diary	Renescure Steenvoorde	01/06/1915	08/06/1915
War Diary	Renescure	09/06/1915	30/06/1915
Heading	3rd Cavalry Division Hd Qrs ASC. 3rd Cavy Divn Vol VIII July 1915		
War Diary	Renescure	01/07/1915	13/07/1915
War Diary	Lespinoy	14/07/1915	31/07/1915
Heading	3rd Cavalry Division OC. ASC. 3rd Cavy Division Vol IX From 1st To 31st August 1915		
War Diary	Lespinoy	01/08/1915	06/08/1915
War Diary	Fauquembergues	07/08/1915	31/08/1915
Heading	3rd Cavalry Division Hd Qrs. ASC. 3rd Cavy Division Vol X Sept 15		
War Diary	Fauquembergues	01/09/1915	21/09/1915
War Diary	Westrehem	22/09/1915	25/09/1915
War Diary	Moulin De Compte And Rincq	26/09/1915	26/09/1915
War Diary	Rincq Moulin Le Compte	27/09/1915	30/09/1915
Miscellaneous	Camp Orders By Major C.E. Hills.	22/09/1915	22/09/1915
Miscellaneous	Camp Orders By Major C.E. Hills	22/09/1915	22/09/1915
Miscellaneous	Camp Orders By Major C.E. Hills	23/09/1915	23/09/1915
Miscellaneous	Camp Orders by Major C.E. Hills	24/09/1915	24/09/1915
Miscellaneous	Camp Orders by Major C.E. Hills	26/09/1915	26/09/1915
Miscellaneous	Camp Orders by Major C.E. Hills	27/09/1915	27/09/1915
Miscellaneous	Camp Orders by Major C.E. Hills	28/09/1915	28/09/1915
Miscellaneous	Camp Orders by Major C.E. Hills	30/09/1915	30/09/1915

Type	Description	Start	End
Heading	3rd Cavalry Division O.C. ASC. 3rd Cavalry Division Vol XI Oct 15		
Miscellaneous		01/10/1915	01/10/1915
Heading	War Diary of The Officer Commanding, Army Service Corps, 3rd Cavalry Division for month of October 1915		
War Diary	Rincq Moulin Le Comte	01/10/1915	04/10/1915
War Diary	Moulin Le Comte	03/10/1915	19/10/1915
War Diary	Fruges	20/10/1915	31/10/1915
Miscellaneous	Camp Orders by Lieut' Colonel C.E. Hills.	01/10/1915	01/10/1915
Miscellaneous	Camp Orders by Lieut' Colonel C.E. Hills.	03/10/1915	03/10/1915
Miscellaneous	Camp Orders by Lieut' Colonel C.E. Hills.	05/10/1915	05/10/1915
Miscellaneous	Camp Orders by Lieut' Colonel C.E. Hills.	06/10/1915	06/10/1915
Miscellaneous	Camp Orders by Lieut' Colonel C.E. Hills.	09/10/1915	09/10/1915
Miscellaneous	Camp Orders by Lieut' Colonel C.E. Hills.	12/10/1915	12/10/1915
Heading	O.C. A.S.C. 3rd Cav Div Nov 1915 Vol XII		
War Diary	Fruges	01/11/1915	30/11/1915
Heading	H.Q. A.S.C. 3rd Cav Div Dec Vol XIII Dec 1915		
Heading	War Diary Of Head Quarters, 3rd Cavalry Divisional A.S.C. for December 1915		
War Diary	Fruges	01/12/1915	31/12/1915
Heading	H.Q 3rd Cav Div Asc Jan 1916 Vol XIV		
War Diary		01/01/1916	02/01/1916
War Diary	Fruges	03/01/1916	31/01/1916
Heading	Feb 1916		
War Diary	Fruges	01/02/1916	24/06/1916
War Diary	Fontrine S/maye	25/06/1916	25/06/1916
War Diary	Domart En Ponthieu	26/06/1916	26/06/1916
War Diary	Le Neville	27/06/1916	30/06/1916
War Diary	Le Neville Somme	01/07/1916	01/07/1916
War Diary	Le Neville	02/07/1916	04/07/1916
War Diary	Hallencourt Somme	05/07/1916	08/07/1916
War Diary	Daours Somme	09/07/1916	09/07/1916
War Diary	Daours	10/07/1916	31/07/1916
War Diary	Daours Somme	01/08/1916	01/08/1916
War Diary	Le Quesnoy Somme	02/08/1916	02/08/1916
War Diary	St Riquier Somme	03/08/1916	03/08/1916
War Diary	St Riquier	04/08/1916	04/08/1916
War Diary	Ligescourt	05/08/1916	05/08/1916
War Diary	Fruges	06/08/1916	31/08/1916
Miscellaneous	AA Q.N.G. 3rd Cav Div	01/10/1916	01/10/1916
War Diary	Fruges	01/09/1916	10/09/1916
War Diary	Dompierre	11/09/1916	11/09/1916
War Diary	Gueschart.	12/09/1916	12/09/1916
War Diary	Belloy	13/09/1915	14/09/1915
War Diary	Daours	15/09/1916	22/09/1916
War Diary	Le Quesnoy	23/09/1916	23/09/1916
War Diary	Frohen Le Grande	24/09/1915	24/09/1915
War Diary	Capelle	25/09/1916	25/09/1916
War Diary	Tortefontaine	26/09/1916	30/09/1916
Miscellaneous	Memorandum	01/10/1916	01/10/1916
War Diary	Tortefontaine	01/10/1916	14/10/1916
War Diary	1/2 Mile S. of Last E in Torte Fontaine (Sheet 14 1/100,000)	15/10/1916	19/10/1916
War Diary	Wailly	20/10/1916	17/12/1916
War Diary	Trepied	18/12/1916	05/04/1917
War Diary	Maresquel	06/04/1917	07/04/1917

War Diary	Monchel	08/04/1917	08/04/1917
War Diary	Boubers Sur Canche	09/04/1917	10/04/1917
War Diary	Etree Wamin	11/04/1917	12/04/1917
War Diary	Gouy En Artois	13/04/1917	16/04/1917
War Diary	Wavans	17/04/1917	19/04/1917
War Diary	Regnauville	20/04/1917	13/05/1917
War Diary	Wavans	14/05/1917	14/05/1917
War Diary	Talmas	15/05/1917	15/05/1917
War Diary	Querrieu	16/05/1917	17/05/1917
War Diary	La Motte En Santerre	18/05/1917	19/05/1917
War Diary	Flamicourt	20/05/1917	30/06/1917
War Diary	Flamicourt Peronne	01/07/1917	02/07/1917
War Diary	Flamicourt	03/07/1917	04/07/1917
War Diary	Treux	05/07/1917	05/07/1917
War Diary	Doullens	06/07/1917	06/07/1917
War Diary	Framecourt	07/07/1917	07/07/1917
War Diary	Pernes	08/07/1917	16/07/1917
War Diary	Busnes	17/07/1917	31/08/1917
Heading	War Diary for September 1917 H. Qrs 3rd Cavalry Divisional Ale Vol 34		
War Diary	Busnes	01/09/1917	30/09/1917
Heading	War Diary of Headquarters, 3rd Cavalry Divisional A.S.C. For October 1917 Vol 35		
War Diary	Busnes	01/10/1917	17/10/1917
War Diary	Pernes	18/10/1917	22/10/1917
War Diary	Houvin Houvigneul	23/10/1917	23/10/1917
War Diary	Domart En Ponthieu	24/10/1917	29/10/1917
War Diary	Domart	30/10/1917	31/10/1917
Heading	War Diary H. Qrs. 3rd Cavalry Divl A.S.C. November 1917 Vol 36		
War Diary	Domart En Ponthieu	01/11/1917	18/11/1917
War Diary	Suzanne	19/11/1917	23/11/1917
War Diary	Beauquesnes	24/11/1917	29/11/1917
War Diary	Corbie	30/11/1917	04/12/1917
War Diary	Corbie Somme	05/12/1917	10/12/1917
War Diary	Corbie	11/12/1917	21/12/1917
War Diary	Domart En Ponthieu	22/12/1917	30/01/1918
War Diary	Monchy Lagache	31/01/1918	31/01/1918
Heading	War Diary of H. Qrs. 3rd Cavalry Divl A.S.C. February 1918 Vol 39		
War Diary	Monchy Lagache	01/02/1918	15/03/1918
War Diary	Athies	14/03/1918	22/03/1918
War Diary	Varesnes	23/03/1918	23/03/1918
War Diary	Carlepont	24/03/1918	25/03/1918
War Diary	Ollenpont	26/03/1918	26/03/1918
War Diary	Compiegne Forest	27/03/1918	29/03/1918
War Diary	Les Carignons	30/03/1918	30/03/1918
War Diary	Wailly	31/03/1918	01/04/1918
War Diary	Pont De Metz	02/04/1918	06/04/1918
War Diary	Rivery	07/04/1918	11/04/1918
War Diary	Long	12/04/1918	12/04/1918
War Diary	Vaulx	13/04/1918	17/04/1918
War Diary	Pernes	18/04/1918	04/05/1918
War Diary	Wail	05/05/1918	05/05/1918
War Diary	Yvrench	06/05/1918	06/05/1918
War Diary	Contay	07/05/1918	17/05/1918

War Diary	Yzeux	18/05/1918	31/05/1918
Heading	War Diary Of HQ. 3rd Cav Divl A.S.C. June 1918		
War Diary	Yzeux	01/06/1918	30/06/1918
War Diary	Yzeux (Amiens-Abbeville) Road	01/07/1918	10/07/1918
War Diary	Yzeux	11/07/1918	06/08/1918
War Diary	Pont De Metz	07/08/1918	08/08/1918
War Diary	Near Domart Sur Luce	09/08/1918	10/08/1918
War Diary	Cayeux	11/08/1918	11/08/1918
War Diary	Boves Wood	12/08/1918	13/08/1918
War Diary	Sains En Amenois	14/08/1918	15/08/1918
War Diary	Yzeux	16/08/1918	25/08/1918
War Diary	Cherienne	26/08/1918	26/08/1918
War Diary	Wail	27/08/1918	06/09/1918
War Diary	Cherienne	07/09/1918	25/09/1918
War Diary	Marieux	26/09/1918	27/09/1918
War Diary	Near Clery	28/09/1918	28/09/1918
War Diary	Near Clery H.4.d.4.5 6.20	29/09/1918	29/09/1918
War Diary	Poeuilly	30/09/1918	30/09/1918
War Diary	Poeuilly	01/10/1918	08/10/1918
War Diary	Maissy Et Fosse	09/10/1918	09/10/1918
War Diary	U.26.b.8.0	10/10/1918	10/10/1918
War Diary	O.11.b.5.4	11/10/1918	12/10/1918
War Diary	Elincourt	15/10/1918	15/10/1918
War Diary	Hennois Wood	14/10/1918	08/11/1918
War Diary	Sainghin	09/11/1918	09/11/1918
War Diary	Antaing	10/11/1918	17/11/1918
War Diary	Bassilly	18/11/1918	18/11/1918
War Diary	Enghien	19/11/1918	21/11/1918
War Diary	Waterloo	22/11/1918	22/11/1918
War Diary	Perwez	23/11/1918	24/11/1918
War Diary	Baleres St Barie Wastines	25/11/1918	25/11/1918
War Diary	Maleves Ste Marie Wastines	26/11/1918	30/11/1918
War Diary	Maleves Ste Marie Wastines Odenge	01/12/1918	09/12/1918
War Diary	Odenge	10/12/1918	16/12/1918
War Diary	Tinlot	17/12/1918	31/12/1918
War Diary	Headquarters, 3rd Cavalry Division R.A.S.C. War Diary, January, 1919		
War Diary	Tinlot	01/01/1919	31/01/1919
Heading	War Diary for February 1919 HQ 3rd Cavalry Divl B.A.S.W Vol 51		
War Diary	Soheit Tinlot	01/02/1919	01/02/1919
War Diary	Liege Belgium	01/02/1919	12/02/1919
War Diary	Sheet Einlet	01/02/1919	28/02/1919
War Diary	Tinlot	01/03/1919	31/03/1919
Heading	April 1919 War Diary H. Qrs 3rd Cav Div B.A.S.E.		
War Diary	Tinlot	01/04/1919	01/04/1919
War Diary	Aux Houx	02/04/1919	10/04/1919
War Diary	Warfusee	10/04/1919	30/06/1919

No ads || so ||

B.E.F. FRANCE & FLANDERS.

3 CAVALRY DIV. TROOPS.

H.Q. 3 CAVALRY DIVISIONAL
ARMY SERVICE CORPS.
(81 COY A.S.C.)
1914 SEPT TO 1919 JUNE.

3 CAVALRY SUPPLY COLUMN.
(73 COY A.S.C.)
1914 OCT TO 1919 JUNE.

B.E.F. FRANCE & FLANDERS.

3 CAVALRY DIV. TROOPS.

H.Q. 3 CAVALRY DIVISIONAL
ARMY SERVICE CORPS.
(81 COY A.S.C.)
1914 SEPT TO 1919 JUNE.

3 CAVALRY SUPPLY COLUMN.
(73 COY A.S.C.)
1914 OCT TO 1919 JUNE.

1150

1914-1919
3RD CAVALRY DIVISION

HQ

3RD CAVALRY DIVL. A.S.C.

SEP 1914 - JUN 1919

(81 Coy ASC)

W 74—664 250,000 3/15 L.S. & Co.

5/France/1

Army Form W. 3091.

Cover for Documents.

Nature of Enclosures.

*Historical Account
of
Headquarters, 3rd Cavalry Div. A.S.C.
(81 H.T. Coy. A.S.C.)*

Notes, or Letters written.

1150

121/4193

Confidential

War Diary
of
O.C. 3rd Cavalry Supply Column.

From 3rd October 1914 to 3rd December 1914.

(Volume I)

June 1919

COPY.

EARLY RECORDS OF 81 COY. A.S.C.

81 Coy. A.S.C. was ordered to be formed at Kensington Barracks on 6th September 1914. Major Swabey the O.C., however, arranged for a Camp to be pitched in Kensington Gardens where the Park authorities gave every help and assistance, laying on water and clearing refuse. The little Camp with its horse lines and men at drill provided the public with a counter-attraction to boat sailing on the Round Pond near by. A few Reservists leavened the newly enlisted recruits and with the help of a good class of Regular N.C.O. the Company was in fair shape in a fortnight. On 1st October the Unit marched for LUDGERSHALL completing the journey in 2 days, where it joined as Headquarters A.S.C. the 3rd Cavalry Division, Commanded by Major-General Hon. Julian Byng, C.B. M.V.O.

Two days later the whole Division entrained for SOUTHAMPTON and embarked under sealed orders. 81 Company were on S.S. ------------ with "K" Battery R.H.A. and the Divisional Signal Company. Destination proved to be OSTEND where part of the Division disembarked, remainder at ZEEBRUGGE. Disembarkation of "K" Battery R.H.A. and other Units was effected very rapidly considering that no ramps were available but had to be hastily improvised with timber found in the Docks and a few carpenters tools and nails which the Signal Coy. fortunately had with them. Refugees were beginning to arrive at OSTEND, and the road from there to BRUGES was full of them. Belgian Infantry were amongst them in a complete state of disorganization. Concentration of the Division was effected at BRUGES on 9th October. The 7th Infantry Division were under Major-General Capper were a day ahead, and this with our weak Cavalry Division (2 Brigades) formed the formidable Corps under Sir Henry Rawlinson which landed with the object of relieving ANTWERP !

Fortunately for us ANTWERP had capitulated on 7th October, and orders from the War Office were received to march in a south-westerly direction to join Sir John French's force, then on the left flank of the advancing Allies. Our Supply Column (73 Coy. A.S.C.) under Captain Archibald first fed the Division at BRUGES on 10th October, having landed and filled at OSTEND the previous day. This Column had many adventures as the German Uhlans were spread over the country and with a little more enterprise could have captured our convoys. What the result would have been had they done this is difficult to estimate. Certainly the juncture effected with French at WYTSCHAETE on 14th October would have been still more difficult than it actually was. We were based for 2 days on OSTEND, after the evacuation of this place on DUNKERQUE for 3 days, and finally on BOULOGNE. The march from BRUGES to WYTSCHAETE via THOUROUT, ROULERS and YPRES took a week, and was attended with many exciting incidents daily. Commander Samson with his armoured cars scoured all roads and brought in many prisoners. Spies, dressed some in Belgian uniforms, swarmed and sent out messages to Germans a few miles away. Many of the Belgian inhabitants were pro-German; Patrol actions took place daily but no serious pressure was felt from the Germans until we were in the neighbourhood of YPRES. After getting in touch with French the Division commenced to advance on his left flank and fought a sharp action near MOORSLEDE on 19th October. During this action

Colonel Swabey was ordered to put the village in a state of defence. This provided an unaccustomed role for A.S.C. drivers. The Division had considerable casualties and retired to POELCAPELLE and ZONNEBEKE. A Division of French Territorials were holding a line covering this village but its unexpected and sudden disappearance during the night in the direction of YPRES left the Cavalry exposed to attack by a German Corps. Next day at ZONNEBEKE 81 Coy. A.S.C. first came under rifle fire. Touch with troops fighting had been lost so it was decided to retire towards YPRES. General Munro's 2nd Infantry Division provided safe shelter at ST JEAN, and further retirement of Cavalry next day brought the Company again to its Headquarters. In subsequent operations whilst the 3rd Cavalry Division made history in holding the line at GHELUVELT 81 Coy. were close behind in the shell torn village of ZILLEBEKE. The feeding of the Division by Supply Column lorries (73 Coy. A.S.C.) was nearly always carried out under shell fire, and under arrangements of Major A.R.Liddell the Senior Supply Officer.

On 20th November the 3rd Cavalry Division was sent into rest at HAZEBROUCK and this ended a phase of the campaign in which 81 Company had a unique experience. Colonel Swabey was awarded the C.M.G. and there were many mentions of other A.S.C. Officers and men in recognition of their services.

The G.O.C. in conveying to all ranks of the Division on 23rd November 1914 his gratitude and appreciation of their conduct stated that the A.S.C. had more than maintained its reputation.

OFFICERS of 81 COMPANY HEADQUARTERS OF 3rd CAVALRY DIVISIONAL A.S.C.

Commander. Lt-Col. W.S.SWABEY.
Adjutant. Lieut. RUSSELL.
Senior Supply Officer. Major A.R. LIDDELL.
Supply Officer. Capt. A. BERGER.
Requisition Officer. T/Lieut. J.A.H.WATERS.

6th CAVALRY BRIGADE.

Supply Officer. Captain F.C.CORFIELD.
Requisition Officer. Capt. H.W.PEEBLES, R.of O.
Transport Officer. Capt. R.FITZ G.GLYN, R.of O.
Royal Dragoons.

7th CAVALRY BRIGADE.

Supply Officer. Capt. W.M.ROYSTON-PIGOTT.
Requisition Officer. Lieut. C.R.MOLYNEUX,
R. of O., X Hussars

Transport Officer. Capt. Hon. E.B.Mead, R.of O
X Hussars

COPY. 6/France/1.

EARLY RECORDS OF 81 COY.

CONFIDENTIAL
A.S.C. Records
4 AUG 1917
Reg. No. 865

81 Coy. A.S.C. was ordered to be formed at Kensington Barracks on 6th September 1914. Major Swabey the O.C., however, arranged for a Camp to be pitched in Kensington Gardens where the Park authorities gave every help and assistance, laying on water and clearing refuse. The little Camp with its horse lines and men at drill provided the public with a counter-attraction to boat sailing on the Round Pond near by. A few Reservists leavened the newly enlisted recruits and with the help of a good class of Regular N.C.O. the Company was in fair shape in a fortnight. On 1st October the Unit marched for LUDGERSHALL completing the journey in 2 days, where it joined as Headquarters A.S.C. the 3rd Cavalry Division, Commanded by Major-General Hon. Julian Byng, C.B. M.V.O.

Two days later the whole Division entrained for SOUTHAMPTON and embarked under sealed orders. 81 Company were on S.S. ------------ with "K" Battery R.H.A. and the Divisional Signal Company. Destination proved to be OSTEND where part of the Division disembarked, remainder at ZEEBRUGGE. Disembarkation of "K" Battery R.H.A. and other Units was effected very rapidly considering that no ramps were available but had to be hastily improvised with timber found in the Docks and a few carpenters tools and nails which the Signal Coy. fortunately had with them. Refugees were beginning to arrive at OSTEND, and the road from there to BRUGES was full of them. Belgian Infantry were amongst them in a complete state of disorganization. Concentration of the Division was effected at BRUGES on 9th October. The 7th Infantry Division were under Major-General Capper were a day ahead, and this with our weak Cavalry Division (2 Brigades) formed the formidable Corps under Sir Henry Rawlinson which landed with the object of relieving ANTWERP !

Fortunately for us ANTWERP had capitulated on 7th October, and orders from the War Office were received to march in a south-westerly direction to join Sir John French's force, then on the left flank of the advancing Allies. Our Supply Column (73 Coy. A.S.C.) under Captain Archibald first fed the Division at BRUGES on 10th October, having landed and filled at OSTEND the previous day. This Column had many adventures as the German Uhlans were spread over the country and with a little more enterprise could have captured our convoys. What the result would have been had they done this is difficult to estimate. Certainly the juncture effected with French at WYTSCHAETE on 14th October would have been still more difficult than it actually was. We were based for 2 days on OSTEND, after the evacuation of this place on DUNKERQUE for 3 days, and finally on BOULOGNE. The march from BRUGES to WYTSCHAETE via THOUROUT, ROULERS and YPRES took a week, and was attended with many exciting incidents daily. Commander Samson with his armoured cars scoured all roads and brought in many prisoners. Spies, dressed some in Belgian uniforms, swarmed and sent out messages to Germans a few miles away. Many of the Belgian inhabitants were pro-German; Patrol actions took place daily but no serious pressure was felt from the Germans until we were in the neighbourhood of YPRES. After getting in touch with French the Division commenced to advance on his left flank and fought a sharp action near MOORSLEDE on 19th October. During this action

Colonel Swabey was ordered to put the village in a state of defence. This provided an unaccustomed role for A.S.C. drivers. The Division had considerable casualties and retired to POELCAPELLE and ZONNEBEKE. A Division of French Territorials were holding a line covering this village but its unexpected and sudden disappearance during the night in the direction of YPRES left the Cavalry exposed to attack by a German Corps. Next day at ZONNEBEKE 81 Coy. A.S.C. first came under rifle fire. Touch with troops fighting had been lost so it was decided to retire towards YPRES. General Munro's 2nd Infantry Division provided safe shelter at ST JEAN, and further retirement of Cavalry next day brought the Company again to its Headquarters. In subsequent operations whilst the 3rd Cavalry Division made history in holding the line at GHELUVELT 81 Coy. were close behind in the shell torn village of ZILLEBEKE. The feeding of the Division by Supply Column lorries (73 Coy. A.S.C.) was nearly always carried out under shell fire, and under arrangements of Major A.R.Liddell the Senior Supply Officer.

On 20th November the 3rd Cavalry Division was sent into rest at HAZEBROUCK and this ended a phase of the campaign in which 81 Company had a unique experience. Colonel Swabey was awarded the C.M.G. and there were many mentions of other A.S.C. Officers and men in recognition of their services.

The G.O.C. in conveying to all ranks of the Division on 23rd November 1914 his gratitude and appreciation of their conduct stated that the A.S.C. had more than maintained its reputation.

OFFICERS of 81 COMPANY HEADQUARTERS OF 3rd CAVALRY DIVISIONAL A.S.C.

    Commander.   Lt-Col. W.S.SWABEY.
    Adjutant.   Lieut. RUSSELL.
    Senior Supply Officer.   Major A.R. LIDDELL.
    Supply Officer.   Capt. A. BERGER.
    Requisition Officer.   T/Lieut. J.A.H.WATERS.

6th CAVALRY BRIGADE.

    Supply Officer.   Captain F.C.CORFIELD.
    Requisition Officer.   Capt. H.W.PEEBLES, R.of O.
    Transport Officer.   Capt. R.FITZ G.GLYN, R.of O.
                             Royal Dragoons.

7th CAVALRY BRIGADE.

    Supply Officer.   Capt. W.M.ROYSTON-PIGOTT.
    Requisition Officer.   Lieut. C.R.MOLYNEUX,
                             R. of O., X Hussars

    Transport Officer.   Capt. Hon. E.B.Mead, R.of O
                             X Hussars

"From this time onward the duties and activities of the Company became of a more settled order.

In subsequent operations around YPRES in the spring and summer of 1915, the Division took its place in the trenches. The Headquarters of the Company remained in the vicinity of HAZEBROUCK and detachments of Supply Personnel were sent up to the vicinity of the line to carry carry out the feeding of the Division.

There is nothing of importance to note in connection with these operations nor indeed was there any further event of importance in the history of the Company until the Battale of LOOS in September, 1915. With the Company Headquarters near AIRE and advanced detachments at MAZINGARBE, a busy time was passed until the Division again returned to Rest Billets at FRUGES on 19th October, 1915.

A Dismounted Brigade was formed in February 1916 but the Company was not employed and remained in billets at FRUGES till 24/6/16 when it proceeded with Divisional Headquarters to LA NEUVILLE (SOMME) in readiness for the operations which took place early in July. The Division was not however employed and was withdrawn to a Back Area till 8th July when it again went forward and 81 Co was billetted at DAOURS with Divisional Headquarters where it remained till the 1st August when it returned to FRUGES. On 10th Spetember the Division again went forwatd to the SOMME Area and the company was encamped on the banks of the SOMME. No Cavalry Operations took place however and on 22nd September we left the forward area and Headquarters and 81 Co finally settled down into winter quarters at TREPIED, where they remained till April 1917.

In April 1917 the Division again went forward to ARRAS. 81 Company remained with the B Echelon of the Division. On the 8th April the Division went into action at TILLOY and MONCHY LE PREUX. It suffered severely and was withdrawn on the 11th April - when B Echelon was ordered to rejoin Brigades and Divisional Headquarters went into billets at GOUY en ARTOIS. Here we reamined until 16th April when the whole Division withdrew to a back area in the neighbourhood of HESDIN to refit, 81 Company being allotted billets at REGNAUVILLE. Here we remained till yhe middle of May - when the Division once more went forward to the PERONNE Area, where dismounted it had held a sector of the line South of EPEHY, 81 Company being accommodated in the ruined village of FLAMICOURT a suburb of PERONNE, where we remained until the 4th July when the Division again moved back and took up their quarters in and around BUSNES. We remained here until the middle of October when again the Division moved forward to take part in the surprise attack on CAMBRAI. The Division was in reserve and remained in billets in the BRAY area and was not called upon to act as Cavalry. We withdrew to the CORBIE area where a Dismounted Division was formed and was went into the line. Horses and spare men and 81 Company withdrew to an area round DOMART en PONTHIEU in which village 81 Co was installed.

From the end of November 1914 to the end of 1917

From this time onward the duties and activities of the Company became of a more settled order.

In subsequent operations around YPRES in the spring and summer of 1915, the Division took its place in the trenches. The Headquarters of the Company remained in the vicinity of HAZEBROUK and detachments of supply personnel were sent up to the vicinity of the line to carry out the feeding of the Division.

There is nothing of importance to note in connection with these operations nor indeed was there any further event of importance in the history of the Company until the battle of LOOS in September, 1915. With the Company Headquarters near AIRE and advanced detachments at MAZINGARBE, a busy time was passed until the Division again returned to rest billets at HUCHES on 10th October, 1915.

A Dismounted Brigade was formed in February 1916 but the Company was not employed and remained in billets at HUCHES till 24/6/16 when it proceeded with Divisional Headquarters to LA NEUVILLE (SOMME) in readiness for the operations which took place early in July. The Division was not however employed and was withdrawn to a back Area till 5th July when it again went forward and 81 Co was billetted at DAOURS with Divisional Headquarters where it remained till the 1st August when it returned to HUCHES. On 10th September the Division again went forward to the SOMME Area and the company was encamped on the banks of the SOMME. No Cavalry Operations took place however and on 22nd September we left the forward area and Headquarters and 81 Co finally settled down into winter quarters at TREPIED, where they remained till April 1917.

In April 1917 the Division again went forward to ARRAS. 81 Company remained with the B Echelon of the Division. On the 9th April the Division went into action at TILLOY and MONCHY LE PREUX. It suffered severely and was withdrawn on the 11th April - when B Echelon was ordered to rejoin Brigades and Divisional Headquarters went into billets at COUY en ARTOIS. Here we remained until 14th April when the whole Division withdrew to a back area in the neighbourhood of FRSDIN to refit, 81 Company being allotted billets at BECQUAUVILLE. Here we remained till the middle of May - when the Division once more went forward to the PERONNE Area, where dismounted it bed held a sector of the line South of YPRES, 81 Company being accommodated in the ruined village of FLAMICOURT a suburb of PERONNE, where we remained until the 4th July when the Division again moved back and took up their quarters in and around LUSHMS. We remained here until the middle of October when again the Division moved forward to take part in the surprise attack on CAMBRAI. The Division was in reserve and remained in billets in the FRAY area and was not called upon to act as Cavalry. We withdrew to the GOMMIE area where a Dismounted Division was formed and was went into the line. Horses and spare men and 81 Company withdrew to an area round DOMART en PONTHIEU in which village 81 Co was installed.

From the end of November 1914 to the end of 1917

1917. owing probably to the activity of Cavalry as an army bring so limited., the experiences of the Company cannot compare with those of the early days of the war - it must not be supposed thet they were idle. The constant moves and various places of operations necessitated many changes in the method of delivering rations to the troops and the Horse Transport, including 81 Co., the 3rd Cavalry Reserve Park and the Auxiliary Horse Transport Co., took their full share of all this work - especially during the month of December 1917 when owing to the almost Arctic conditions, Mechanical Transport was practically incapacitated.

1917. owing probably to the activity of Cavalry as an army being so limited., the experiences of the Company cannot compare with those of the early days of the war - it must not be supposed that they were idle. The constant moves and various places of operations necessitated many changes in the method of delivering rations to the troops and the Horse Transport, including 81 Co., the 3rd Cavalry Reserve Park and the Auxiliary Horse Transport Co., took their full share of all this work - especially during the month of December 1917 when owing to the almost Arctic conditions, Mechanical Transport was practically incapacitated.

8TH CAVALRY FIELD AMBULANCE.

No. .... Date. 30/9/17.

O.C., A.S.C.,
3rd Cavalry Division.

Reference your letter No.2379 dated 26th.inst., there is very little that one can report in this connection.

This Unit has been employed in every big engagement since February 1915:-

    2nd battle of Ypres.
    Neuve Capelle. (standing by)
    Ypres. (May & June 1915)
    Loos.
    Dismounted Composite Regiment. (Jan & Feb 1916)
    Somme. (standing by)
    Arras & Monchy le Preux.

In all these engagements the A.S.C.Personnel have always been most anxious to give their services for the rapid collection and evacuation of sick without any personal consideration whatever: both H.T and M.T men.

During the 2nd battle of Ypres the motor ambulance drivers especially did good service, working both day and night. One man kept to the driving wheel for 70 hours continuous work.

At the Loos battle also they did good work, but they were then working under Divisional arrangements.

                                                Capt.R.A.M.C.
                                   O.C, 8th Cav. Field Ambulance.

SUPPLY OFFICE,
7th
CAVALRY BRIGADE.
A.S. 760

O.C. A.S.C.
3rd. Cavalry Division.

In reply to your No.2379 of the 29th. September, I beg to enclose a short record of the work done by the 7th. Cavalry Brigade Supply Detachment in France.

EJ Dale
Captain A.S.C.
S.O. 7th. Cavalry Brigade.

30/9/17

1914

The first Supply Detachment of the 7th. Cavalry Brigade was mobilised at LUDGERSHALL CAMP and sailed with the Brigade on the 6th. October to OSTEND and ZEEBRUGGE. Captain Molyneux was Supply Officer with Captain Piggot as Requisitioning Officer.

From the day they landed until the 20th. November, when the Brigade went into rest billets, the Detachment did most splendid work under great hardships. Most of the time they were under shell fire and work was seldom finished before midnight. During all this time the Brigade never once went without rations and the noticeable fact is that the rations were always delivered at Units' billets, though civilian carts had often to be requisitioned to enable this to be done.

An incident worthy of note is when the Supply Detachment went into the trenches at PASSCHENDALE under Captain Piggot, where they remained until relieved by French infantry.

The remainder of the year was spent in winter billets. In November Captain Piggot was relieved by 2nd. Lieutenant Riley.

1915

The first part of this year was spent in winter billets. At the end of April Captain Molyneux left the Brigade and was replaced by Lieutenant Cotton. 2nd. Lieut. Lake took the place of 2nd. Lieutenant Riley as Requisitioning Officer.

At the end of April and the beginning of May, the Brigade moved up to the 2nd. battle of YPRES. During this battle, however, the hardships were not as great as those suffered in 1914. The Detachment came under shell fire at VLAMERTINGE but met with no casualties.

During the remainder of the year the Brigade did nothing of importance affecting the supply personnel.

In July Lieutenant Davey relieved Lieutenant Cotton as Supply Officer.

In September part of the Detachment went up to ration a digging party of the Brigade at ARMENTIERS.

In October Lieutenant Johnston relieved Lieutenant Davey as Supply Officer.

1 9 1 6

The first part of 1916 was spent in winter billets. In January the Brigade sent up a Dismounted Party to hold a part of the line round BETHUNE. A few men of this Detachment were sent up to assist in the issue of rations.

In April Lieutenant Johnston left the Brigade to join the 35th. Divisional Train, and was replaced as Supply Officer by Captain Lake. 2nd. Lieutenant Emby joined as Requisitioning Officer.

In May the Brigade with the exception of "B" Echelon went to the surroundings of ABBEVILLE for two weeks' training. Captain Lake proceeded with this party taking the whole detachment with the exception of two men who were left behind with 2nd. Lieutenant Emby to ration "B Echelon".

In June the Brigade left winter billets and proceeded up to the first battle of the SOMME. The whole detachment was with the Brigade. The Brigade, however, did not go into action and returned to billets in August. This was the first time since May 1915 that the Detachment as a whole was in the environments of the Front and their work was carried out in a very satisfactory way.

In September the Brigade went up for the 2nd. Battle of the SOMME, and again they did not go into action, but returned to billets at the end of the month. The weather was extremely bad and the men suffered great discomfort.

1 9 1 6   (page 2)

At the end of December, SS/1054 Sergeant Sheppard, who had been with the Detachment since they left England in 1914, left to take a commission in the Argyle & Sutherland Highlanders.   Sergeant Wrigley became Senior Sergeant of the Detachment.

Nothing of any importance occurred during the remainder of the year.

1917

The Brigade was in winter billets until the commencement of April, when they moved up to the battle of ARRAS. During this battle the Detachment did not move up with the Brigade beyond ARRAS, but remained behind with the Rear Divisional Headquarters, with the exception of 2nd. Lieutenant Emby and two men who were with Brigade Headquarters,. The weather was deplorable, and the mud and heavy rain and snow put great difficulties in the way of issuing rations.

The Brigade returned to rest billets after a few days, and remained there until May, when they moved to the Peronne Area. They remained in this district until the commencement of July, when the Brigade moved to rest billets behind the line.

OC ASC 3rd Cav Div

Ref Your 2379 A/76/9/17

I regret there are no records in this Office to furnish required information. The only hearsay evidence we could collect would probably be slightly inaccurate and undoubtedly many points would be missed that should be recorded.

Oct 5/17

J. M. Powell Capt
for OFFICER COMMANDING
No 6 CAVALRY FIELD AMBULANCE

O.C. A.S.C., 1st Cavalry Divn.
O.C. A.S.C., 2nd Cavalry Divn.
O.C. A.S.C., 3rd Cavalry Divn.
O.C. A.S.C., 4th Cavalry Divn.
O.C. A.S.C., 5th Cavalry Divn.

The attached memo from the Director of ....
is forwarded for information.

Every effort should be made for this information to be available when required, and assistance given to the Officer collecting the information.

Lieutenant Colonel,
A.D.S.& T., Cavalry Corps.

23/7/17.

D.D.S.T., First Army.
D.D.S.T., Second Army.
D.D.S.T., Third Army.
D.D.S.T., Fourth Army.
D.D.S.T., Fifth Army.
A.D.S.T., Cav. Corps.
D. D. T., Northern.
D. D. T., Southern.
D.A.D.S.T., G.H.Q.Tps.
=============================

In order to enable the Historical Records of A.S.C. Units to be compiled in as complete a form as possible and more or less on the same lines, I have appointed a Recording Officer who will visit units in turn and obtain from the Commanding Officers all information which is procurable.

He will then from this information write a history of the Unit, in conjunction with the Commanding Officer, and will transmit it in duplicate to my representatives with Army Headqrs., Cavalry Corps, G.H.Q. Troops, or L. of C., as the case may be, who will, after satisfying themselves of its general correctness, forward it to my office in duplicate in order that I may transmit it to the War Office.

The War Establishments of 1914, which were drawn up in time of peace, provided for certain units with well defined functions, and the conditions obtaining in France corresponded very nearly to those which the establishments were framed to meet.

We ought to endeavour, I think, in the Historical Records to show how these functions were fulfilled, the changes which the actual conditions of War rendered necessary together with full reasons for and a full description of such changes.

The records should also contain some picture of the activities of the A.S.C., the diversity of the work, the conditions under which it was carried out, the difficulties which had to be met and overcome, and the various improvisations and expedients which from time to time had to be made.

King's Regulations Para.1931 lay down the particulars which should be contained in the Historical Record of a Unit, which are for convenience sake repeated herein, viz:

(1) The circumstance of its original formation.

(2) Any unusual means by which it has been recruited.

(3) The stations at which it has been employed, and the date of its arrival at and departure from such stations.

(4) The military operations in which it has been engaged and its achievements.

(5) The names of all Officers killed or wounded, and the name of any Officer or soldier who has specially distinguished himself in action.

(6) The badges and devices which it has been permitted to bear, and the reason for which such badges and devices, or other marks of distinction, were granted, together with the date and authority for the same.

/(7).

F.

(2)

(7) Alterations in the clothing, arms, accoutrements, colours or horse furniture, with date and authority for the same.

(8) Any other important matter relating to its regimental administration, such as changes in peace establishments and terms of service.

(9) Drafts received and despatched, their strength, dates of their arrival or departure, and names of the Officers who accompanied them.

Drafts numerically weaker than an officer's party should not be separately specified.

(10) Any other matter which may be considered of historical importance.

Of the above Nos. 1, 3, 4, 5, 8, 9 & 10 are the most important.

In order to enable the Historical Records to be readily revised from time to time, it is advisable that statistical information should be given in the forms of appendices to the main body of the History. The appendices can then be added to from time to time by the Recording Officer from information which has been compiled and kept up to date by the Officer Commanding the Unit.

In such a variety of units as comprise the A.S.C., it is difficult to lay down the exact nature of the statistics which will be of interest for Record purposes, but they should certainly include the following:

(A) Date of formation of the Unit.

(B) Name and rank of successive Commanding Officers and date of their appointment to and transfer from the Unit.

(C) Honours, Rewards or Mention in Despatches, which have been conferred on individuals and the date thereof in the London Gazette.

(D) Work performed each month by the Unit under the headings of: average daily mileage; tons carried; patients carried.

(E) Number of solid tyres fitted per month, in the case of Tyre Press Detachments.

(F) Number of derelict vehicles extricated and repaired in the case of Mobile Repair Units.

(G) Estimated number of tons of stores received each month into Base and Advanced M.T. Depots; total number of packages or cases despatched daily to Units.

(H) Approximate number of demands received each month in Base and Advanced M.T. Depots.

(I) Number of vehicles each month received into and despatched from Reserve Vehicle Parks.

(J) Total number of gallons of water dealt with each month by Water Tank Companies or Water Lorry Companies.

(K) Number of vehicles which have been evacuated monthly/to Heavy Repair Shops for complete overhaul.

/(L).

DIRECTOR OF TRANSPORT,
GENERAL HEADQUARTERS.

12521.

(L) Number of vehicles which have been destroyed or damaged by shell fire.

(M) Number of lorries, Ambulances or Cars, Motor Bicycles, repaired each month in the case of Heavy Repair Shops.

(N) Value of spare parts retrieved each month, in the case of Heavy Repair Shops with a Retrieving Section attached.

----- * -----

The Recording Officer has now completed the Units on the Northern Line of Communication, and has commenced work on the Southern Line. He will then proceed to Armies, etc., in rotation, but it will facilitate his task and enable the Records to be completed more rapidly if Officers Commanding A.S.C. Units will prepare in advance all the information which they desire to be included in the History of their Units.

G.H.Q.,
19/7/17.

Major General,
DIRECTOR of TRANSPORT.

O.C. A.S.C. 3rd Cav Divn.   A.D.S.&T. Cav Corps
                                              No 672

The attached memo from the Director of Transport
is forwarded for information.

Every effort should be made for this information to be
available when required, and assistance given to the officer
collecting the information.

                                              (sd) Lt Cranage, Director

28/7/17   A.D.S.&T. Cav Corps

3rd Cav. Supply Column
3rd Cav. Ammn. Park
3rd Cav. Aux. H.T. Co.
3rd Cav. Reserve Park

        ———————

for information necessary action —

                                    S.E. Currie Lt Colonel.
26/7/17   O.C. A.S.C. 3rd Cavalry Division

A.D.S.T., A.S. No 1512
D of T. G.H.Q.
12521.

A.D.S.T.
Cavalry Corps

In order to enable the Historical Records of A.S.C. Units to be compiled in as complete a form as possible and more or less on the same lines, I have appointed a Recording Officer who will visit units in turn and obtain from the Commanding Officers all information which is procurable.

He will then from this information write a history of the Unit, in conjunction with the Commanding Officers, and will transmit it in duplicate to my representatives with Army Headquarters, Cavalry Corps, L. of C. Troops, or Base, as the case may be, who will, after satisfying themselves of its general correctness, forward it to my office in duplicate in order that I may transmit it to the War Office.

The War Establishments of 1914, which were drawn up in time of peace, provided for certain units with well defined functions, and the conditions obtaining in France corresponded very nearly to those which the establishments were framed to meet.

We ought to endeavour, I think, in the Historical Records to show how these functions were fulfilled, the changes which the actual conditions of War rendered necessary, together with full reasons for and a full description of such changes.

The records should also contain some picture of the activities of the A.S.C., the diversity of the work, the conditions under which it is carried out, the difficulties which had to be met and overcome, and the various improvisations and expedients which from time to time had to be made.

King's Regulation Para. 1921 lay down the particulars which should be contained in the Historical Record of a Unit, which are for convenience sake, repeated herein, viz:-

(1). The circumstance of its original formation.
(2). Any unusual means by which it has been recruited.
(3). The stations at which it has been employed, and the date of its arrival at and departure from such stations.
(4). The military operations in which it has been engaged and its achievements.
(5). The names of all Officers killed or wounded, and the names of any Officer or Soldier who has specially distinguished himself in action.
(6). The badges and devices which it has been permitted to bear, and the reason for which such badges and devices or other marks of distinction, were granted, together with the date and authority for the same.
(7). Alterations in the clothing, arms, accoutrements, colours or horse furniture, with date and authority for the same.
(8). Any other important matter relating to its regimental administration, such as changes in peace establishments and terms of service.
(9). Drafts received and despatched, their strength, dates of their arrival or departure, and names of the Officers who accompanied them.

Drafts numerically weaker than an officer's party should not be separately specified.

(r) Any other matter which may be considered of historical importance.

Of the above Nos. 1, 3, 4, 5, 8, 9, & 10 are the most important.

In order to enable the Historical Records to be readily revised from time to time, it is advisable that statistical information should be given in the form of appendices to the main body of the History. The appendices can then be added to from time to time by the Recording Officer from information which has been compiled and kept up to date by the Officer Commanding the Unit.

In such a variety of units as comprise the A.S.C. it is difficult to lay down the exact nature of the statistics which will be of interest for Record purposes, but they should certainly include the following:—

(a) Date of formation of the Unit.

(b) Name and rank of successive Commanding Officers and date of their appointment to and transfer from the Unit.

(c) Honours, Rewards or Mention in Despatches, which have been conferred on individuals and the dates thereof in the London Gazette.

(d) Work performed each month by the Unit under the headings of: average daily mileage; tons carried; ration carried.

(e) Number of solid tyres fitted per month, in the case of Tyre Press Detachments.

(f) Number of derelict vehicles extricated and repaired in the Mobile Repair Unit.

(g) Estimated number of tons or stores received each month into Base and Advanced M.T. Depots; total number of packages or cases despatched daily to Units.

(h) Approximate number of demands received each month in Base and Advanced M.T. Depots.

(i) Number of vehicles each month received into and despatched from Reserve Vehicle Parks.

(j) Total number of gallons of water dealt with each month by Water Tank Companies or Water Ferry Companies.

(k) Number of vehicles which have been evacuated monthly to Heavy Repair Shops for complete overhaul.

(l) Number of vehicles which have been destroyed or damaged by shell fire.

(m) Number of Lorries, Ambulances or Cars, Motor Bicycles, repaired each month in the case of Heavy Repair Shops.

(n) Value of spare parts retrieved each month, in the case of Heavy Repair Shops with a Retrieving Section attached.

The Recording Officer has now completed the Units on the Northern Line of Communications, and has commenced work on the Southern Line. He will then proceed to Armies, etc, in rotation, but it will facilitate his task and enable the Records to be completed more rapidly if Officers Commanding A.S.C. Units will prepare in advance all the information which they desire to be included in the History of their Unit.

W. C. Boyce
Major General
Director of Transport

18/7/17

A.A.A.G., 3rd Brig. Divn.   A.A.A.G. 3rd Cav. Bgd.
                                        m/676

The attached comes from the Director of Transports
so forwarded for information.

Every effort should be made to convert this information to be
available when required, and assistance given to the Officers
collecting the information.

A.C. & T. Department

By order Brig. General

Copy to

3rd Tons. Supply Column.
3rd Bar. Ammn. Parr.
3rd Bar. Ann. H. T. C.
3rd Bar. Reserve Parr.

for information necessary action —

S.A. Murray, Col.
A.C. 3rd Cavalry Division

A.S.C. HEADQUARTERS
3rd CAVALRY DIVISION
Ab/379

A.D.S.T., A.C. No 1512
D of T. G.H.Q.
12521.

A. D. S. T.
  Cavalry Corps

In order to enable the Historical Records of A.S.C. Units to be compiled in as complete a form as possible and more or less on the same lines, I have appointed a Recording Officer who will visit units in turn and obtain from the Commanding Officers all information which is procurable.

He will then from this information write a history of the Unit, in conjunction with the Commanding Officers, and will transmit it in duplicate to my representatives with Army Headquarters, Cavalry Corps, G.H.Q. Troops, or L of C, as the case may be; who will, after satisfying themselves of its general correctness, forward it to my office in duplicate in order that I may transmit it to the War Office.

The War Establishment of 1914, which were drawn up in time of peace, provided for certain units with well defined functions, and the conditions obtaining in France corresponded very nearly to those which the establishments were framed to meet.

We ought to endeavour, I think, in the Historical Records to show how these functions were fulfilled, the changes which the actual conditions of War rendered necessary together with full reasons for and a full description of such changes.

The records should also contain some picture of the activities of the A.S.C., the diversity of the work, the conditions under which it is carried out, the difficulties which had to be met and overcome, and the various improvisations and expedients which from time to time had to be made.

King's Regulations Para. 1921 lay down the particulars which should be contained in the Historical Record of a Unit, which are for convenience sake, repeated herein, viz:-

(1). The circumstance of its original formation.
(2). Any unusual means by which it has been recruited.
(3). The stations at which it has been employed, and the date of its arrival at and departure from such stations.
(4). The military operations in which it has been engaged and its achievements.
(5). The names of all Officers killed or wounded, and the name of any Officer or Soldier who has specially distinguished himself in action.
(6). The badges and devices which it has been permitted to bear, and the reason for which such badges and devices, or other marks of distinction, were granted, together with the date and authority for the same.
(7). Alterations in the clothing, arms, accoutrements, colours or horse furniture, with date and authority for the same.
(8). Any other important matter relating to its regimental administration, such as changes in peace establishments and terms of service.
(9). Drafts received and despatched, their strength, dates of their arrival or departure, and names of the Officers who accompanied them.

Drafts numerically weaker than an officer party should not be separately specified.
(o) Any other matter which may be considered of historical importance.

Of the above Nos. 1, 2, 4, 6, 8, 9, & 10 are the most important.

In order to enable the Historical Records to be readily accessed for ... it is advised that historical information should be given in the form of appendices to the main body of the History. New appendices can then be added from time to time by the Record Office from material which has been compiled and sent in by the Officer Commanding the Unit.

It is not possible to wait or compile the A.S.C., it is difficult to lay down the exact nos. of the matters which will be of interest for Record purposes, but they should certainly include the following:—

(a) Date of formation of the Unit.
(b) Names and ranks of successive Commanding Officers and ... of admissions to and transfers from the Unit.
(c) Honors, Awards, or Mention in Dispatches which have been conferred on individuals, and the deeds done in the Service Field.
(d) Distinguished work by the Unit under the Command of average ... of villages; &c. in convoys; indents issued.
(e) Number of artist types filled per month, in the case of ... Detachments.
(f) Number of derelict vehicles extricated and repaired in the ...
(g) Estimated number of tons or cases received each month into Base and delivered to M. Depot. Total number of packages received ... daily at Base.
(h) Approximate number of animals received each month on Base and delivered to M. Depot.
(i) Number of vehicles each month received into and despatched from Reserve Vehicle Parks.
(j) Total number of gallons of water distilled each month by Water Tank Companies on Water Barge Companies.
(k) Number of vehicles which have been evacuated monthly to Heavy Repair Shops for complete overhaul.
(l) Number of vehicles which have been destroyed or damaged by hostile fire.
(m) Number of ... Ambulances or Cars, Motor Bicycles, repaired each month in the case of Heavy Repair Shops.
(n) Value of stores returned each month, in the case of Heavy Repair Shops with a Returning Section attached.

The Recording Officer is now compiling the Unit Histories for the Northern Line of Communication, and has commenced work with the Southern Line. He will then proceed to Canvas, &c. in rotation, but it will facilitate his task and enable the Records to be completed more rapidly if Officers Commanding A.S.C. Units will prepare in advance all the information which they desire to be included in the History of their Unit.

COs
  Major (afterwards Lt Col) W.S. Swabey from formation to 1.2.15
  Major D.C.E. Grose from 1.2.15 to 7.6.15
  Major (afterwards Lt.Col) C.E. Hills from 7.6.15 to
  Lt Colonel A.E. Cuming from

Rewards
  Lt Col. W.S. Swabey - CMG
  Capt & Maj. H.W. Peebles - Despatches (since DSO)
  Major. A.R. Liddell - Despatches (since DSO)
  T. Major E.T. Carver. Despatches
  Sergt. C.H. Hanson. Despatches.

S.SOs
  Major A.R. Liddell from formation to 1.2.15
  ~~Major D.C.E. Grose from~~
  Capt & Maj. F.C. Corfield 13.2.15. to 2.5.15
    "   "   H.W. Peebles 3.5.15.
  T.Maj. E.T. Carver.

Adjt. Lieut. R.V. Russell from formation to 5.11.14.
  1. Lt. J.A.H. Waters 5.11.14 to
  T.Lt. R. Coyle

Date of formation of Coy

S.O. 6th Cav. Bde.   B.S.O. 8th Cav. Bde.
S.O. 7th Cav. Bde.   B.S.O. 7th Cav. Bde.
S.O. 8th Cav. Bde.   O.C. 6th C.F.A.
O.C. 7th C.F.A.   O.C. 8th C.F.A.

Copy

At the request of the Officer i/c A.S.C. Records, I am compiling a Historical Record of the 3rd Cavalry Division A.S.C. and I am anxious that the work of A.S.C. personnel with the Cavalry Brigades should be adequately represented therein.

With this end in view, I shall be glad if A.S.C. Officers with Brigades and O.C. Field Ambulances will send me a short history of their units with particular reference to the work of their A.S.C. personnel.

Lt. Colonel,
O.C. A.S.C. 3rd Cavalry Divn.

26.9.17.

O.C. ASC.
3rd Cav. Divn.

Reference to your 2379 of 3rd July 1917 and G.R/29591/R/1, A.D. of S&T. Cav. Corps, M.1512, the attached are true copies of letters received by Captain C.S.R. Weller referring to the work done by his Company then under his command, on the SOMME, during operations of 1916, mentioned in my communication of 11-7-17.

W N Buckley
Captain
Comdg. 3 Cav. Div. Aux. H.T. Co. ASC

6/ /

XIV Corps.
No. Q/1207.

H.Q. 3 C.D.
No. 4753.

A.S.C 3 CD
1616.

3rd Cavalry Division

The 3rd Cavalry Div. Aux. H.T. Company has been attached to XIV Corps since the 16th August, and has been employed carrying water forward to the neighbourhood of BERNAFAY Wood.

This company commanded by Captain. Weller A.S.C. has performed most excellent work usually under adverse circumstances and has done all in its power to keep the forward troops supplied with water. I regret that its services have had to be withdrawn from me.

Cavan. Lieut. General.
Commanding XIV. Corps.

15/9/16

O.C. A.S.C.   2.
          1. For information.
Please pass this to Captain Weller for his retention. The G.O.C was very pleased to get such a good report.

Sgd. W.A Featherstonhaugh
Lieut Colonel
A.A & Q.M.G. 3 Cav Division
16/9/16

3.
Capt. Weller. A.S.C.
Passed to you, for retention.
Sgd. D. Glynn
19/9/16

XIV Corps
Q.1207.

D.14.

14th Corps Q.

After a tour in the line I should like to report that the arrangements made for sending up drinking water in G.S. Wagons to BERNAFAY WOOD and the BRIQUETERIE worked well and reflect credit on officers and detachment of A.S.C. concerned. I hope that their conduct may meet with official approbation.

Sgd. J.E. Capper.
Major General.
Comdg. 24th Division

22/8/16.

O.C. 3rd Cav. Div. Aux. H.T. Coy.

The Corps Commander is much gratified at receiving this report which reflects great credit on the good work done by your company.

Sgd B H Cooke Brig General
D.A.&Q.M.G. 14th Corps

26/8/16.

O.C. A.S.C.
    3rd Cav. Div.

    Attached is a brief outline of the work of this Coy in response to your 2379 of 1/7.

    I have written to the late O.C. Coy for a copy of the letter from G.O.C. 14th Corps.

    W. N. Buckley
        Capt

11/7 cdg 3rd Cav. Div. Aux H.T.Co.

O.C. A.S.C.
3rd Cav. Div.

Reference letter from A.D.S.T. Cav. Corps. dated 29.6.17 I am submitting a brief outline of the work of this Coy since its formation.

The 3rd Cav. Div. Aux H.T. Coy. was formed at ABBEVILLE in September 1915 with teams of horses and civilian pattern wagons, for the purpose of carrying "horse rugs" for the Cavalry during the winter months, on the basis of one wagon per squadron and R.H.A. Battery.

The civilian pattern wagons were found unsatisfactory as they were unable to stand the rough usage, furthermore there were difficulties in effecting necessary repairs.

In the Spring of 1916 G.S. wagons were supplied.

The Coy. was detached from the Cavalry about June 1916 for the purpose of carrying water on the SOMME during the heavy fighting which took place in the ensuing Summer.

Water tanks with a carrying capacity of about 200 G.

O.C. A.S.C. 3rd Cav. Div. (cont)

were fitted for this duty.

The Coy was first attached to the 13th Corps, and then the 14th Corps, where good work was done under adverse conditions, recognition of the same being received in writing from the Earl of Cavan, then G.O.C. 14th Corps, on its return to the Cavalry in September 1916.

During the winter of 1916/1917 the wagons were sent out to the Regiments, whilst in billets.

In April 1916 the Coy was collected together for the purpose of carrying ammunition as a Park during the cavalry operations around ARRAS, and the wagons were again sent out to the Regiments on their return to billets.

One section was employed cutting hay in June around PERONNE district.

The work on the SOMME was rather exceptional, otherwise the Coy has been employed in the usual A.S.C. transport duties.

W.A. Buckley

G. Aylward

O/C A.S.C. Records,
Woolwich Dockyard.

[Stamp: A.S.C. RECORDS WOOLWICH DOCKYARD 28 JUL. 1917 REGᴅ Nº]
[Stamp: A.S.C. HEADQUARTERS 3rd CAVALRY DIVISION — A/6/2312]

I should be much obliged if you would forward the War Diary (duplicate) of H.Qrs. 3rd Cavalry Divisional A.S.C. for reference and return to you.

It is now in your possession (vide your R/1299 d/12.4.17) and it is required in connection with the anticipated visit of the A.S.C. Recording Officer.

I understand that you have the Historical Record of this unit, compiled by ~~Colonel~~ SWABEY, lately in command of 3rd Cav. Div. A.S.C. If at all possible, I should like to have this also.

S.E. Cumming Lt. Colonel
Comdg. 3rd Cavalry Div. A.S.C.

26/7/17

SEPT - DEC - 1914

Confidential   121/3971

War Diary
of
Head Quarters, 3rd Cavalry Divisional A.S.C.

From 4th September 1914   To 31st December 1914

(Volume 1)

1st to
June 1919

H.C. Sherborn
Lt Col
ASC
Comdg. HdQrs 3 Cav Div A.S.C

Army Form C. 2118.

WAR DIARY
or
INTELLIGENCE SUMMARY
(Erase heading not required.)

Instructions regarding War Diaries and Intelligence Summaries are contained in F. S. Regs., Part II. and the Staff Manual respectively. Title pages will be prepared in manuscript.

Hour, Date, Place	Summary of Events and Information	Remarks and references to Appendices
4.9.14 LONDON	Order received for formation of 81 Coy Army Sn Corps	
5.9.14 LONDON	Notification of appointment of Senior Supply Officer, 2 Transport Officers received. 6 Clerks joined from ALDERSHOT.	
7.9.14 LONDON	Captain ROYSTON PIGOTT joined for duty as Adjutant.	
10.9.14 LONDON	Major LIDDELL and Captain BERGER joined, also parties from BRADFORD (21 H.T. N.C.Os & men) & 16 M.T. Drivers) ALDERSHOT (23 H.T. N.C.Os & men & 16 M.T. Drivers) and acting Qr. Mr. Sergt. from WOOLWICH.	
11.9.14 LONDON	Camp pitched in KENSINGTON GARDENS. 25 Specially Enlisted Clerks arrived from ALDERSHOT	
12.9.14 LONDON	—	
13.9.14 LONDON		
14.9.14 LONDON	84 men (H.T.) and 10 Draught horses from ISLINGTON	

Army Form C. 2118.

WAR DIARY
or
INTELLIGENCE SUMMARY
(Erase heading not required.)

Instructions regarding War Diaries and Intelligence Summaries are contained in F. S. Regs., Part II. and the Staff Manual respectively. Title pages will be prepared in manuscript.

Hour, Date, Place	Summary of Events and Information	Remarks and references to Appendices
15.9.14 LONDON	—	
16.9.14 — do —	Informed over telephone by C.O.O London District that Establishment of Company had been altered, and that only Peace Equipment as shewn in G.1098-54 should be drawn. Requisition accordingly submitted.	
17.9.14 — do —	—	
18.9.14 — do —	Peace Equipment drawn from TOWER. Orders received for Major LIDDEL and Captain BERGER to report to WAR OFFICE 10 a.m. 19.9.1914.	
19.9.14 — do —	—	
20.9.14 — do —	—	
21.9.14 — do —	—	
22.9.14 — do —	—	

Army Form C. 2118.

WAR DIARY
or
INTELLIGENCE SUMMARY

(Erase heading not required.)

Instructions regarding War Diaries and Intelligence Summaries are contained in F. S. Regs., Part II. and the Staff Manual respectively. Title pages will be prepared in manuscript.

Hour, Date, Place	Summary of Events and Information	Remarks and references to Appendices
23.9.14 LONDON	Major SNABEY visited WAR OFFICE. Information obtained re move of Company to WINDMILL HILL Camp. Horses Exchanged. (Riding and draught.)	
24.9.14 -do-	Farrier Staff Sergeant, Acting Company Quarter Master Sergeant Shoeing Smith, 5 Drivers and 12 N. J. Drivers to Head Quarters 3rd Cavalry Division. Captain PIGOTT, Clerk, and two Issuers to 7th Cavalry Brigade.	
25.9.14 -do-	Orders received for Unit to go by March Route to WINDMILL HILL Camp. Captain CORFIELD arrived. Lieutenant RUSSELL arrived.	
26-9-14 -do-	—	
27-9-14 -do-	—	
28-9-14 -do-	—	
29-9-14 -do-	3 Officers, 131 other ranks, 13 draught horses, 5 riding horses, 2 waggons, 3 carts and 1 water cart to LUDGERSHALL by march route. Started at 8.45 am	

1247 W 3299 200,000 (E) 8/14 J.B.C. & A. Forms/C. 2118/11.

Army Form C. 2118.

WAR DIARY
or
INTELLIGENCE SUMMARY

(Erase heading not required.)

Instructions regarding War Diaries and Intelligence Summaries are contained in F. S. Regs., Part II. and the Staff Manual respectively. Title pages will be prepared in manuscript.

Hour, Date, Place		Summary of Events and Information	Remarks and references to Appendices
30-9-14	LONDON	Camp at KENSINGTON closed, 3 NCO and 15 men proceeded to WINDMILL HILL CAMP by 2-10 pm train	WL
1-10-14	WINDMILL CAMP P.	Major SWABEY and Major LIDDELL arrived by road – framing company en route	WL WL
3-10-14	-"-	Company arrived by road from LONDON about 6-30 pm	WL
3-10-14	-"-	50 NCO and men (Horse Transport) posted to "C" Coy: Role 7A, 9 clerks and issue number to "3" Coy Supply Off, 6 Cav. Bde: 6 clerks and 1 SSt NCO to Supply Officer 4 Cavalry Bde to complete requirements. Officer and two (2) NCO proceeded from the Res 3rd Cav Bde before to PORTSMOUTH & draw mobilization equipment.	WL WL WL
4-10-14	-"-	Mobilization equipment drawn from Ordnance readiness received about 11 am for unit to be in readiness to entrain at short notice.	WL
5-10-14	-"-	Orders received for company to entrain at 4-30 am 6-10-14	WL
-"- 12 men			WL
3/3-0am 6/7/4	WINDMILL HILL	Company left camp, and entrained at LUDGERSHALL about 7am arrived SOUTHAMPTON & embarked on SS "MINNESOTA" about 3 pm	WL
4am 7/7/4	SOUTHAMPTON	Sailed from SOUTHAMPTON.	WL
8/10/4	OSTENDE	Arrived OSTENDE disembarked, horses kept on slept for the night.	WL
9am 9/7/4	BELGIUM	Left OSTEND by march route for BRUGES. Detail	WL

1247 W 3299 200,000 (E) 8/14 J.B.C. & A. Forms/C. 2118/11.

WAR DIARY or INTELLIGENCE SUMMARY

Army Form C. 2118.

(Erase heading not required.)

Instructions regarding War Diaries and Intelligence Summaries are contained in F.S. Regs., Part II. and the Staff Manual respectively. Title pages will be prepared in manuscript.

Hour, Date, Place	Summary of Events and Information	Remarks and references to Appendices
9/10/14	Details of 1 NCO and 11 men left at OSTEND. Marching strength — 5 Officers, 89 other ranks, 15 horses & G.S. waggon, 1 tank, 2 cars	ky
9/10/14 3pm BRUGES 10/10/14 4pm	arrived and billeted at CASTIER PERSYN. MARCHE DE VENDREDI. Left BRUGES by march route for OOSTCAMP. Reached there about 6 pm. Men stores billets in Officers in house opposite.	ky ky
9 am 11/10/14	Left OOSTCAMP by march route. Arrived and bivouacked at Damme, Oostcamp, THOUROUT. Luftpen Colonne 4 hours late	ky
10 am 12/10/14 THOUROUT	Left by march route for ROULERS. Remained 3.30 pm billeted at watermen — n.a. Domicile	ky
10.30am 13/10/14 ROULERS	Left billets about 10/30 am. March en route to Iseghem. Reached at 4 pm that n. march t ISEGHEM	ky
5.15 am 14/10/14 ISEGHEM	Marched movement at 5.15 am. Reached WYTHOCAETE. After short wait then marched to WYTHOCAETE 2 am 15. Luftpen Colonne did not arrive until 3 am 15.	ky
15/10/14 WYTHCHAETE	Remained at WYTNNCHAETE all day. Luftpen Colonne arrived 10/30 am 15/10/14	ky
10.30am 16/10/14	Left in column at 11.30 am directed 5 am during afternoon. Reached ZONNEBEKE for about Bivouac at Cafe du Commerce. Luftpen Colonne 3 am 17/10/14 leaves march on Graveystein for ST JULIEN for about	ky

1247 W 3290 200,000 (E) 8/14 J.B.C. & A. forms/C. 2118/11.

WAR DIARY or INTELLIGENCE SUMMARY

(Erase heading not required.)

Army Form C. 2118.

Instructions regarding War Diaries and Intelligence Summaries are contained in F.S. Regs, Part II. and the Staff Manual respectively. Title pages will be prepared in manuscript.

Hour, Date, Place		Summary of Events and Information	Remarks and references to Appendices
ZONNEBEKE	17-10-14	Remained in billets all day. Supply Column arrived 3-10 pm	
"	18-10-14	Remained at ZONNEBEKE all day. Supply Column arrived 4-30 pm	
"	19-10-14	Left at 10 am for PASSCHENDALE. Division in action. Returned to ZONNEBEKE in evening. Supply Column arrived 11 pm	
"	20-10-14	Left ZONNEBEKE at 3 pm, we halted on road outside to ST JEAN. Billeted there for 2 hours, then marched to ST JEAN. Billeted Supply Column did not arrive before YPRES this night owing to battle.	Left Zonnebeke — Constant stream of shells & bullets falling in from Zonnebeke on fire even
ST JEAN	3 am 21-10-14	Marched at 4 am to YPRES & again nothing then on to MENIN Road. Action fought by Division. Column then marched to VOORMEZEELE. Column Rationed. Supply Column arrived 10 pm. R. 9-30 pm S.W. YPRES - DICKEBUSCH - BAILLEUL Road. 1 tun.	
VOORMEZEELE	22-10-14	R. came as for 21/10/14. Column left for ZILLEBEKE 5 pm. arrived 9 pm. Supply Column arrived in town. Billeted.	
ZILLEBEKE	23-10-14	Remained in billets all day. R. came on first. Supply Column arrived 3-30 pm. Village shelled at night by enemy at intervals of ½ an hour.	
"	24-10-14	Transport Column left ZILLEBEKE about 11 am owing to disturbance of return and horses not bearing up. YPRES noon. Returned to ZILLEBEKE about 6 pm. R. came as for 21/2. German arrived. Thus a few shells sent at us by enemy during the night	
"	25-10-14	Remained in billet at ZILLEBEKE all day. Supply Column arrived 3-36 pm. R. 1 mile W. of YPRES at 1 pm.	

WAR DIARY or INTELLIGENCE SUMMARY

Army Form C. 2118.

(Erase heading not required.)

Instructions regarding War Diaries and Intelligence Summaries are contained in F. S. Regs., Part II. and the Staff Manual respectively. Title pages will be prepared in manuscript.

Hour, Date, Place	Summary of Events and Information	Remarks and references to Appendices
26-10-14. ZILLEBEKE	Remained in billets all day. R came in for 25". Luffey Column arrived 3.30 p.m.	M/
27-10-14 — do —	Remained in billets all day. R same as for 25". Luffey Column arrived 3.30 p.m. No wagon made up as only 3 Teams went received much artillery fire outside of town.	M/
28-10-14 — do —	Remained in billets all day. R same as for 25". Luffey Column arrived 3 p.m. Village shelled at 4 p.m.	M/
29-10-14 — do —	In billets all day. R 1 mile S.W. of YPRES on BAILLEUL Road. 1 hr. Luffey Column arrived 3 p.m.	M/
30-10-14 — do —	Column left ZILLEBEKE about 10.30 a.m. owing to development of engagement. Heard there was not but 4 miles on. Passed another line of column fire at YPRES at railway. Passed another Battery came in 1.30 p.m. who were from Corps. No casualties. R came to 100 to 300 yards for 39. 6-4.5 in. Same as made at for 39. 1 German armoured column moved at Kemmel Road. Accommodated at Chateau Beau Sejour, YPRES.	L/
31-10-14. CHATEAU BEAU SEJOUR.	Remained at Chateau all day. R same as for 39.¢. Column arrived about a few minutes ago.	M/
1 ? 1-11-14 — " —	Remained at Chateau all day very fire engagement and transport was got ready to move in several directions as far as R. Column arrived 8 p.m. Same as Cross Road on before	M/

1247 W 3299 200,000 (E) 8/14 J.B.C. & A. Forms/C. 2118/11.

Army Form C. 2118.

WAR DIARY
or
INTELLIGENCE SUMMARY
(Erase heading not required.)

Instructions regarding War Diaries and Intelligence Summaries are contained in F.S. Regs., Part II. and the Staff Manual respectively. Title pages will be prepared in manuscript.

Hour, Date, Place	Summary of Events and Information	Remarks and references to Appendices
2-11-14. CHATEAU BEAU SEJOUR YPRES.	Left Chateau in column at 9.30am. Proceeded to Chateau at FREZENBERG about 1½ miles from last major events. Chateau being occupied by women and children. Sent men on for B9". Hd Qrs of Echelon B transport is in field at this farm. Lances numbers at YPRES station about 4 from.	W/
3-11-14. FREZENBERG. (YPRES).	Received in billets & bivouacs acc. plans. Baynes received for Lieutenant RUSSELL to go to 2nd Divisional train for duty. Pte GILLESPIE PRIOR posted for duty under 2.O. "B" Cav. Bde R ao for temporary duty. Leons. (Dufferey) arrives at about 2.30pm but owing to detention whilst being fought against was not would under after dark much shelling	W/
4-11-14. — do —	Luffey Column arrives 2.30am. some firing in neighby leaves not completed until 5pm. R. 1 mile S.W. of YPRES — BAILLEUL R. ao f Divisional Train, YPRES. Lieut. RUSSELL enemy all day	W/
5-11-14. — do —	R ao fo 4th Luffey Column arrived at 1am. R.P. as yesterday, left chateau and proceeded to bivouac 500 yards further down road (from YPRES). Fire in town everafter laymen on to 'Carlile' 3 a/c men killed — 4 wounded	W/
6-11-14 — do —	In bivouac all day. Pandd R.P. as yesterday. Burial of Cpl HENNEY Dr SEARLEY — who with in Ypres last night found ammund and placed under convoy	W/

1247 W 3299 200,000 (E) 8/14 J.B.C. & A. Forms/C.2118/11

Army Form C. 2118.

WAR DIARY
or
INTELLIGENCE SUMMARY

(Erase heading not required.)

Instructions regarding War Diaries and Intelligence Summaries are contained in F. S. Regs., Part II. and the Staff Manual respectively. Title pages will be prepared in manuscript.

Hour, Date, Place		Summary of Events and Information	Remarks and references to Appendices
6-11-14	YPRES.	Supply Column arrives 5pm	MJ
7-11-14	-do-	In bivouac all day. Ration Column arrives 3pm.	MJ
8-11-14	-do-	Remained at bivouac all day. R. knocks S.W. of YPRES on BAILEUL Road, yesterday. HENNEY & SEARLEY trench found.	MJ
9-11-14	-do-	HENNEY & SEARLEY tried by F.G.C.M. — both for "when on active service being drunk on duty post." at 11am transport moved back to Chateau we left on Thursday last. Men bivouacked in trenches made by French. R.R.P. on for yesterday. Supply Column arrives 4pm	MJ
10-11-14	-do-	At Chateau all day. HENNEY sentenced to 5 years hard labour. SEARLEY sentenced to (5 years remitted) R&RP as yesterday. Men 2 yours [?] came on.	MJ
11-11-14	-do-	Remained at Chateau and bivouac all day. R.R.P. as yesterday. Supply Column arrived 3pm.	MJ
12-11-14	-do-	Same arrangements as yesterday. Lieut RILEY joined today. R.R.P. as yesterday.	MJ

Army Form C. 2118.

WAR DIARY
or
INTELLIGENCE SUMMARY

(Erase heading not required.)

Instructions regarding War Diaries and Intelligence Summaries are contained in F. S. Regs., Part II. and the Staff Manual respectively. Title pages will be prepared in manuscript.

Hour, Date, Place		Summary of Events and Information	Remarks and references to Appendices
13-11-14.	YPRES	Still at Chateau and bivouac. R.R.P. as yesterday. Supply Column arrived 2 p.m.	M/
14-11-14	- do -	R.R.P. as before. Also accommodation. Supply Column arrived about 3-30 p.m.	M/
15-11-14	- do -	Accommodation, R.R.P. as yesterday which sleeping of the French Supply Column activates lines. Supply Column arrived 3 p.m. in lieu of 3 return buses issued today — much appreciated by the men.	M/
16-11-14	- do -	Still at Chateau & R.R.P. as yesterday. Supply Column arrived 2 p.m. first convoy of supplies after six times and tubes received today.	M/
17-11-14	- do -	At Chateau bivouac as day yesterday. Supply Column arrived 3 p.m. Driver HILL HORNE and HOPKINS arrived today.	M/
18-11-14	- do -	R.R.P. & accommodation as yesterday. Column arrived 2 p.m. Hill return to Captain CORFIELD	M/
19-11-14	- do -	R.R.P. accommodation as yesterday. Snow today for first time. Move to HAZEBROUCK tomorrow morning.	M/

Army Form C. 2118.

WAR DIARY
or
INTELLIGENCE SUMMARY

(Erase heading not required.)

Instructions regarding War Diaries and Intelligence Summaries are contained in F. S. Regs, Part II. and the Staff Manual respectively. Title pages will be prepared in manuscript.

Hour, Date, Place		Summary of Events and Information	Remarks and references to Appendices
30-11-14	YPRES.	Reveille at 4.30 a.m. Marched at 6 a.m. in column to HAZEBROUCK commencing march on roads in horse piquetting. Arriving at HAZEBROUCK at 9 a.m. Billeted at farm from A.S. MERVILLE Road. No leave today owing to unsettled nature of billets.	
31-11-14	HAZEBROUCK	Leave made above from Units — R — MORBECQUE — R.R's — Div A.S.C. – 3rd at billets of 6 Bty R.H.A. – but Southern delivered direct to some units. Those Batteries of R.H.A. now with Divisional Troops.	M/
22-11-14	— do —	R — MORBECQUE, R.R's as yesterday. Came went to ST OMER Transport to 6 Bulgarian movement tonight. Biscuits gone.	M/
23-11-14	— do —	R.R's + accommodation as yesterday. Redistribution of affairs suspended in supply duties & accommodation today, mica affairs from tomorrow. Lieut RILEY posted to 7 Sub Park as Regimentmaster.	M/
24-11-14	— do —	R.R.'s + accommodation as yesterday. Captain Friggatt invalided home yesterday & another took over duties today. Regn. affair working.	M/

Supply affairs
Capt J.A. CORFIELD
C/(Lt H. PEEBLES
Capt H. MOLYNEUX
Lieut J.E. KEECHER

Regimenting affairs
2/Lt J.A.H. WATERS
2/Lt E. KLINGENSTEIN
Lieut M.D. RILEY
2/Lieut J.B. TREND

WAR DIARY
or
INTELLIGENCE SUMMARY

(Erase heading not required.)

Army Form C. 2118.

Hour, Date, Place		Summary of Events and Information	Remarks and references to Appendices
25-11-14	HAZEBROUCK	R.R.P. and accommodation unsettled. Lt SWEENEY C.S. sharp eng.- about 7 town.	H/
26-11-14	— do —	R.R.P. and Cavalry Brigade accommodation same. Transport for 2" Cavalry Brigade sent to that Brigade today. Pte GRIESBACH to rept Depot ROUEN.	H/
27-11-14	— do —	Accommodation, R.R.P. as before.	H/
28-11-14	— do —	Lt (A/Capt) Detonie - 1 Nco and 5 men joined to 6th Cavalry Brigade. Capt RUSSELL returned with cook book. No news with part of men getting R.R.P. and accommodation same.	H/
29-11-14	— do —	Orders received for Captains BERGER & ROYSTON PIGOTT to proceed to Enlargement on arrival. Drivers HORNE & HOPKINS emp/here to announce sent to announce. M.T. Depot ROUEN - also 4 M.T. Drivers surplus to requirements of 6th Cavalry Bde. R.R.P. &c. remain the same	H/
30-11-14	— do —	8 Htrs surplus requirements & Cav Bde to announce H.T. Depot ROUEN. 1 N.C.O. & Drivers in places of Griesbach arrived today. R.R.P. and Billets same as yesterday	H/
1-12-14	— do —	3 Can Rein notified of their inspection to-day also. R.R.P. &c as before. Drivers training for inspection by H.M. the King tomorrow at 9 am.	H/

WAR DIARY
or
INTELLIGENCE SUMMARY

(Erase heading not required.)

Army Form C. 2118.

Instructions regarding War Diaries and Intelligence Summaries are contained in F. S. Regs., Part II. and the Staff Manual respectively. Title pages will be prepared in manuscript.

Hour, Date, Place	Summary of Events and Information	Remarks and references to Appendices
2-12-14. HAZEBROUCK.	R. 2 p.m. MORBECQUE. R.P. Sheets arrived. Inspection by H.M. The King. Captain BRANDER proceeded to No. 1 Depot ROUEN for duty. Capt. E.T. SAVAGE joined and assumed command. Ammunition Park. Transport of Supply column of 7 Division joined today, twice be reviewed 10 am tomorrow.	W
3-12-14 —"—	R. 11 am MORBECQUE 11 am R.P. Sheets arrived. Yesterday Transport review to unite with option of those for 1st Life Guards.	W
4-12-14 —"—	Captain A. BERGER A.S.C. left today on leave pending examination to met. motor car of D.D.M.S. 2nd Army Corps found in attaching new little driver & another man found unconscious. Acting Sergt WALTHUIS A.S.C. found under arrest (drunk).	W
5-12-14 —"—	R. R.P. Sheets arrived. Kent for 1st Life Guards were promoted.	W
6-12-14 —"—	R. R.P. Sheets arrived. Received STEENBECQUE	W

1247 W 3299 200,000 (E) 8/14 J.B.C. & A. Forms/C. 2118/11.

Army Form C. 2118.

WAR DIARY
or
INTELLIGENCE SUMMARY

(Erase heading not required.)

Instructions regarding War Diaries and Intelligence Summaries are contained in F. S. Regs., Part II. and the Staff Manual respectively. Title pages will be prepared in manuscript.

Hour, Date, Place	Summary of Events and Information	Remarks and references to Appendices
7-12-14. HAZEBROUCK	R.R.Ps & billets same along on Mr Sgt Foley & 3 men evidence at F.G.C.M at MERVILLE.	W
8-12-14. " "	R. 10am MORBECQUE R. Ps billets same at late WALTHUIS taken by F.G.C.M + requisition	W
9-12-14. " "	R. R. P. & billets same	W
10-12-14. " "		
11-12-14. " "	R.R.Ps billets same Lce Cpl.S. A.S.C. (Clerk in the Coy appointed to Base.	W
12-12-14. " "	R. R. Ps & billets same. Pte ESTICK sent to the Base.	W
13-12-14. " "	R,R,Ps & billets same. Driver SLACK & ROWLINGS + 5 men from Field Ambulances Amylrea to Armoured H.T. Depôt. Driver DRAPER & RIDDLE joined no change billets tomorrow	W
14-12-14. " "	Left billets 10·15am proceeded via LA MOTTE- VIEUX BERQUIN- BAILLEUL & ST JANS CAPPEL. arrived to new billets & 1 mile W of BAILLEUL on CAESTRE Rd. R.P. in centre of village	W

Army Form C. 2118.

WAR DIARY
or
INTELLIGENCE SUMMARY
(Erase heading not required.)

Instructions regarding War Diaries and Intelligence Summaries are contained in F. S. Regs., Part II. and the Staff Manual respectively. Title pages will be prepared in manuscript.

Hour, Date, Place	Summary of Events and Information	Remarks and references to Appendices
15-12-14. ST JAN'S CAPPEL	Billets, R & R.Ps as yesterday. Orders received to return to HAZEBROUCK tomorrow.	
16-12-14 "	Left in column at 8.15am. Arrived HAZEBROUCK 3pm & occupied old billets. R. MORBECQUE 3 men. R.Ps as before - 1y at units' quarters &	
17-12-14 HAZEBROUCK	R.R.P. Billets same	
18-12-14 "	R. R.Ps Billets same. Leave for the Division re-opened.	
19-12-14 "	R. R.Ps & Billets same.	
20-12-14 "	— " —	
21-12-14 "	— " —	
22-12-14 "	— " —	
23-12-14 "	— " —	
24-12-14 "	— " —	
25-12-14 "	— " —	
26-12-14 "	— " —	
27-12-14 "	— " — Princess Mary's gift distributed	
28-12-14 "	— " —	

WAR DIARY
or
INTELLIGENCE SUMMARY

Army Form C. 2118.

(Erase heading not required.)

Hour, Date, Place	Summary of Events and Information	Remarks and references to Appendices
29-12-14. HAZEBROUCK	R.R.P° Biscuits jam	
30-12-14 "	Rouchan chouqent to EBBLINGHEM. R.R.P° ann Biscuits jam.	
31-12-14 "	R. R. P° + biscuits jam.	

War Diaries

of

Divisional A.S.C

3rd Cavalry Division

January 1915 to December 1915

Jan 1915

121/4194

H⁰Qrs A.S.C. 2nd Cavalry Division.

Vol II. 1 - 31.1.15

Ad Oro 1 Corps
3rd Cavalry Division

Army Form C. 2118.

WAR DIARY
or
INTELLIGENCE SUMMARY
(Erase heading not required.)

Instructions regarding War Diaries and Intelligence Summaries are contained in F.S. Regs., Part II. and the Staff Manual respectively. Title pages will be prepared in manuscript.

Hour, Date, Place	Summary of Events and Information	Remarks and references to Appendices
1st Jan, 1915 – HAZEBROUCK	Rendezvous – MORBECQUE. Refilling Point, Farm Belbecq. HAZEBROUCK. Billet, Farm Belbecq, HAZEBROUCK.	RV
2nd Jan, 1915 – " –	R. R. P. billets the same.	RV
3rd Jan, 1915 – " –	R. R. P. billets the same. Temp. Lieuts. R. CLIBBON, S.F.S. JOHNSON, and E.W. BAKER reported at HQrs. 3rd Cav.Div. These officers are A.S.C. and were sent to 3rd Cav.Div. Supply Column who reported their arrival. Driver WOODLEY brought from 6th Cav. Field Amb. under arrest for desertion.	NV
4th Jan, 1915 – " –	R. R. P. billets the same. Orders received for MAJOR N.R. LIDDELL to take up duties as O.C. A.S.C. 2nd Cav. Div. A.S.C. MAJOR D.C.E. GROSE, A.S.C. appointed S.S.O. 3rd Cav. Div. in place of MAJOR LIDDELL. Communication from D.A.D.T. to the effect that one of the three officers who joined yesterday should be appointed Requisition Officer, consequent on LIEUT. JAH. WATERS doing duty as Adjutant.	RV
5th Jan, 1915 – " –	R. R. P. billets the same. – do –	RV
6th Jan, 1915 – " –	STEENBECQUE. Railhead changed to	RV

Army Form C. 2118.

WAR DIARY
or
INTELLIGENCE SUMMARY

(Erase heading not required.)

Hd Qrs 2 Corps
2nd Army

Instructions regarding War Diaries and Intelligence Summaries are contained in F. S. Regs, Part II. and the Staff Manual respectively. Title pages will be prepared in manuscript.

Hour, Date, Place	Summary of Events and Information	Remarks and references to Appendices
7th Jan, 1915. HAZEBROUCK	R. R.F. billets same. Temp. Lieut. CLIBBON posted to 6th CAV. BDE. as Brigade Transport Officer. Temp Lieut E.W. BAKER posted to 8th Cav. Bde. as B.T.O.	N/-
8th Jan, 1915. — —	R. R.F. billets same. Driver Woodley sentenced to six months hard labour for desertion. Medically inspected handed over to the A.P.M. Temp. Lieut. S.T.S. JOHNSON appointed Requisition Officer vice Temp. Lieut. J.A.H. WATERS.	N/-
9th Jan, 1915 — —	R. R.F. + billets the same. Notification from D. of S. that CAPT. CORFIELD will shortly be sent home.	N/-
10th Jan, 1915 — —	R. R.F. billets the same. Lieut. PUGH admitted Hosp. 9th =	N/-
11th Jan, 1915 — —	R. R.F. billets the same.	N/-
12th Jan, 1915 — —	— do —	N/-
13th Jan, 1915 — —	— do — . MAJOR D.C.E. GROSE reported for duty.	N/-
14th Jan, 1915 — —	— do —	N/-
15th Jan, 1915 — —	— do — . CAPT. F.A. CORFIELD + CAPT. C.K. ARCHIBALD appointed Temporary Majors.	N/-
16th Jan, 1915 — —	R. R.F. billets the same.	N/-
17th Jan, 1915 — —	— do —	N/-

Army Form C. 2118.

Hone Albert
3rd Cav D.

WAR DIARY
or
INTELLIGENCE SUMMARY

(Erase heading not required.)

Instructions regarding War Diaries and Intelligence Summaries are contained in F. S. Regs., Part II. and the Staff Manual respectively. Title pages will be prepared in manuscript.

Hour, Date, Place	Summary of Events and Information	Remarks and references to Appendices
18th Jan., '15. HAZEBROUCK.	R. R.F. + billets the same. Temp. Lieut. DURNFORD to go from Ammunition Park to ISBERGUES to superintend hire price. Temp. Lieut. R. JOHNSON-TAIT, R.A.M.C. joined Supply Column as Medical Officer in charge. 17-1-15.	KH
19th " "	R. R.F. + billets the same.	KH
20th " "	— do — Temp. Lieut. BENTLEY, A.S.C. posted to 6th Cavalry Brigade to understudy CAPT. PEEBLES. 3 A.S.C. drivers surplus to Establishment 1st Cav. Field Ambulance to Horse Transport Depot, ABBEVILLE.	KH
21st " "	R. R.F. billets the same.	KH
22nd " "	— do —	KH
23rd " "	— do — Lt. CAMPBELL A.S.C. joined 3rd Cav. Divl. Ammunition Park for duty. R. R.F. billets the same. Temp. LIEUT. G. KLINGENSTEIN	KH
24th " "	A.S.C. lift 6th Cav. Bde. (R.O.4.) proceeded to G.H.Q. for duty with D.D. of S.	KH
25th " "	R. R.F. billets the same.	KH
26th " "	— do — Notification of Inspection by G. in - C.	KH

HQrs A.S.C.
3rd Cav Div

WAR DIARY
or
INTELLIGENCE SUMMARY
(Erase heading not required.)

Army Form C. 2118.

Instructions regarding War Diaries and Intelligence Summaries are contained in F. S. Regs., Part II. and the Staff Manual respectively. Title pages will be prepared in manuscript.

Hour, Date, Place	Summary of Events and Information	Remarks and references to Appendices
27 Jan '15. HAZEBROUCK.	R.R.F. killed the same. 3rd Cav Divl. A.S.C. (HQrs. Supply Column & Ammunition Park) inspected by Sir John French, C. in C., in the field to the right of the HAZEBROUCK — SOUVERAIN ROAD (Map ST. OMER H — 1/50,000) at 12 noon. The C. in C. expressed his approval of the work performed by the A.S.C. particularly in this Div. Temp. Lieut. C. COTTON, A.S.C. joins as Requisitioning Officer, 6th Cav. Bde.	
28th Jan '15	R.R.F. billets the same.	
29th " "	" " "	
30th " "	" " "	
31st " "	R.R.F. billets the same.	

Feb. 1915

121/4506

Hd Qrs. A.C. 3rd Cavalry Division.

Vol III. 1 – 28.2.15

Army Form C. 2118.

WAR DIARY
or
INTELLIGENCE SUMMARY
(Erase heading not required.)

Instructions regarding War Diaries and Intelligence Summaries are contained in F. S. Regs., Part II. and the Staff Manual respectively. Title pages will be prepared in manuscript.

Hour, Date, Place	Summary of Events and Information	Remarks and references to Appendices
1st Feby, 1915. HAZEBROUCK.	Rendezvous the same (MORBECQUE) - Refilling Point the same (FARM DELBECQ, HAZEBROUCK). Billet the same (FARM DELBECQ, HAZEBROUCK.) LIEUT. COLONEL W.S. SWABEY taken over duties of A.D. of S.+T., Cavalry Corps and MAJOR A.R. LIDDELL those of D.A.D. of S+T., Cav Corps. Also to Cavalry Corps Hd. Qrs. 5 other ranks. 2 O.R. taken on strength. MAJOR D.C.E. GROSE assume duties of Commandant	
2nd Feby, 1915. — " —	R.R.P. + billets the same. 2nd Lieut. A.S.C. 2/Lt. TERRILL appd. Sup Off. 2/Lt. O'MALLEY and 2/Lt. DRAPER appd. Supr. for that	
3rd Feby, 1915. — " — AND POPERINGHE.	Part of Division (about one half) proceeded to YPRES to take over section of trench line for 10 days. Marched in two echeloups via STEENVOORDE, POPERINGHE, and VLAMERTINGHE to YPRES. Proceeded from here MAJOR F.A. CORFIELD + one other rank, with 1 car + 1 lorry. R.R.P. + billets the same for HAZEBROUCK. For that part of Division in YPRES area Refilling Point at POPERINGHE (10.30 a.m.). A.S.C. billet at POPERINGHE.	
4th Feby, 1915. — " —	R. + billets the same. Refilling Point same place at 2.30 p.m.	
5th Feby, 1915. — " —	R.R.P. + billets the same.	
6th Feby, 1915. — " —	— do —	
7th Feby, 1915. — " —	— do —	

Army Form C. 2118.

H.Qrs. 3rd Cav. Div. A.Q.

WAR DIARY
or
INTELLIGENCE SUMMARY

(Erase heading not required.)

Instructions regarding War Diaries and Intelligence Summaries are contained in F. S. Regs., Part II. and the Staff Manual respectively. Title pages will be prepared in manuscript.

Hour, Date, Place	Summary of Events and Information	Remarks and references to Appendices
8th Feby., 1915. HAZEBROUCK & POPERINGHE	R. R. P. & billets the same.	
9th Feby., 1915 " — " —	" — " —	
10th Feby., 1915 " — " —	R. & billets the same. POPERINGHE R. S. changed to ST. JANS TER BIEZEN.	
11th Feby., 1915 " — " —	R. R. P. billets the same, as 10th.	
12th Feby., 1915. HAZEBROUCK	— do — . MAJOR F.A. CORFIELD and Party	
13th Feby. " — " —	return to HAZEBROUCK	
" — " —	Rendezvous MORBECQUE. Re-filling point, HAZEBROUCK. Billets HAZEBROUCK, on return of Division from trenches. Re-filling point billet changed from FARM DELBECQ, (FERME DELRUYNE) HAZEBROUCK, to farm of M. DESIRE DAVID, RUE DE BIRCUS, HZ.BRK. MAJOR F.A. CORFIELD takes over duties of Senior Supply Officer, 3rd Cavalry Division. CAPT. H.W. PEEBLES joins up Supply Officer, Divisional Troops. Temp. Lieut. P.H. BENTLEY taking the place of CAPT. PEEBLES as Supply Officer, 6th Cavalry Bde.	
14th Feby. " — " —	R. R. P. billets the same.	
15th Feby. " — " —	— do —	

1247 W 3299 200,000 (E) 8/14 J.B.C. & A. Forms/C. 2118/11.

Army Form C. 2118.

WAR DIARY
or
INTELLIGENCE SUMMARY
(Erase heading not required.)

Instructions regarding War Diaries and Intelligence Summaries are contained in F. S. Regs., Part II. and the Staff Manual respectively. Title pages will be prepared in manuscript.

3rd Cav. D. Amb. Col.

Hour, Date, Place	Summary of Events and Information	Remarks and references to Appendices
1915		
16th Feby. HAZEBROUCK	R.A.P. & billets the same.	N.Y.
17th Feby. — " —	— do — Capt. C.J. MARTIN, A.S.C. posted as O.C. 3rd Cav.A.P. Divisional Ammunition Park.	N.Y.
18th Feby. — " —	R.A.P. & billets the same. Lieut. C.C.H. KING, A.S.C. joins 3rd Cavalry Divisional Supply Column for duty.	N.Y.
19th Feby. — " —	R.A.P. & billets the same.	N.Y.
20th Feby. — " —	"	N.Y.
21st " — " —	— do —	N.Y.
22nd " — " —	— do — 3 Supply details joined from 3rd Cav.Supply Col.	N.Y.
23rd " — " —	— do — 1 Sgt. T. driver joined from B.H.T.D. LE HAVRE	N.Y.
24th " — " —	— do —	N.Y.
25th " — " —	— do — Capt. C.J. MARTIN joins as O.C. 3rd Cav. Div. Ammunition Park.	N.Y.
26th " — " —	— do —	N.Y.
27th " — " —	— do —	N.Y.
28th " — " —	— do —	N.Y.

March 1915.

Hd. Qrs. ASC. 3rd Cavalry Division

Vol IV 1 – 31.3.15.

Army Form C. 2118.

WAR DIARY
or
INTELLIGENCE SUMMARY   Hayes. Col. 3/ Cav D--

(Erase heading not required.)

Instructions regarding War Diaries and Intelligence Summaries are contained in F. S. Regs., Part II. and the Staff Manual respectively. Title pages will be prepared in manuscript.

Hour, Date, Place	Summary of Events and Information	Remarks and references to Appendices
1st. March-1915.- HAZEBROUCK.	Rendezvous MORBECQUE. Re-filling point HAZEBROUCK. billets at FERME DELRUYNE, RUE DE SIRCUS, HAZEBROUCK. One H.T. driver from 7th Cavalry Brigade.	NYY
2nd. -"-	R. A. F. + billets same. 1 Supplies School from Hazgo.	NYY
-"-	2 H.T. drivers from B. H.T.D. LE HAVRE. 1 Officer's Charger + 1 light draught horse arrived.	of
3rd. -"-	R. A. F. + billets same. (1 H.T. driver to A.H.T.D. ABBEVILLE. 4-3-15.)	NYY
4. -"-	- do -	NYY
5. -"-	- do -	NYY
6. -"-	- do - 1 H.T. driver to 4th Cav Bde. Lce. Browne sent from 6th Car Bde. to 3rd Div. Train. 1 Riding Horse transferred to Col. Major D.C.E. GROSE. invalided.	NYY
-"-	NORTH SOMERSET YEOMANRY. Ot transport of NTH. SOMERSET YEOMANRY.	off
7. -"-	R. A. F. + billets same.	NYY
8. -"-	- do - O.C. A.S.C. inspected transport of	NYY
-"-	3RD DRAGOON GUARDS. Pt. FIRMAN confined for drunk on sentry. Pte. SCOTT B Echelon transport to MORBECQUE to take car M1501 to GENNEVILLERS.	
9. -"-	- do - R. A. F. billets same.	
10. -"-	- do - Orders received for Division to concentrate at Aviatorial Rendezvous, BOIS D'AVAL at 7am on 11th B Echelon transport to assemble at same hour in present billets. Dr. FIRMAN remanded for F. G. C. M.	NYY
11. -"-	Reveille at 4 am. Ready to march at 7am but no orders received. Remained hooked in until	NYY

1247 W 3299 200,000 (E) 8/14 J.B.C. & A.   Forms/C. 2118/11.

Army Form C. 2118.

WAR DIARY
or
INTELLIGENCE SUMMARY
(Erase heading not required.)

Adjgs A.a. 3rd Cavalry Division

Instructions regarding War Diaries and Intelligence Summaries are contained in F. S. Regs., Part II. and the Staff Manual respectively. Title pages will be prepared in manuscript.

Hour, Date, Place	Summary of Events and Information	Remarks and references to Appendices
11th March '15 (continued)	about 3-30 p.m. - Supply Column came up to Refilling Point at 4-30 p.m. Lt. FIRMAN tried by Field General Court Martial on charge of omission on sentry and sentenced to six months imprisonment with hard labor.	MDy
12th March '15. HAZEBROUCK.	Lt. NOLAN admitted Hospital. R.H.Q. billets same. 'B' Echelon transport of Brigade received orders to move up to Regts. Divisional troops to stand fast for present. Column (Supply) came up about 2 p.m.	MDy MDy MDy
13th March, 1915.	R.H.Q. billets same. Lt. FIRMAN handed over A.P.M. S/2005B Pte. G. MOORE, 6th Car.Bde. committed suicide 10 a.m. To be ready to move at 1 hour & 40 minutes notice.	MDy
14th " "	- do -	
15th " "	R.H.Q. billets same. Capt. JOSEPH called about 11 a.m. with orders to be prepared to move at one hour after 1 a.m. "Degree of readiness" afterwards made 1 hour & 40 minutes. Lt. NOLAN sent from Hospital to Base.	MDy
16th " "	R.H.Q. billets same. Degree of Readiness altered to 3 hours & 40 min.	MDy
17th " "	- do - See WALTHUIS & WALL proceeded to report	MDy
18th " "	on duty at office of D.A.A.G. (Cav.) R.H.Q. billets same. O.C. A.S.C. inspects 'B' Echelon transport of CFAS.	MDy
19th & 20th & 21st "	- do - Lt. HIBBERT sent from 6th Cav.Bde. to Indian Corps Troops Supply Column 204	MDy
22nd " "	- do - R.H.A. Brigade moved up to firing line. Refilling Point at crossroads ½ mile N.W. of ST. JANS CAPPEL for R.H.A.	MDy

WAR DIARY or INTELLIGENCE SUMMARY

Army Form C. 2118.

Hdqrs. 3rd Cav. Bde. A.S.C.

Hour, Date, Place	Summary of Events and Information	Remarks and references to Appendices
23.3.15. HAZEBROUCK.	R.R. & billet the same. Re-filling points for R.H.A. Amm. Column same (ST JANS CAPPEL) & "L" & "H" Batteries at LOCRE. Lt WEATHERLEY sent to 3rd Cav. Mechvt. Anvl. train from 1st Cav.R.	NVY
24.3.15 "	R.R. & billet same. Artillery Re-filling points same. Lieut. E.G.M. LAKE arrived with one O.R. & proceeded to 7th Cavalry Brigade same day. (from Supply Depot, BOULOGNE)	NVY
25.3.15 "	R.R. & billet same. Artillery Re-filling point same. Major D.C.E. GROSE, O.C. A.S.C. inspected transport of Essex Yeomanry	NVY
26.3.15 "	R.R. & billet same. Artillery Re-filling point same. O.C. A.S.C. inspected "A" Echelon transport as follows:— 7th Cavalry Field Ambulance at RENESCURE 10 am. " " " BLERINGHAM 10.45 am. " " " BOESEGHEM 11.45 am.	NVY
27.3.15. "	R.R. & billet the same. R.H.A. Re-filling point same. Following changes in duties of A.S.C. Officers in the Division took place on this day:— Temp. Capt. C.R. MOLYNEUX from S.O., 7th Cav. Bde. reported to O.C. 1st Divisional Train for duty. Temp. Lieut. C. COTTON, from R.O. 6th Cav. Bde. to S.O., 7th Cav. Bde. Temp. Lieut. N.D. RILEY, from R.O., 7th Cav. Bde. to R.O., 6th Cav. Bde. Lieut. E.G.M. LAKE, from Supply Depot, BOULOGNE to R.O., 7th Cav. Bde. These changes to date from 25-3-15.	NVY

Army Form C. 2118.

WAR DIARY
or
INTELLIGENCE SUMMARY
(Erase heading not required.)

Hazen Brigade Dvl ASC

Hour, Date, Place	Summary of Events and Information	Remarks and references to Appendices
28-3-15. HAZEBROUCK.	R. L. P. & billet the same. R.H.A. L.L. filling limit same.	NIY.
29-3-15	R. L. P. & billet the same. R.H.A. R.L. as follow Amm & Column same (ST JANS CAPPEL). "E" & "K" Batteries at LOCRE. "G" Battery at LA CLYTTE. Lts. HUDSON and GRIFFITH from 1st Cav Bde. to 4th Divisional train for duty.	NIY. NIY.
30-3-15.	R. L. P. & billet the same. R.H.A. L.L. same.	
31-3-15.	No change.	

121/5099.

April 1915
Apl 5

HdQrs A.V.C. 3rd Cavalry Division

Vol V 1-30.4.15

Army Form C. 2118.

WAR DIARY
or
INTELLIGENCE SUMMARY
(Erase heading not required.)

Headqrs.
3rd Cav. Divl. A.S.C.

Instructions regarding War Diaries and Intelligence Summaries are contained in F.S. Regs, Part II. and the Staff Manual respectively. Title pages will be prepared in manuscript.

Hour, Date, Place	Summary of Events and Information	Remarks and references to Appendices
HAZEBROUCK 1-4-15	Rendezvous – MORBECQUE. Re filling point HAZEBROUCK. Billet at farm of DESIRÉ DAVID, RUE DE SIRCUS, HAZEBROUCK. Refilling points for R.H.A. Ammunition Column at ST JAN CAPPEL – "G" & "K" Batteries at LOCRE.	MY
" 2-4-15	R.R.Ps. & Billets the same.	MY
" 3-4-15	– do – O.C. A.S.C. MAJOR D.C.E. GROSE, inspected transport of the First Royal Dragoons.	MY
" 4-4-15	R.R.Ps. & Billets the same.	MY
" 5-4-15	– do –	MY
" 6-4-15	– do –	MY
" 7-4-15	– do – . . . S.S.M. NICHOLLS from 7th Cav. Field Ambulance & G.H.Q. troops train, on promotion. 2 Butchers & 6 Bakers joined from HAVRE. 2nd Lieut. L.J.B. DURNFORD, 3rd Cav. Ammunition Park, to 4th Divisional Supply Column. (8-4-15).	MY
" 8-4-15	R.R.Ps. & Billets the same. Stos. MEE & WESTERN to 6th Cav.Bde., TREBLE & DIMMOCK to 7th Cav.Bde. MAXWELL & HARRISON to 8th Cav.Bde for duty with Supply Officers.	MY
" 9-4-15	R.R.Ps. & Billets the same.	MY
" 10-4-15	– do – . Sto. YOUNIE proceeds from 6th Cav.Bde to HAVRE, being surplus to Establishment of Clerks.	MY

Army Form C. 2118.

WAR DIARY
or
INTELLIGENCE SUMMARY

(*Erase heading not required.*)

Head Qrs. 3rd Cav Brd. Art.

Instructions regarding War Diaries and Intelligence Summaries are contained in F. S. Regs, Part II. and the Staff Manual respectively. Title pages will be prepared in manuscript.

Hour, Date, Place		Summary of Events and Information	Remarks and references to Appendices
11-4-15	HAZEBROUCK.	R. R. G's. Billets the same.	MY
12-4-15	"	-do- 6th Cav. Field Ambulance. Pte Bleasdale and Lawton joined from	MY
13-4-15	"	R. R. G's. Billets same. Pte. Wright to 3rd Cav Supply Column. Pts. Morgan and Manthorpe from Havre. 3 KT drivers surplus to Establishment 6th Cav. Field Ambulance sent to A.H.T.D. Abbeville.	MY
14-4-15	"	R. R. G's. Billets same.	MY
15-4-15	"	-do- 2 sits. 2nd Life Guards rendezvous at A.S.C. Billets. 2 G.S. Wagon turnouts 1st Life Guards. handed over to 1st Cav. Brd. Col.	MY
16-4-15	"	R. R. G's. Billets same. Pte. Lovett and Beasley from 7th Cav Bde. to B.A.T.D. Havre, being surplus to Establishment of Elévers.	MY
17-4-15	"	R. R. G's. Billets same. Sen. C.O. H.S. Spracklan, arrived from HQrs. 5th Cav Bde. + sent to 7th Cav Bde. Ambce.	MY
18-4-15	"	R. R. G's. Billets same. -do-	MY
19-4-15	"	R. R. G's. Billets same. Major Corfield on leave.	MY

WAR DIARY or INTELLIGENCE SUMMARY

Army Form C. 2118.

HQrs. 3rd Cav. Bde. A&Q

Hour, Date, Place	Summary of Events and Information	Remarks and references to Appendices
20.4.15. HAZEBROUCK	R. R'ts. & Billets the same. 22 G.S. Wagons (horse drawn wagons) are handed over to the 2nd Line Divisional Train at MERVILLE.	VBY
21.4.15 — " —	R. R'ts. & Billets the same.	VBY
22.4.15 — " —	— do —	VBY
23.4.15. — " —	Notification recd. 9.30 am from G.S. that Division likely to move this morning at very short notice. Operation order at 11.30 am. Brigade to march from Rendezvous as rat times stated. "B" Echelon Transport to remain ready to move in present billets. Major Copeland recently from leave. A.A. & Q.M.G. forwarded copy of Cav. Corps telegram directing 3rd Cav. Supply Columns to proceed in rear of its fighting troops + return South via ABEELE, cross roads on frontier due north of GODEWAERSVELDE through this town MEECKIS.	VBY

WAR DIARY

or

INTELLIGENCE SUMMARY

Army Form C. 2118.

Hqrs. 3rd Cav Bde. cal

(Erase heading not required.)

Hour, Date, Place	Summary of Events and Information	Remarks and references to Appendices
24.4.15 HAZEBROUCK &c.	R. RF's Billets the same for "B" Eschelon, also for R. JTY. for "A" Eschelon various points in the vicinity of GODEWAERSVELDE. Notification from GHQ at 7pm that "B" Eschelon must be ready to move at one hour's notice. 2nd O. R.Q. Shracklan from 1st Cav Eschelon Comb, to H.Qrs. 3rd Cav.?	MY
25.4.15 HAZEBROUCK & STEENVOORDE.	R. RF's Billets the same for "B" Eschelon & R.H.A. " " " " "A" Eschelon at various points in the vicinity of STEENVOORDE. Major CORFIELD, S.S.O, Capt. PEEBLES, S.O. Sril. Troops, + 2nd Lieut JOHNSTON, with 4 O.R move up to STEENVOORDE. MY	MY
26.4.15 " "	R. RF's Billets same as for 25". 2nd C. S. M. J. FOLEY confirmed in his provisional rank. transferred to Eng Comd for duty with new Divin.	MY
27.4.15 " "	R. RF's Billets same	MY
28-30.4.15 " "	— do —	MY

May 1915

121/5482

H.Q.rs A.C. 3rd Cav: Division

Vol VI 1 — 31.5.15

Army Form C. 2118.

Hodges, Sirl, L.S.C.
Butler, Sirl, L.S.C.

WAR DIARY
INTELLIGENCE SUMMARY
(Erase heading not required.)

Instructions regarding War Diaries and Intelligence Summaries are contained in F. S. Regs., Part II. and the Staff Manual respectively. Title pages will be prepared in manuscript.

Hour, Date, Place	Summary of Events and Information	Remarks and references to Appendices
1st May, 1915. HAZEBROUCK & STEENVOORDE	E. Echelon — Rendezvous at MORBECQUE — Refilling point at Billets, i.e. farm of DESIRE DAVID, RUE DE SIRCUS, HAZEBROUCK. A. Echelon in the vicinity of STEENVOORDE. Billets for O.C. at GRANDE PLACE, STEENVOORDE. R.H.Q. Refilling point at LOCRE.	MJ
2nd May/15 — do —	No change in L.R.G's or Billets. Major F.A. CORFIELD leaves for England to take up appointment at War Office.	MJ
3rd May/15 — do —	No change in L.R.G's or Billets. Notification received from G.S. at 4 a.m. that "B" Echelon must be ready to move at 6.30 am 4th May. This move was cancelled at 1 pm. Capt. J.B. PEEBLES takes over the duties of Senior Supply Officer, 3rd Cavalry Division.	MJ
4 May, 1915 — do —	No change in L.R.G's — Billets.	MJ

1247 W 3290 200,000 (E) 8/14 J.B.C. & A. Forms/C. 2118/11.

WAR DIARY or INTELLIGENCE SUMMARY

Army Form C. 2118.

HQrs. 3rd Cav. Div: A.S.C.

Hour, Date, Place	Summary of Events and Information	Remarks and references to Appendices
5th May, 1915. HAZEBROUCK & STEENVOORDE	No change in R.H.Q's or Billets.	WJ
6th " "	— do —	WJ
7th " "	The Division moved back to permanent billets in the vicinity of HAZEBROUCK. Capt. A.L. STEWART, R.S.O, Cav. Corps Railhead, reports for duty. Lt. GATRELL joins from Cav. Corps Railhead ("S" Depot Unit of Supplies) Ref. A.J. 5/MS from B.A.T.D. HAVRE. Two Draught horses evacuated to Mobile Veterinary Section - one lame and one mare in foal. Refilling	WJ
8th " "	Rendezvous for Division at MORBECQUE. Refilling Points at billets of the various Units in the vicinity of HAZEBROUCK. Capt. STEWART takes over duties of Supply Officer, Divisional Troops.	WJ
9th " " HAZEBROUCK	The Division again moved up to firing line. Capt. Peebles, S.S.O, Capt STEWART. S.O, Divl Troops, & Lt. JOHNSTON, with 5 O.R. moved up to XXXXX STEENVOORDE. "B" Echelon remains behind in billets at HAZEBROUCK. Refilling Points at various hours in the vicinity of STEENVOORDE and POPERINGHE.	WJ

Army Form C. 2118.

WAR DIARY
or
INTELLIGENCE SUMMARY
Headqrs. 3rd Cav. Divl. A.S.C.

(Erase heading not required.)

Hour, Date, Place	Summary of Events and Information	Remarks and references to Appendices
10th May 1915. HAZEBROUCK & STEENVOORDE	No change in R.R.'s or Billets. The Serv's to 1st Cav. Bde. on transfer of one trucker (Pte Knight) from that Bde. to 8th Cav Bde.	MY.
11th " "	R.R. & Billets the same. Took over forage cart turnout from 2nd Cav. Field Ambulance, 2nd Cav: Div: Lt. 107. Wright sent to Cav. Corps Railhead for duty with "D" Depot	MY.
12th " "	R.R. & Billets the same.	MY.
13th " "	- do -	MY.
14th " "	- do -	MY.
15th " "	- do -	MY.
16th " "	- do -	MY.
17th " "	- do - Took over two light draught horses from the Field Remount Depot at THIENNES.	MY.
18th to 20th " "	No change in R.R. & Billets	MY.

WAR DIARY
or
INTELLIGENCE SUMMARY

Army Form C. 2118.

Hour, Date, Place	Summary of Events and Information	Remarks and references to Appendices
21st May 1915. HAZEBROUCK STEENVOORDE &c	A R.E. + Billets the same. Our light draught horses sent to field remount depôt, THIENNES. Our heavier reported from base Horse transport Depôt. Have in reply to our letter (?) + S.G. (enquire) who are to be sent to (By. T. & Jo. E.) Souvre.	
22nd " "	R.E. + Billets the same. Capt. H.W. PEEBLES appointed Temporary Major. Temp. Lieut. J.A.H. WATERS appointed Temp. Capt. 2nd Lieut. Estcourt — Temp. Lieut. 2nd Lieut. S.F.S. JOHNSTON appointed Temp. Lieut. All to date from 26th March, 1915. London Gazette 21-5-15. Two Joiners (Everett & Hankin) to I. Coy Cole; two carpenters (Brown & Smith) & two Joiners (Gossitt & Wilson) to 8th Cav. Bde. rice two Joiners (Hobson & Galt) The Division moves back to permanent billets in the vicinity of HAZEBROUCK.	NY
23rd " "	Rendezvous MORBECQUE. Shifting down Billets in the vicinity of HAZEBROUCK. Divisional Headquarters move to RENESCURE — Major PEEBLES + Lieut. S. JOHNSTON take up Billets at RENESCURE.	NY

Army Form C. 2118.

WAR DIARY
or
INTELLIGENCE SUMMARY
(Erase heading not required.)

Hodgson
3rd Cav: Div: A.S. Corps

Instructions regarding War Diaries and Intelligence Summaries are contained in F. S. Regs., Part II. and the Staff Manual respectively. Title pages will be prepared in manuscript.

Hour, Date, Place		Summary of Events and Information	Remarks and references to Appendices
May, 1915.	HAZEBROUCK	R.R.G. + Billets the same, except for 2nd N. Oro.	
25th May, 1915	"	R.R.B. of which moved RENESCURE. Orange Cart H.Q. base on establishment for postal services attached to 2nd Sqdrn.	MY
26th	"	R.R.G. + Billets the same.	MY
27th	"	- do -	MY
	RENESCURE	- do - Hqrs. A.S.C. move to RENESCURE at farm 250 yds north of Railway crossing on the RENESCURE - LE NIEPPE road.	MY
28th	"	No change in R.R.G. or billets.	MY
29th	"	3rd Cav: Div: goes up to the trenches east of YPRES in relief of 2nd Cav.Div. Capt. Stewart Supply Officer 3rd Cav. troops takes up billet at STEENVOORDE. "B" Echelon remains behind	
	STEENVOORDE	in billets at RENESCURE +c.	MY
30th	"	R.R.G. + Billets the same.	MY
31st	"	- do -	MY

June 1915

121/5829

3rd Cavalry Division

HdQrs. R.E. 3rd Cav: Division

WAR DIARY or INTELLIGENCE SUMMARY

Army Form C. 2118.

H/qtrs. 3rd Can Bn. A.S.C.

Hour, Date, Place	Summary of Events and Information	Remarks and references to Appendices
1st June, 1915. RENESCURE STEENVOORDE	Rendezvous & Refilling points same as for 31st. Billet changed to farm of M. FELIX DE SERARTE, RUE D'OUDOF, RENESCURE.	C/4
2nd — " —	R.R.P. & Billets unchanged. L.A.P.M.R. reports (on 2nd inst.) M/40043 Pte H. PAYNE (6.C.F.A.) Killed, M/408135 Pte G.P. HORSFALL (6.C.F.A.) wounded, and M/9714 Pte L. BUSHELL (8.C.F.A.) wounded, all on 2/5-	C/4 (on 2nd inst.) C/4
3rd — " —	R.R.P. & Billets same as on 2nd.	C/4
4th — " —	— do —	
5th — " —	— do —	
6th — " —	Division moved back to Billets in HAZEBROUCK area. Leave to England commencing.	C/4
7th — " —	Rendezvous at MORBECQUE. Refilling point Billets at various places in the vicinity of HAZEBROUCK. Major D.C.E. GROSE proceeds to England and Major G.E. HILLS takes over command of 3rd Can. Div. Col.	C/4
8th — " —	R.R.P. & Billets the same. 7/19.75 L.Cpl. Hasscard (ionied for duty for Base with H.Qrs.)	C/4

WAR DIARY
or
INTELLIGENCE SUMMARY

(Erase heading not required.)

Army Form C. 2118.

Headqrs. 2nd Cav. Divl. J.S.C.

Instructions regarding War Diaries and Intelligence Summaries are contained in F.S. Regs., Part II. and the Staff Manual respectively. Title pages will be prepared in manuscript.

Hour, Date, Place	Summary of Events and Information	Remarks and references to Appendices
9th June, 1915. RENESCURE	H.Qs. + Billets unchanged. Lieut. Johnston proceeds on 5 days leave to England.	CN
10th — —	No change in H.Qs. or Billets. T/Sub Lt. N.S. Clifford to 5th Reserve Regt. 7/3/15 N. Nesants to 6th Cav. Bde. H.Qs. + Billets same.	
11th — —	— do —	
12th — —	— do —	
13th — —	Maj. Stills proceeds on 3 days leave to England. Orders received for Capt. A.S. Stewart to take up duties of S.S.O. 1st Cav. Dn. 2nd Lieut. J. Johnston to be appointed Supply Officer, Divisional Troops, vice Capt. Stewart	CN
14th — —	H.Qs. + Billets the same. 2nd Cavalry Division to be inspected by the Commander-in-Chief on Wednesday, 16th inst.	CN
15th — —	H.Qs. + Billets as for 14th. Commander-in-Chief's inspection now postponed to a later date not yet fixed. Notification that Temp. Lieut. C.E.G. NYE from Supply has been ordered to report for duty as Regtl. Off. 2nd Cav. Divl. Troops, vice Lieut. Johnston.	CN

WAR DIARY
or
INTELLIGENCE SUMMARY

(Erase heading not required.)

Army Form C. 2118.

Hd.Qrs. 3rd Cav: Divl: ASC

Hour, Date, Place	Summary of Events and Information	Remarks and references to Appendices
16th June, 1915 Renescure	H.Q. & Billets unchanged. Lieut. C.C.H. KING, A.S.C. Supply Column, evacuated sick	CM
17th June, 1915 - " -	H.Q. & Billets unchanged. $ - 16th S/Lieut. A.L. STEWART proceeded to 1st Cavalry Division as Senior Supply Officer. + 1/Lieut. S.T.S. JOHNSTON, A.S.C, took over duties of Supply Officer, 3rd Cavalry Divisional Troops, 3rd Cav. Divn: vice Capt. STEWART. S/22209 Sgt. P. GATRELL, 1st Cav.Divl. Col. 17th - Two Leavers. No. S4/07285 Pte. S. BROWN, & No. S4/07071 Pte. H. MARA from No. 3 B.S. T Sqdt, HARRIE. Capt/Actg.Capt. WATERS to England on 3 days leave.	CM
18th June 1915 - " -	H.Q. & Billets the same. Commander- in-Chief inspected 3rd Cavalry Division. Parade state A.S.C. - 5 Officers Off 100 O.R. Maj. PEEBLES to England on 3 days leave.	CM
19th - " -	H.Q. & Billets the same. Major C.E. HILLS, O.C. A.S.C. inspected transport of Essex Yeomanry. Echelon. A.	

Army Form C. 2118.

WAR DIARY
or
INTELLIGENCE SUMMARY   HQrs 3rd Cav Bde A.C.

(Erase heading not required.)

Instructions regarding War Diaries and Intelligence Summaries are contained in F. S. Regs., Part II. and the Staff Manual respectively. Title pages will be prepared in manuscript.

Hour, Date, Place	Summary of Events and Information	Remarks and references to Appendices
20th June, 1915, RENESCURE	R.R.S. + Billets the same. Temp Lieut. C.E.G. NYE A.S.C. joins as Requisitioning Officer. Divisional Troops S. Capt. R. DAVIES, A.S.C. Ammunition Park, to go to Royal Flying Corps, + will be relieved by Temp Lieut. KIRKE, A.S.C.	CM
21st - " - - " -	R.R.S. + Billets unchanged. Temp. Lieut. P.G.S. CLARKE, R.S.C. ordered to join 3rd Cav Bde Supply Column to complete establishment.	CM
22nd - " - - " -	No change in R.R.S. or Billets.	CM
23rd - " - - " -	- do - S/Lieut. KIRKE joins 30L Cavalry Ammunition Park.	CM
24th - " - - " -	R.R.S. + Billets unchanged. No. 6 A.C. inspected. Transport of 3rd Dragoon Guards. Ech. "A" + "B", + that of "B" Echelon, 7th Cap: Field Ambulance + Billets same.	CM
25th - " - - " -	R. Cap. "A" S. Transport of the 1st Royal Dragoons Ech. + Billets same.	CM
26th - " - - " -	R.R.S. + Billets same. 1st Cav Bde. Transport M.T. "B" Ech. inspected by the O.C. A.C.	CM

Army Form C. 2118.

WAR DIARY
or
INTELLIGENCE SUMMARY
(Erase heading not required.)

Hd Qrs 3rd Cav. Bde. AC1

Hour, Date, Place	Summary of Events and Information	Remarks and references to Appendices
27th June '15. RENESCURE.	R.R.G. & Billets as for 26th	CA
28th " "	— do —	CA
29th " "	— do —	CA
30th " "	— do —	CA

E.J. Stokes Major
D.A.A.G.
3 C.D.

July 1915
2m/5
6

3rd Cavalry Division

51/6160

H'd Q'rs A.S.C. 3rd Cavy. Div'n

Vol VIII

G

July 1915

Army Form C. 2118.

WAR DIARY
or
INTELLIGENCE SUMMARY

Headqrs. 3rd Cav. Bde. AR-6

(Erase heading not required.)

Instructions regarding War Diaries and Intelligence Summaries are contained in F. S. Regs., Part II. and the Staff Manual respectively. Title pages will be prepared in manuscript.

Hour, Date, Place	Summary of Events and Information	Remarks and references to Appendices
1st July 1915, Reresscure	In same billets. T/Lt. Myg A.S.C. on leave to England. O.C. A.S.C. Lt.Col. Somerset. Inspected A & B Echelons of ammunition Yeomanry and visited 3rd Fed. Sqn. in evening with D.A.D.O.S. to hold experiment with brakes on G.S. limbers	ELL
2nd "	In same billets. O.C. A.S.C. Inspected Transport of H.Q. son 3 Cav. Bde. A.S.C., and visited Director of Supplies at G.H.Q, in evening.	CH
3rd "	In same billets. O.C. A.S.C. proceeded to Tournehem, and on to Hevres on duty.	CH
4th "	In same billets. O.C. A.S.C. visited M.W. Imp. Yeomanry, and again inspected G.S. limbers (C Sqn. only). The Qr. master of 3" D GS do arranged, brought a complete G.S. limber outfit for demonstration purposes. Lieuts. Bromham, and Jesse visited Hd. Qrs. 3 Cav. Bde. A.S.C. T/Major H. Peebles, A.S.C. on leave to England.	CH

Army Form C. 2118.

WAR DIARY
or
INTELLIGENCE SUMMARY

(Erase heading not required.)

Headqrs 3rd Cav. Div: A.P.6.

Instructions regarding War Diaries and Intelligence Summaries are contained in F.S. Regs., Part II. and the Staff Manual respectively. Title pages will be prepared in manuscript.

Hour, Date, Place	Summary of Events and Information	Remarks and references to Appendices
5th July 1915. RENESCURE.	In same billets. O.C. M.S.C. visited D. of S. G.H.Q. on duty. A.D.M.S. (Col. Hardy) visited 3 Cav. Div. H.Q. on A.S.C. visited C.C. workshops at STEENBECQUE. Then proceeded to WILLIAM WARDRECQUES & and made arrangements to inspect Transport of 7th Cav. Bde — /CAPTA. H. WATERS (ADJUTANT) attended a "Sanitary lecture" at WARDRECQUES - by A.D. M.S. 3 CAV. DIV.	
6th July 1915. "	In same billets. O.C. M.S.C. visited 7th Cav. Bde — and inspected Transport of H.Q. Sqn — also "A" Echelon 7th Cav. Res, Auble —	Ct
7th " "	In same billets. O.C. M.S.C. inspected A. & B. Echelons Transport of 2nd Life Guards, and Leicstir Yeomanry. Lieut: Lieut: C.W. DAVEY joined from HAVRE for duty with 7th Cav. Brigade:	Ct
8th " "	No change in Rendezvous. Re filling Lorries or Billers. Inspected A & B Echelon 1st Life Gds.:	Ct
9th " "	R.P. Billeer the same. O.C. A.R.C. inspected, at LA PIERRE, "A" Echelon Transport of the 8th Cavalry Brigade as under :—	Ct

WAR DIARY or INTELLIGENCE SUMMARY

Army Form C. 2118.

Headqrs. 3rd Cav. Divl. A.S.C.

(Erase heading not required.)

Hour, Date, Place		Summary of Events and Information	Remarks and references to Appendices
9th July 1915 (continued)		Escort Germany at 9.30 a.m. R. Horse Gds. at 10.15 a.m.	CM
10th July 1915	RENESCURE	10th Hussars at 11 a.m. Temp. Lieut. C. COTTON to Base Supply Dept. HAVRE, on being relieved by 2/Lt. R.P.O. — Billets same as on 9th. 2nd Temp. Lieut. G.W. Savery	CM
11th	— " —	No change in Rendezvous, Refilling Points or Billets.	CM
12th	— " —	—do— Received 4 forage cart turnout (mules) from 9th B.F.A., in anticipation of 3 artificers being added to Est.	CM
13th	— " —	—do— OC Adv[anced] H Echelon Transport of 9th Cav. Field Ambulance.	CM
14th	LESPINOY	Billets changed to LESPINOY. OC A.S.C. takes over charge of the M.Or. motor cars from the A.P.M.	CM
15th	LESPINOY	R.P.O. — Billets as to 14th i.e. Refilling point for Arl. HQrs. at HEURINGHEM, for "B" Echelon of HQ. Ambcs, Divnl. tc. at HAZEBROUCK, & working parties at NEUVE EGLISE and SAILLY SUR LA LYS.	CM

Army Form C. 2118.

WAR DIARY
or
INTELLIGENCE SUMMARY

(Erase heading not required.)

Hd. Qrs. 3rd Cav: Bri'l. Arm

Hour, Date, Place	Summary of Events and Information	Remarks and references to Appendices
15th July (continued)	06. A.S.C. inspected, in morning, 1st Echelon 6th Cav. Field Ambulance.	CA
16th July 1915. LESPINOY	No change as regards 1st R.P. or billets.	CA
17th — " —	— do —	
18th — " —	— do —	
19th & 20th — " —	— do — 20. 06. A.S.C. inspected 2nd Echelon 6th Cav. Field Ambulance. 8. Ech. 8th Amb. Hd. Qr. Transport, 6th Cav. Bde. North Somerset Yeomanry.	CA
21st " "	R.R.F's & billets unchanged. No.NCB/7625 Pte CHERRY, R.M., to stay to 6th Cav Bde. to take over Daimler Car M #23, then being driven by an N.C.O. of R.E.	CA
22nd " "	R.R.F's & billets same. Temp. Lieut. C.E.G. NYE transferred to Chemical Branch.	CA

Army Form C. 2118.

WAR DIARY
or
INTELLIGENCE SUMMARY
(Erase heading not required.)

Head qrs. 3rd Cav. Bde. A.C.

Hour, Date, Place	Summary of Events and Information	Remarks and references to Appendices
23rd July 1915. LESPINOY	Rendezvous. Re-filling points hitted as for 22nd.	C4
24th " "	Temp. 2/Lt. H.V. LISTER joins 3rd Cav. Bde. Supply Column for duty vice Temp. Capt. J.S. TEULON.	C4
" "	R.R. of Billets unchanged. Temp. Capt. A.P. WILLIAMS, A.S.C., 3rd Cav. Bde. Ammunition Park departs for England for duty with New Armies and Temp. Lieut. R.H. STEVENS arrives for duty in relief. Board of Officers assembled at WARDRECQUES to enquire into loss of W.D. bicycle (folding pattern) No. 19009. They find bicycle was stolen by some person or persons unknown.	C4
25th " "	No change in R., R.P. or Billets.	C4
26th " "	— do —	C4
27th " "	— do —	C4
28th " "	— do — One mule evacuated to 14th M. Vet. Sect. with broken knee.	C4
29th " "	— do —	C4
30th " "	— do — Notification that 2/Lieut. (S.R.) C.D. ROTCH, A.S.C. has been ordered to join I relief of 2/Lt. NYE.	C4
31st " "	— do —	C4

121/6550

Aug- 1915

3rd Cavalry Division

O.C. A.S.C. 3rd Cav. Division

Vol IX

from 1st to 31st August 1915

Army Form C. 2118.

Hargis, 3rd Cav.
Divnl. 226.

WAR DIARY
or
INTELLIGENCE SUMMARY

(Erase heading not required.)

Instructions regarding War Diaries and Intelligence Summaries are contained in F. S. Regs., Part II. and the Staff Manual respectively. Title pages will be prepared in manuscript.

Hour, Date, Place	Summary of Events and Information	Remarks and references to Appendices
1st August, 1915. LESPINOY.	Rendezvous, Refilling Points, Billets same as for 31st. Notification from A.D.S.+T. that from 3rd August, Railhead will be changed to ARQUES. Temp. Offic. r/Lieut. M.A. TOOMEY joins 3rd Cav. Div. Supply Column.	
2nd " "	R. R, & Billets unchanged. Temp: Lieut: (S.R.) C.D. ROTCH, A.S.C. reports from 1st Cav. Div. Supply Column for duty as Requisitioning Officer, Divisional Troops. One H/Shft driver (M/T 34721 S/SMART, J.W.) accompanied this officer.	CM
3rd " "	R. R. & Billets unchanged. 7/29329 Dr DUGGAN, D. admitted Hospital. (Rheumatism). Railhead changed to ARQUES and Rendezvous	CM
4th " "	R. R. & Billets as 3rd. Temp. 2/Lt. H.V. LISTER, A.S.C. leaves 3rd Cav. Div. Supply Column for No. 8 Ammn Sub Park. 3rd Cav. Ammnt. Park moved to ENQUIN LES MINES.	CM
5th " "	No change in Rendezvous, Refilling Points or Billets.	CM

Army Form C. 2118.

WAR DIARY
or
INTELLIGENCE SUMMARY

(Erase heading not required.)

Hd. Qrs.
3rd Cav. Div. A.S.C.

Hour, Date, Place	Summary of Events and Information	Remarks and references to Appendices
6th Aug. 1915. LESPINOY.	Proceeded to CAPELLE-SUR-LA-LYS but billets there being found unsuitable, proceeded to FAUQUEMBERQUES where suitable accommodation was found.	CH
7th Aug. 1915. FAUQUEMBERQUES.	Rendezvous unchanged. Refilling point in FAUQUEMBERQUES vicinity. Billets for A.6. Hd. Qrs. at FAUQUEMBERQUES. Car No. 1796 broken down, sent to F.A.W. Unit for thorough overhaul repair.	CH
8th - " -	R.R.S. Billets unchanged. Hd.Qrs. of Supply Col. changes to Mairie, ARQUES.	CH
9th - " -	- do -	CH
10th - " -	- do -	CH

WAR DIARY or INTELLIGENCE SUMMARY

Army Form C. 2118.

Headquarters
3rd Cav. Divl: A.S.C.

Hour, Date, Place	Summary of Events and Information	Remarks and references to Appendices
11th Aug, 1915. FAUQUEMBERQUES	Rendezvous. Refilling points & billets unchanged. T/29329 Lt: Duggan, S. discharged from hospital.	C/1
12th " "	R.A.S.C. Billets unchanged. Lt Col Duggan, D, surplus to establishment of H.Q.rs. 3rd. Cav. Divl Col to Supply Officer, 7th Cavalry Brigade to complete Est. - Lieutenant Officer i/c of S.O. Ion. Who to 3rd Cav. Col. Workshop Temporarily attached. Car for thorough overhaul. Repair. Ford car	C/1
13th " "	R.A.S.C. Billets unchanged. Temp. Lieut. J.A.L. CAESAR from 3rd Cav. Dn. Supply Column to G.H.Q. Troops Supply Column. 700 men from Division to Armentieres for trench digging. Lt Bentley S.O. 6 Bde posted to that place for supply duties. Rations for French digging parties to be drawn from 1st Army rail head La Gorgue.	C/1

Army Form C. 2118.

WAR DIARY
or
INTELLIGENCE SUMMARY
(Erase heading not required.)

Headquarters
3rd Cavalry Divisional A.S.C.

Instructions regarding War Diaries and Intelligence Summaries are contained in F.S. Regs., Part II. and the Staff Manual respectively. Title pages will be prepared in manuscript.

Hour, Date, Place	Summary of Events and Information	Remarks and references to Appendices
14th Aug 1915. FAUQUEMBERGUES	A.R.F. & fleet unchanged. 7/5056 Dr Barrett, J. admitted Hospital.	CA
15th "	A.R.S. & fleet unchanged. Approval received for the addition of 3 artificers (1 Shoeing Cpl, 1 Saddler & 1 S.rC.S.) with Mallow Cart & horse to Establishment of A.S.C. Helps. to the purpose of carrying out light running repairs to vehicles & harness &c. (Authy: W.O. ltr. 131/6080 of 11/8/15.)	CA
16th "	No change in A.R.F. & fleet.	CA
"	— do —	CA
17th "	Cr. No 1796 returned from D.A.W. Unit thoroughly retested & repaired. Accident to 9.9.t Co. no fault of driver. Mansiff Ambulance broken axle on road had the team in.	CA

1247 W 8299 200,000 (E) 8/14 J.B.C. & A. Forms/C. 2118/11.

Army Form C. 2118.

Headquarters
3rd Cavalry Divisional A.S.C.

WAR DIARY
or
INTELLIGENCE SUMMARY

(Erase heading not required.)

Instructions regarding War Diaries and Intelligence Summaries are contained in F. S. Regs., Part II. and the Staff Manual respectively. Title pages will be prepared in manuscript.

Hour, Date, Place	Summary of Events and Information	Remarks and references to Appendices
18th Aug. 1915. FAUQUEMBERGUES.	R. R. S. & fields unchanged.	C/I
19th " "	— do —	C/I
20th " "	— do —	C/I
21st " "	— do — Major C.E. Hills, A.P.C., on 70 days leave to England.	C/I
22nd " "	No change in R. R. F. & o. Billets.	C/I
23rd " "	— do —	

1247 W 3299 200,000 (E) 8/14 J.B.C. & A. Forms/C. 2118/11.

Army Form C. 2118.

WAR DIARY
or
INTELLIGENCE SUMMARY
(Erase heading not required.)

Headquarters,
3rd Cavalry Divisional, A.S.C.

Instructions regarding War Diaries and Intelligence Summaries are contained in F. S. Regs., Part II. and the Staff Manual respectively. Title pages will be prepared in manuscript.

Hour, Date, Place	Summary of Events and Information	Remarks and references to Appendices
24th Aug. 1915. FAUQUEMBERGUES.	L.R.F. & Billets unchanged. Received one heavy Draught horse from Base Germany. Wrote to D.A.D.S.R., Cavalry Corps for instructions as to disposal of two surplus mules now with unit.	CM
25th Aug. 15. -"-	R.R.F. & Billets unchanged.	CM
26th " -"-	- do -	
27th " -"-	- do - One L.D. mule to 1st Cav. Field Ambulance through No. 8 Mobile Veterinary Section & one L.D. mule to 1st Army Field Remount Section through No. 9 Mobile Veterinary Section. Both these animals were surplus to establishment. Author. A.A.D.R. Cav. Corps 448, d/. 26.6.15. Receipts for the two mules forwarded to D.A.D.R. Cav. Corps on 28th Aug. Cav 57s F.T.A.N.A. A taking down & transporting	CM

1247 W 3299 200,000 (E) 8/14 J.B.C. & A. Forms/C. 2118/11.

Army Form C. 2118.

WAR DIARY
or
INTELLIGENCE SUMMARY

(Erase heading not required.)

Headquarters
3rd Cavalry Divisional A.S.C.

Instructions regarding War Diaries and Intelligence Summaries are contained in F. S. Regs., Part II. and the Staff Manual respectively. Title pages will be prepared in manuscript.

Hour, Date, Place	Summary of Events and Information	Remarks and references to Appendices
28th Aug. 1915. FAUQUEMBERGUES	Lt. R.J. Phillips unchanged.	A
29 " "	do	A
30 " "	do	A
31 " "	do	A

3rd Cavalry Division

Hd Qrs ASC. 3rd Cavy: Division

Vol X

Sept. 15.

Army Form C. 2118.

WAR DIARY
or
INTELLIGENCE SUMMARY
(Erase heading not required.)

Headquarters,
3rd Cavalry Divisional A.S.C.

Instructions regarding War Diaries and Intelligence Summaries are contained in F.S. Regs., Part II. and the Staff Manual respectively. Title pages will be prepared in manuscript.

Hour, Date, Place	Summary of Events and Information	Remarks and references to Appendices
1st Sept. 1915. FAUQUEMBERGUES	Rendezvous, Refilling points & Billets as p/r 31st Aug/15. G.H.A. is lent to 1st Army, his batteries by 3rd Car. Bde. Lieut. Lewis A.S.C. doing duty as Ferrier Supply Officer. 2/Lt. Roberts Cav. Corps. R.O.	A.
2nd " "	R.P. & Billets the same. 1 Capt. & hoy & Baters on 7 days leave to England. Car No W 1252 sent to G.H.Q. as unserviceable.	"
3rd " "	R.P. & fields unchanged. 22941 L/Saddler Whittaker J. — STR 662 Farrier Johnson fb. reported from Havre to duty with H.Qn. 3rd Cav. Brit. A.P.C.	A.
4th " "	— do — Sniping parties returned	—
" " "	from ARMENTIERES. Wood cutting parties from LA MERPE Lambs car M 111 received & replaces No M 1582 attached H.Qn. 8th Cav Bde.	A.
5th " "	R.P. & Billets unchanged. No 18626 Sergt. Armstrong reported at H.Q. 7th Cav. Bde. from Base. No 55/327 2/Lt Owens H.Q. arrived from base & was sent to General Staff Office for duty.	A.

Army Form C. 2118.

WAR DIARY
or
INTELLIGENCE SUMMARY
(Erase heading not required.)

Headquarters 3rd Cavalry Divisional A.S.C.

Hour, Date, Place	Summary of Events and Information	Remarks and references to Appendices
6. Sept. '15. Tavquemberques	R.R.F. - Billets unchanged. Instructions received to send No. 2/T6062 Sergt. Killeen, A.T. from G.S. Office to the 1st Cav. Bde.	CM
7. Sept. '15. -"-	R.R.F. - Billets the same. No. 2/T6062 Sergt. Killeen A.T. from G.S. office to 1st Cav. Bde. No. 3/T5686 Sergt. Armstrong, V.C. reported H.Qrs. 7th Cav. Bde.	CM
8. " " " -"-	R. R.R. - Billets as for 7th. Sunbeam M. 604 to G.H.Q. as unserviceable. Temp'y. Lt. Johnson on 10 days leave to England. 7th 575 Sept. rec.	
9. " " "	-do- Car No M 15373 received to replace M1804 (Supply Officer, 7th Cav. Bde.) 15686. Sgt. Armstrong K. evacuated to base sick. (8/9/15)	CM
10. " " "	R. R.R. - Billets unchanged. Car M.575 returned from repairs at workshop of 1st Cav. Bde.	CM

WAR DIARY or **INTELLIGENCE SUMMARY** Hdqrs. 3rd Can. Div. Sig. Coy.

Army Form C. 2118.

Hour, Date, Place	Summary of Events and Information	Remarks and references to Appendices
11th Sept. 15. FAUQUEMBERGUES.	R. R.G. & Billets unchanged. Car № 1793 to workshops of 3C.D.A.C. for repair.	
12th " "	R. R.G. & Billets the same.	
13th " "	R. R.G. & Billets the same. 33266 Actg. Corporal Kitchens from 1st Can. Div. office to G.S. office. 78666 Sergt. Armstrong reported on discharge from Hospital. Arrangements made to send him to G.S. office for instruction.	
14th " "	R. R.G. & Billets the same. Sergt. Armstrong sent to G.S. office.	
15th " "	R. R.G. & Billets unchanged.	

WAR DIARY
or
INTELLIGENCE SUMMARY

Army Form C. 2118.

Hdqrs. Indian Cav. Div. A.S.C.

Hour, Date, Place	Summary of Events and Information	Remarks and references to Appendices
16. Sept. 15. FAUQUEMBERQUES.	Lt. R.G. Willets the same. S.Sgt. 35/5330u S.Sgt. R.E. Williams + 35/5346 Sgt. C.S. Reid arrive for instruction in staff office work. Williams sent to G.S. Office and Reid to "Q" Office. Reports to be rendered to A.S.C. Records in a month as to their capabilities. 9705 Sgt. J. Armstrong is taken off into office of O.C. A.S.C. for temporary duty. Car No M559 broken down at G Ome (steering arm &c.) taken to Supply Column for repairs. Supply lorries detached with R.H.A. to load at AIRE up to 6 and including 17th inst. then rejoining Supply Column to loading on under as under normal conditions from 18th inst.	
17th Sept. 15. " "	Lt. R.G. Willets unchanged. Temp. Lieuts. T.E. COBBOLD + C.H. SENDELL, A.S.C. joined for duty. These officers are posted in anticipation of the formation of an Auxiliary Horse Transport Company which will provide for the conveyance of winter blankets and horse rugs.	

WAR DIARY or INTELLIGENCE SUMMARY

Army Form C. 2118.

Head quarters
3rd Cav. Divisional A.S.C.

Hour, Date, Place	Summary of Events and Information	Remarks and references to Appendices
18th September, 1915. FAVQUEMBERGUES	R.E.'s Billets unchanged.	OK
19th "	— do —	OK
20th "	— do — 7.C.B. with B. Echelon Tpt attached to II Army with portion of supply Col. S.E. billets HAZEBROUCK ST SYLVESTRE Ruleing CAESTRE. OK Refilling points at billets in Zaupuemberques vicinity.	
21st "	"B" Echelon transport of 6th Cav. Bde., 6th Cav. Bde., 6th Cav. Field Amb. + Div. +A.S.C. H.Qr. left billets about 1 pm., concentrating under the command of Major C.E. HILLS, H.A.S.C. on the ground East of the river at WESTREHEM, N.E. of DELETTE, and bivouacked. "B" Echelon transport of the 7th Cavalry Brigade, including 7th Cav. Field Ambulance to accompany its Brigade when it moves. Major Hill O.C. A.S.C. took over the duties of Camp Commandant, 3rd Cav. Bn. from Capt. BLATAM FORTH, before leaving FAVQUEMBERGUES 6+8 C.Bs with A Echelon k LABUSIÈRE	OK

Army Form C. 2118.

HdQrs. 3rd Cav. Bde. Sup. Col.
Camp Commandant, Lt. Col. ......

WAR DIARY
or
INTELLIGENCE SUMMARY
(Erase heading not required.)

Hour, Date, Place	Summary of Events and Information	Remarks and references to Appendices
22nd Sept 1915. WESTREHEM.	"B" Echelon remained in Bivouacs at WESTREHEM. Refilling point for "B" Echelon at WESTREHEM. Railhead at ARCQUES. 6 & 6 C.B. & Div. Troops come under I Army.	Camp orders Nos. 1 to 9 issued. Copies are appended. CB
23rd " "	Accommodation Refilling point for "B" Echelon at Westrehem. M.S.V.S. retain also 3 M.M.S proceed to Advanced H.Qrs. at 7 a.m. RAILHEAD ARCQUES. Supply Echelon of S. Col. of 6+6 CB moved to new billet LILLERS, CHOQUES Rd.	Camp orders Nos. 10-12. CB
24th " "	Accommodation refilling point for "B" Echelon as for 23rd. On arrivals redeparture from "B" Echelon see camp orders. Railhead 8 CB + Divisional Troops AIRE " " 6 CB. CHOQUES. Ammunition Park moved to AUCHEL.	Camp orders Nos. 13-16 CB

WAR DIARY
or
INTELLIGENCE SUMMARY

Army Form C. 2118.

O.C. A.S.C. Camp Commandant, 3rd Cavalry Division

Hour, Date, Place	Summary of Events and Information	Remarks and references to Appendices
25th Sept. 1915. WESTREHEM.	"B" Echelon left WESTREHEM at 10 am & arrived at RINCQ at 12.30 p.m. The Echelon bivouacked in the field to the right of the road from that place to MOULIN DE COMTE. T/927 Acting Farrier Sergeant OFFENBURG, W.T., A.S.C. from Divisional Head Quarters to the Advanced Horse Transport Depot at ABBEVILLE, for duty with one of the new Cavalry Divisional Auxiliary Horse Transport Cos., to retain his acting rank. Authority:— A.P.C. Section, Base, No 6232 of 22.9.15 Railheads Same as for 24th :- Rendez-vous on VERMELLES LOOS Rd 11 P.m. 6 & F C.B. in LOOS.	Camp orders 17.22. Refilling point for "B" Echelon at RINCQ. O.C. A.S.C. office established at the Moulin de Comte
26th Sept. 1915. MOULIN DE COMTE and RINCQ.	"B" Echelon remained in bivouac as occupied on 25th. A.S.C. H.Qrs. evacuated one draught & riding horses to 13th M.V. Section & draught horse to H.Q. 3rd Cav. Dn. Rail head 6 C.B. moved to NOEUX LES MINES	

WAR DIARY
or
INTELLIGENCE SUMMARY

(Erase heading not required.)

Army Form C. 2118.

O.C. A.S.C. Camp Commandant, Trafalgar.

Hour, Date, Place	Summary of Events and Information	Remarks and references to Appendices
27th Sept. 15. RINQ – MOULIN LE COMPTE	Re. filling point & accommodation for "B" Echelon as yesterday. Lieut. Roth joins "A" Echelon. (Relieved 25th) Railheads same as for 27th.	Camp Orders 23-24 issued
28th " "	Refilling point & accommodation for "B" Echelon as yesterday. Ptes Hill + Davies b Advanced HQrs at LA BUISSIÈRE. Lt BAKER sent to MAZINGARBE & report to HQrs on duty.	Camp Orders 25 & 26.
29 "	Refilling pt & accomn. 15 lchs. on 28th 6 & 8 C.B. relieved from trenches & Cavalry Amn at Jachin to refit this replaced from G.H.Q. B. Mobile amm. Refilling pt & accomn S. Feb. on 29. & Railhead for 6 & 8. C.B. & Div Troops & ROZIN & Les MINES 6 & 7 C.B. in Billets. Cav 1789 to the Stuhalk.	
30 "		

C. Stubbs Major
O.C A.K.3C.D.

CAMP ORDERS by MAJOR C.E.HILLS.

22nd September, 1915.

1. No horses are to be stabled in any farms or outbuildings in WESTREHEM, owing to mange being prevalent.

2. Estaminets are closed to all troops except between the hours of 11 a.m. and 1 p.m., and 6 p.m. to 8 p.m. All men proceeding to the village will be properly dressed, wearing bandoliers or side-arms.

3. Exercise will take place on the EAST side of the river only - all roads to be kept clear.

4. Orderly Room will be at 9 a.m. daily.

5. Sanitary arrangements will be made by the O.C., Sanitary Sect.

6. Roll Call will be at 8.15 p.m. Lights out 8.45 p.m. Orderly Corporals will parade for orders at 6 p.m. daily.

C. E. H I L L S, Major.
O.C., A.S.C., and Camp Commandant.

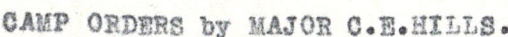

CAMP ORDERS by MAJOR C.E.HILLS.

22nd September, 1915.

7. DEPARTURES.

3 M.M.P., Head Quarters, 3rd Cavalry Division, also A.D.V.S. and staff, will proceed to Advanced Head Quarters at 7 a.m. tomorrow. Current days rations to be taken.

8. POSTAL ARRANGEMENTS.

POST leaves at 10 a.m. and 6 p.m. O's C. Units, "B" Echelon, will arrange to have all letters censored and delivered to the Post Office by 9 a.m. and 5 p.m., where they will be stamped. Deliveries take place at 11 a.m. and 7 p.m.

9. DRINKING WATER.

Great care must be taken over drinking water and no water should be drunk unless treated by the Medical Authorities or boiled.

C. E. H I L L S, Major.

O.C., A.S.C., and Camp Commandant.

CAMP ORDERS by MAJOR C.E.HILLS.

23rd September, 1915.

10. REVEILLE.

Reveille will be at 5.30 a.m.

11. MANURE.

All manure will be removed and stacked in heaps in the field east of the present horse lines and about 50 yards clear of the lines.

12. PUNISHMENTS!

The following punishments have this day been awarded.

Corps	Regtl.No.	Rank & Name	Offence	Punishment
A.S.C.	T/4/071253	Pte.Harrison G.	When on Active Service - drunkeness	28 days Field Punishment No:1.
1/R.Dns.	3243	Pte.McFarlane F.	1. Whilst on Active Service disobeying an order. 2. Entering a cafe during prohibited hours.	14 days Field Punishment No:1.

C.E.HILLS, Major.
O.C., A.S.C., and Camp Commandant.

CAMP ORDERS by MAJOR C.E.HILLS.

24th September, 1915.

13. CAMP ORDERS.

Camp Orders will be issued to O's C., "B" Echelons of the 6th Cavalry Brigade, 6th Cavalry Brigade, R.A.M.C., and Divisional Head Quarters.
These Units will detail a N.C.O. to receive orders at 6 p.m. daily as directed in Camp Order No:6 of 22nd instant.

14. ARRIVALS.

The following arrivals are taken on the strength from the dates stated:-

23.9.15.	3rd Signal Squadron.	3 O.R.	2 horses.
	A.S.C., 6th Cav.Bde.	2	..

15. DEPARTURES.

The following departures are struck off the strength from the dates stated:-

23.9.15.	R.E.Postal Service	1 O.R.			
	Royal Horse Guards	6	..		
	N.Somerset Yeomy.	1	..		
24.9.15.	Rev.A.H.Boyd, C.F.	1	..	2 horses	
	Divl. Headquarters	1	..	1	..
	A.S.C.	1	..		
	A.S.C.Headquarters	1	..	2	..
	3rd Field Sqn R.E.	1	..		
	D.A.D.O.S. & staff.				

16. ~~ARR~~ REPORTS - ARRIVALS AND DEPARTURES.

Units will render arrival and departure reports to this office each evening at 6 p.m.

ARTHUR WATERS , Captain and Adjutant

for O.C., A.S.C., and Camp Commandant.

CAMP ORDERS by MAJOR C.E.HILLS.

25th September, 1915.

17. DIVINE SERVICE.

For R.C. and Wesleyan under arrangements to be made by Chaplains concerned.

18. BOUNDS.

The town on AIRE is out of bounds except to men granted special passes, which will be issued by Camp Commandant at 9 a.m. daily to 5% per Unit for a limited period.

19. SANITATION.

The Sanitary Officer will make all necessary arrangements for latrines and camp sanitation and arrange for drinking water.

20. SICK.

All sick will be seen by the Medical Officer at the Medical Inspection Room at 9 a.m.

21. DEPARTURE.

Act. Farrier Sergeant Offenburg, having proceeded to ABBEVILLE, is struck off the strength of Divl.H.Q. from this date.

22. RETURNS.

All Units will render a return by 12 noon tomorrow exact strength of men, horses and vehicles now present with "B" Echelon. All departures and arrivals to be reported daily at 6 p.m. by Orderly Corporals.

C.E.HILLS, Major.

Camp Commandant and O.C., A.S.C.

CAMP ORDERS by MAJOR C.E.HILLS.
───────────────────────────────

27th September, 1915.

23. ARRIVALS.

The following arrived on the date stated and are taken on the strength accordingly:-

26.9.15.	Essex Yeomanry	1 Officer.
		2 O.R.
		4 horses.

24. DEPARTURES.

The following departed on the date stated and are struck off the strength accordingly:-

26.9.15.	H.Qrs., A.S.C.	3 horses.
	N.Somerset Yeomanry	1 O.R.
	Hd.Qrs., 6th Cav.Bde.	1 O.R. (R.E.)
	3rd Dragoon Guards	1 O.R.
	Essex Yeomanry	4 O.R.
		5 horses.

C.E.HILLS, Major,

Camp Commandant and O.C.A.S.C.

CAMP ORDERS by MAJOR C.E.HILLS.
———————————

28th September, 1915.

25. ARRIVALS.

The following arrived on the dates stated and are taken on the strength accordingly:-

26.9.15.	Sanitary Section.		25 O.R.	
27.9.15.	R.Horse Guards.		6 ..	
	13th M.Vet.Sect.		1 ..	
	Essex Yeomanry.	1 Officer		3 horses.
	N.Somerset Yeo.		2 ..	4 ..
28.9.15.	H.Q., 6th Cav.B.		20 ..	
	3rd Dragoon Gds.		5 ..	
	1st R.Dragoons		4 ..	
	N.Somerset Yeo.		16 ..	
	10th R.Hussars.		10 ..	
	Essex Yeomanry.		6 ..	
	R.Horse Guards.		5 ..	
	R.H.A.		1 ..	

26. DEPARTURES.

The following departed on the dates stated and are struck off the strength accordingly:-

26.9.15.	1st R.Dragoons		1 O.R.	
27.9.15.	20th M.Vet.Sect.		19 ..	19 horses.
	N.Somerset Yeo.		1 ..	
	13th M.Vet.Sect.		2 ..	
	Essex Yeomanry	1 Officer	1 ..	
28.9.15.	H.Q., 6th Cav.B.	1 ..	1 ..	3 ..
	H.Q., A.S.C.		2 ..	
	3th C.F.Amb.	1 ..		
	6th C.F.Amb.	2 ..	2 ..	

C.E.HILLS, Major.

Camp Commandant and O.C., A.S.C.

CAMP ORDERS by MAJOR C.E.HILLS.

30th September, 1915.

27. ARRIVALS.

The following arrived on the dates stated and are taken on the strength accordingly:-

29.9.15.	3rd Dragoon Gds.		2 O.R.
	R.Horse Guards.		1 ..
	1st R.Dragoons.		1 ..
	Essex Yeomanry.		2 ..
	H.Q., A.S.C.		1 ..
	13th M.Vet.Sect.		1 ..
	20th M.Vet.Sect.		2 ..
	8th C.F.Amboe.	1 Officer	3 ..
	3rd Field Sqn.		2 ..
	R.H.A.		12 ..
	19th Hussars.		5 ..
	7th C.F.Amboe.		1 ..
	1st Life Guards		4 ..
30.9.15.	H.Q., 8th Cav.B.	1 ..	

28. DEPARTURES.

The following departed on the dates stated and are struck off the strength accordingly:-

30.9.15.	H.Q., A.S.C.	2 O.R.	
	H.Q., 8th Cav.B.		1 horse.

C.E.HILLS, Major.

Camp Commandant and O.C., A.S.C.

3rd Cavalry Division

O.C. W.C. 3rd Cavalry Division

Vol. XL.

Oct /15

WAR DIARY of the Officer Commanding, Army Service Corps, and Camp Commandant, Third Cavalry Division.

1st October, 1915.

WAR DIARY of

The Officer Commanding,

Army Service Corps,

3rd Cavalry Division.

for month of October, 1915.

Army Form C. 2118.

WAR DIARY
or
INTELLIGENCE SUMMARY

(Erase heading not required.)

H.Q. A.S.C. Camp Commandant
3rd Cavalry Division

Hour, Date, Place	Summary of Events and Information	Remarks and references to Appendices
1st Oct., 1915. MOULIN LE COMTE. KING@—	Reconnoitred refilling point for 1st Echelon as yesterday. Railhead for 6 & 8 Cav. & Div. Troops at LILLERS. Wolseley Ambulance of Pt. Cpt. A. evolved a damaged bearing to M. Cav. Gager car broke stub axle & this S.P out of action near side hub wheel. had returned in in the dark from the VERMELLES – LOOS Road. No change in accommodation of refilling points for B. Echelon. Dis. Rlhead 1100Pux LES MINES	Camp Orders 29-31. OK. + Initialled next wire next rec'd. 1st. Supply Column move to Lillers (head at railway agency in west of the town). OK.
2nd " "	" "	Camp Orders 32-33. OK
3rd. " "	Acomdn. H.Q. & B. Ech. unchanged. Roberts G. arrived from 1st Cav. Div. reported to A/Lt/Sgt. 12662 A/Lt/Sgt. Acb. JHQ. Details Divisional JHQ. moved ECQUEDECQUES west of LILLERS. JHQ. 6th Cav. Bde. to TERFAY & JHQ. 8th Cav. Bde. to BURBURE.	OK
4th " "	No change in Recomdn. n R.G — A/L/Sgt. Newman T. reports from H.Q. 2nd Div. Sain & will be retained until arrival of the new Amn. S.R. Co. to which he will be posted. Tsmgr St. Wadeloy F. + admitted Hospital 2/6/15 St. Penningham G. & 1st Cavbde. Pte 73-5 in G. J. Ash, owing to carelessness & driving.	OK

Army Form C. 2118.

WAR DIARY
or
INTELLIGENCE SUMMARY

Camp Commandant
G.H.Q. 3/Edn

(Erase heading not required.)

Instructions regarding War Diaries and Intelligence Summaries are contained in F. S. Regs., Part II. and the Staff Manual respectively. Title pages will be prepared in manuscript.

Hour, Date, Place	Summary of Events and Information	Remarks and references to Appendices
5th Oct. 1915. Moulin le Comte.	No change in accommodation or refilling points for B.Echelon. Major G.F. Archibald O.C. Sig Car Sec. E.Col. on 7 days special leave in England 5th-12th. 3rd Signal Sqn. report four motor bicycles damaged by lorries and one stolen from Signal Office. New Sunbeam Ambulance, 7th Cav. Bde. reported out of action owing to teeth of cross-wheel breaking off. Motorcycles (Rex demand new car tubes) 2nd Army, broken they are still attached. On R.H.Q. NOEUX LES MINES. Supply Col. CHOQUES to PK. ANGEL.	Camp Orders 34 - 35. /CA/
6th "	Refilling point for B.Echelon unchanged. Arriv. H.Q. details & H.Q. A.S.C. move into the vicinity of present camp. "B" Echelon of 1st & 2nd Cav Bdes. move up to their B Echelon. 6th Lt. Murphy J. admitted Hospital. Di R.H.ead in 5th.	Camp Orders 36 - 38. CA/

Army Form C. 2118.

Camp Commandant H.Q. 3rd ~~Cavalry~~ Brown ~~Division~~

WAR DIARY
or
INTELLIGENCE SUMMARY

(Erase heading not required.)

Hour, Date, Place	Summary of Events and Information	Remarks and references to Appendices
7. Oct. 1915: Morchies to Cork.	Accommodation & filling point for "B" Echelon as in use yesterday. "B" Echelon of 3rd Signal Squadron moved up to its "A" Echelon. Sunbeam car M.755 returned from Workshops of I.W.T. Wolseley car M.1793 returned from I.W.T. after repairs to wind-screen. Div R.O. Head CHORGES.	C.H.
8"	R.G. descendes to "B" Echelon. Div. R.O. Ht. as for 7."	C.H.
9" "	Div R.O. Head Qrs. to "B" Echelon & VILLERS & supply Column VILLERS	Cambrai 39–42. C.H.

1247 W 3299 200,000 (E) 8/14 J.B.C. & A. Forms/C. 2118/11.

Army Form C. 2118.

H.Q. and Camp Commandant
3rd Cav. Bde.

WAR DIARY
or
INTELLIGENCE SUMMARY

(Erase heading not required.)

Instructions regarding War Diaries and Intelligence Summaries are contained in F. S. Regs., Part II. and the Staff Manual respectively. Title pages will be prepared in manuscript.

Hour, Date, Place	Summary of Events and Information	Remarks and references to Appendices
10. Oct. 1915. Moulin le Conte.	R.E. harassing parties for 'B' Echelon unchanged. Marched for 'B' Echelon at LILLERS. also for Division	O4
11th	— do —	
12th	— do — Divl. Hdrs. move to BOURECQ. Sergs. Lieut. Kirke, Amn. Park, granted 10 days leave of absence in England. No.796 returned from workshops of 3rd D.T.M.Br.	Camp Orders 43,44. O4
13th	R.C. r Accom. 'B' Echelon as yesterday. also same for Division as yesterday.	O4

1247 W 3299 200,000 (E) 8/14 J.B.C. & A. Forms/C. 2118/11.

Army Form C. 2118.

WAR DIARY
or
INTELLIGENCE SUMMARY

(Erase heading not required.)

O.C. A.S.C. 1 Camp Commandant
2nd Cavalry Division

Hour, Date, Place	Summary of Events and Information	Remarks and references to Appendices
14th Oct., 1916 Moulin le Conte	R.S. raccomm. for "B" Echelon uncharged Division	CM
15th — " —	— do —	CM
16th — " —	— do — T/10/56426 Wheeler Byrne P. + 75/857 Farrier Wilson to join from B.A.T. Depot.	CM
17th — " —	— do —	CM
18th — " —	— do — 75/857 Farrier Wilson M. 6706 Cft. A. to replace 75/6399 Farrier Newman who is sent to Base Hqrs Depot, on being reported upon as inefficient orders for Hola Division From	CM

T.R.H GEO

Army Form C. 2118

H. Col. "Bull" Coast,
1st C. E. Bde, 3rd Cavalry Division

WAR DIARY

or

INTELLIGENCE SUMMARY

(Erase heading not required.)

Hour, Date, Place	Summary of Events and Information	Remarks and references to Appendices
19th Oct 1915. Moulin le Comte.	"B" Echelon left RIMCQ & MOULIN LE COMTE at 9.45 a.m. & marched to FRUGES, there joining up with A Echelon billeting. Intimation received from I.A. & O. Brig. that 3rd Cav. Bde. Auxiliary H.T. will arrive at Fruges on 22nd to report to H.Q. 3 Cav. Divl. Troops replaced at Fruges. Temp. Lieut. C. E. FARRAN on leave to Lt. LILLERS. Divl. H.Q. etc FRUGES.	A
20" -"- FRUGES.	R.R.P. & Billets as yesterday.	A
21" -"- -"-	do -do- Railhead changed to LAMBRES. AIRE. Supply Column moves to LAMBRES. This Divn is on come under Cavalry Corps from this date. 7 Cd refunded from I Army.	A

1247 W 3299 200,000 (E) 8/14 J.B.C. & A. Forms/C. 2118/11.

WAR DIARY
or
INTELLIGENCE SUMMARY H. Q. L. Camp Commandant 3rd Cav. Div.

Army Form C. 2118.

(Erase heading not required.)

Hour, Date, Place	Summary of Events and Information	Remarks and references to Appendices
22nd Oct. 1915. FRUGES.	Rendezvous to 6th Cav.Bde. at ESTREE BLANCHE. + 7th Divisional Troops at HEZECQUE. Temp. Lieut. S.F.S. JOHNSTON to 7th Cavalry Brigade for duty as Supply Officer. Also transferred No. SS/519 S/e. Stevens, P. + No. M6755. S/e. R.Q. Bennie, + can No. M6755. Temp. Capt. G.Y. DAVEY from Supply Officer, 7th Cavalry Brigade to Supply Officer, Div. Troops, bringing with him No. M/036305. Burgess, S/R. + can No. M 15373. Also S4/036309 S/e. West. D. Ammn.R. moved to L/MMBRES.	C.A.
25nd Oct. '15. Fruges.	Lt.Col. Bills. Northcroft as for 22nd. (Colonel C.E. Hills Col. relinquished command of 2nd Cavalry Divisional A.S.C. + proceeded to Havre in charge of base Supply Depot. Major H.W. Riddle. A.S.C. returned temporary command of S.D. A.S.C.	

WAR DIARY
or
INTELLIGENCE SUMMARY

(Erase heading not required.)

Army Form C. 2118.

Hour, Date, Place	Summary of Events and Information	Remarks and references to Appendices
23.10.15 (continued)	Lt. Col. Mills, before proceeding to Havre, handed over the duties of Camp Commandant 2nd Cavalry Division, to Capt. V.E.C. CARNEGY, G.S.O. 3, 2nd Cav. Dn.	J.P.
24.10.15 Dieppe	R'd R.R. Billets & Railhead a/c for 23rd. Capt. Davey granted 7 days leave to U.K.	J.P.
25.10.15 "	Rendezvous, Refilling Points, Billets & Railhead a/c for 24th.	
26.10.15 "	Rendezvous, Refilling Points, Billets, Railhead a/c for 25th. Lieut. Colonel H.E. Cunning arrived to take over duties of O.C. 3rd Cavalry Divisional A.S.C. Supple Sqn. car laid up — telegraphed to Athies Depot for driving level gunion	J.P.

WAR DIARY
INTELLIGENCE SUMMARY

Army Form C. 2118.

H.A.S.C. 3rd Cavalry Divn.

Hour, Date, Place	Summary of Events and Information	Remarks and references to Appendices
27th Oct. 1915 Steenje	Rendezvous, Supplying Points, Railhead &c as for 26th. The three Sections of the line M.T. Co. proceeded at 1 p.m. to join their respective Brigades, carrying rations to & for 26th.	Std
28th	R.R.R. Ella Sellers unchanged. Major H.W. Peebles granted leave to Havre in England from 5.11.15 for 10 days. Instructions received for return of car No 15373 to 9th Cav Bde. Wire received from A.M.T. Depot that spare part required for Sig. Sqn. car will have to be obtained in usual manner, that they cannot give permission transit Depot to obtain part.	Std

WAR DIARY
or
INTELLIGENCE SUMMARY
(Erase heading not required.)

Army Form C. 2118

O.C. 2nd Div. 2nd Kew bn

Instructions regarding War Diaries and Intelligence Summaries are contained in F. S. Regs., Part II. and the Staff Manual respectively. Title pages will be prepared in manuscript.

Hour, Date, Place	Summary of Events and Information	Remarks and references to Appendices
Bruges 29.10.15.	R. R.E. Bldo. + Billets as for 28th. The Auxiliary R.E. Co. moved to CREQUY.	SEL
" 30.10.15.	R. R.E. Bldo., Billets as for 29th. Estimated weekly requirements of Coal sent to A.D.S.T. (65½ tons per week).	AEL
" 31.10.15.	R. R.E. Bldo. Billets unchanged. Digging parties from each Brigade from Field Sqn. to leave tomorrow will be billeted in Lynde. Sereno vicinity. 7/1/2694 D: Warburton. H. 7/30658 D: Hatcherd. J.W. 1-732409 D: Killon. J. Joined from Base Horse Transport Depot, Havre.	SEL

CAMP ORDERS by LEEUT'COLONEL C.E.HILLS.
───────────────────

Q   1st October, 1915.

29. ARRIVALS.

The following arrived on the dates stated and are taken on the strength accordingly:-

28.9.15.	H.Q.6th Cav.B.	1 O.R.	
29.9.15.	do	2 ..	
30.9.15.	H.Q. A.S.C.	1 ..	2 horses.
	13th M.Vet.Sect.	2 ..	
1.10.15.	"C" Battery	3 ..	

30. DEPARTURES.

The following departed on the date stated and are struck off the strength accordingly:-

    1.10.15. "C" Battery   43 O.R.   18 horses.

31. BILLETING.

Any alterations in billets are to be reported to this office the same evening and also to Lieut.Renaud, Interpreter, 8th Cavalry Brigade.

Changes in billets lead to a great deal of work and confusion and billets once taken up should be retained by Units concerned unless it is absolutely necessary to change them for sanitary or other reasons.

        ARTHUR WATERS, Capt.and Adjutant.

          for Camp Commandant and O.C., A.S.C.

CAMP ORDERS by LIEUT.COLONEL C.E.HILLS.
___

3rd October, 1915.

32. ARRIVALS.

The following arrived on the dates stated and are taken on the strength accordingly:-

Date	Unit	Officers	O.R.	Horses
1.10.15.	"C" Battery		4 O.R.	
	6th C.F.A.		1	
2.10.15.	H.Q.6th C.B.		1	2 horses.
	6th C.F.A.	1 Officer	2	
	8th C.F.A.		8	

33. DEPARTURES.

The following departed on the dates stated and are struck off the strength accordingly:-

Date	Unit	Officers	O.R.	Horses
1.10.15.	10th R.Hussars.		10 O.R.	
	Essex Yeomanry.	1 Officer	10	13 horses
	R.Horse Guards.		15	
	H.Q. 6th Cav.B.		1	
2.10.15.	H.Q. A.S.C.		1	
	3rd Dragoon Gds.		11	11
	N.Somerset Yeo.		9	
	13th M.Vet.Sect.		2	
	R.Horse Guards.		4	5
	H.Q.8th Cav.B.		2	
	10th R.Hussars		5	10
	8th C.F.A.		8	
	1st R.Dragoons		8	9

C.E.HILLS, Lieut.Colonel.

Camp Commandant and O.C., A.S.C.

CAMP ORDERS by LIEUT.COLONEL C.E.HILLS.

5th October, 1915.

34. ARRIVALS.

The following arrived on the date stated and are taken on the strength accordingly:-

  3.10.15. 1st R.Dragoons.   1 O.R.
       N.Somerset Yeo.   1 ..
       13th M.Vet.Sect. 1 ..

T/12662 Acting Farrier Sergeant Roberts, G., A.S.C., arrived from 1st Cavalry Division on 3rd instant, and is posted to H.Q.Details.

35. DEPARTURES.

The following departed on the dates stated and are struck off the strength accordingly:-

  3.10.15. 10th R.Hussars   2 horses.
       H.Q.6th Cav.Bde. 1 O.R. 1 ..
       H.Q.8th Cav.Bde. 1 ..
       13th M.Vet.Sect.   4 ..
  4.10.15. H.Q. A.S.C.   2 .. 1 ..
       1st R.Dragoons   6 ..
       H.Q.6th Cav.Bde. 2 ..
       N.Somerset Yeo. 10 ..
       R.Horse Guards.   1 ..
       Essex Yeomanry.   9 .. 2 ..
       3rd Dragoon Gds. 18 ..
       10th R.Hussars.   2 .. 4 ..

C.E.HILLS, Lieut.Colonel.

Camp Commandant and O.C., A.S.C.

CAMP ORDERS by LIEUT. COLONEL C.E.HILLS.

1915.
6th October,

36. WATERING OF HORSES.

Horses are not to be led into water. They must be watered by buckets only. The practice of leading horses into water contaminates the water and leads to disease.

37. ARRIVALS.

The following arrived on the date stated and are taken on the strength accordingly:-

    3.10.15. 3rd Dragoon Gds.   2 O.R.

38. DEPARTURES.

The following departed on the dates stated and are struck off the strength accordingly:-

Date	Unit	Officers	O.R.	Horses
5.10.15.	H.Q.8th Cav.B.		1 O.R.	
	R.Horse Gds.		2	2 horses.
	N.Somerset Yeo.			1
6.10.15.	H.Q.8th Cav.B.		16	16
	13th M.Vet.Sect.		7	7
	3rd Dragoon Gds.		37	46
	1st R.Dragoons		32	39
	N.Somerset Yeo.		34	39
	H.Q. 8th Cav.B. & 20th M.V.S.		19	22
	R.Horse Guards	1 Officer	27	39
	10th R.Hussars	1	13	22
	Essex Yeomanry	1	23	51

C.E.HILLS, Lieut.Colonel.

Camp Commandant and O.C., A.S.C.

CAMP ORDERS by LIEUT.COLONEL C.E.HILLS.

9th October, 1915.

39. DAMAGE TO TREES.

Attention is again drawn to the fact that horses must not be tied to trees. Any trees damaged by horses being tied to them will be paid for by the unit occupying the billet. This order is to be put up in a prominent place in all billets.

40. PASSES.

All passes for AIRE submitted for the signature of the Camp Commandant must bear the initials of the O.C. the unit concerned. *or a officer deputed by him*

41. ARRIVALS.

The following arrived on the date stated and are taken on the strength accordingly:-

```
6.10.15.   "B" Ech.C.F.A.    2 O.R.
8.10.15.   H.Q., A.S.C.      1  ..     1 horse.
```

The latter part of Camp Order No.34 is cancelled and the following substituted:-
No:T/22170 Acting Farrier Sergeant NEWMAN, A.S.C., arrived from Head Quarters, 2nd Divisional Train, on 4th instant, and is posted to Head Quarter Details.

42. DEPARTURES.

The following departed on the dates stated and are struck off the strength accordingly:-

```
5.10.15.   "B" Ech.C.F.A.     1 O.R.
           20th M.Vet.Sect.   1  ..
```

C.E.HILLS, Lieut.Colonel,

Camp Commandant and O.C., A.S.C.

CAMP ORDERS by LIEUT.COLONEL C.E.HILLS.

12th October, 1915.

43. LEAVE.

(1) It is notified for information that, in addition to General and Staff Officers, Officers not below the rank of Lieutenant Colonel, may now travel by the ordinary packet steamers.

(ii) Commencing on the night 15-16 October, 1915, French money of soldiers proceeding on leave will be exchanged at VICTORIA STATION instead of at BOULOGNE as heretofore.

44. DEPARTURE.

1 O.R., 6th C.F.A., proceeded to join "A" Echelon on 10th instant and is struck off the strength accordingly.

C.E.HILLS, Lieut.Colonel,
Camp Commandant and O.C., A.S.C.

Nov-1915

O.C. Adm. 3rd Cav. Bn.

Nov 1915.

Issue XII

WAR DIARY
or
INTELLIGENCE SUMMARY.
(Erase heading not required.)

Army Form C. 2118

Hour, Date, Place	Summary of Events and Information	Remarks and references to Appendices
1st Nov. 1915. FRUGES.	Rendezvous, Rallying points, Billets & Railhead remain as for 31st. T/12694. St. Warburton, W. to 6th Cav. of Punt. T/32400 Dr. Killen, J. to 5th Cav. F.A. to replace Casualties. Digging Party sent to OUDERDOM - Railhead for this party at CAESTRE.	SEL
2nd Nov. 1915. do	R, R.P. billets & Railhead unchanged. Capt. W.O. Campbell, Amm. Park, granted leave of absence to England 4th to 11th	SEL
3rd Nov. 1915. do.	R.R.P. Billets & Railhead as for 2nd. Capt. H.E.H. Daniels, 3rd C.D. Amm. H.T.C. granted leave of absence to England from 4th to 72nd Nov. 15. Further party to Ouderdom for digging	SEL

Army Form C. 2118

O.C. A.S.C. 2nd Cavalry Divn.

WAR DIARY
or
INTELLIGENCE SUMMARY
(Erase heading not required.)

Instructions regarding War Diaries and Intelligence Summaries are contained in F.S. Regs., Part II. and the Staff Manual respectively. Title pages will be prepared in manuscript.

Hour, Date, Place	Summary of Events and Information	Remarks and references to Appendices
4th Nov. 1915. Fruges	Rendezvous, Refilling Points, Billets & Railhead unchanged. Major Little proceeded to England on 10 days leave of absence. Lieut. Borton granted 7 days leave to England.	
5th "	R., R.P., Billets & Railhead unchanged.	See
6th "	R., R.P., Billets & Railhead unchanged. Supple. Party sent to Ordererson for dipping.	See

WAR DIARY
or
INTELLIGENCE SUMMARY

Army Form C. 211

Headquarters
2n Cav. Div. A.S.C.

Hour, Date, Place	Summary of Events and Information	Remarks and references to Appendices
4t Nov 1915. Frupes	Rendezvous, Refilling Points, Billets and Railhead as for 6th.	SEL
6t Nov. 1915 "	R., R.E., Billets & Railhead as for 7th. Lt.Col. H.E. Cuming, O.C. A.S.C. inspected transport of 1st Royal Dragoons at LIGNY LEZ AIRE at 10 a.m. M.268 (Wolseley) car of H.Q. 7th Cav. Bde. broke down at DESVRES level crossing & was towed in.	SEL
9t Nov. 1915 "	R., R.E., Millets & Railhead as for 6th. My 890 car, Bolsoley, broke down near Estrée Blanche. O.C. A.S.C. inspected transport of North Somerset Yeo. also that of H.Qrs. 6th C. Bde.	SEL

1247 W.3299 200,000 (E) 8/14 J.B.C. & A. Forms/C. 2118/11.

Army Form C. 2118

WAR DIARY
or
INTELLIGENCE SUMMARY   A.A.S.C. 2nd Carlton
(Erase heading not required.)

Instructions regarding War Diaries and Intelligence Summaries are contained in F. S. Regs., Part II. and the Staff Manual respectively. Title pages will be prepared in manuscript.

Hour, Date, Place	Summary of Events and Information	Remarks and references to Appendices
10th Nov. 1915. Fouges.	R, R.F. & Billets & Railhead unchanged. 1 S.L. Lance granted 5 days leave from 15 – 19.11.15. 1 S/t – 2 Pte Burlace 7 days leave from 14 – 20 – 11.15.	S/tl
11th Nov. 1915 "	R, R.F. & Billets, Railhead unchanged. 1 Sr. Cpl. Rotch granted 7 days leave from 16 – 22.11.15. S/TA/350 a/Cpl. Jordan, R.B. rejoins from Hospital	S/tl
12th Nov. 1915 "	R, R.F. & Billets & Railhead unchanged. A/Cpl suspected draught of "S" Echelon. 6th Bn. L. Cumb. M268 sent to 7th. Cav. Hole on completion of repairs. Extra shoeing smith authorized for Amm. S.T. Co. joins Hos. company.	N/L

Army Form C. 2118.

WAR DIARY
or
INTELLIGENCE SUMMARY

(Erase heading not required.)

HQ Div Arty
For Res. Divl. Art.

Hour, Date, Place	Summary of Events and Information	Remarks and references to Appendices
13th Nov. 1915. Fruges	R.R. Billets, Railhead unchanged. Intimation received from A.A.Q.M.G. that Railhead will be changed to MARESQUEL on Wednesday next.	SWL
— " —	Revelegoro, Flefelly, Fruges, Billets and Railhead as for 13th.	RWL
15th "	R.R. Billets & Railhead as for 14th. Lt. Colotch proceeded on 7 days leave of absence to England. Divisional Billeting area to be changed from tomorrow. Supply Column to be at Beauvoir-velle and Ammunition Park to Fruges, Divl. HQrs. remaining at Fruges.	AWL

WAR DIARY
or
INTELLIGENCE SUMMARY

(Erase heading not required.)

Army Form C. 2118

Hour, Date, Place	Summary of Events and Information	Remarks and references to Appendices
16th Nov. 1915 Truges	R.E. billets. Railhead as fr. 15th. Moves to new billeting areas carried out — Brigades to change areas tomorrow.	AW
17th Nov. 1915 "	Rendezvous @ 1.30 pm at RIMEUX — VAN DONNE — FAUQUEMBERGUES — FRUGES four cross roads. Billeting points at Billets in new areas. Railhead at MARESQUEL.	AW
18th Nov. 1915 "	Rendezvous 9am @ GUERNINVILLE. Billeting points at billets. Railhead MARESQUEL.	AW

Army Form C. 2118.

WAR DIARY
or
INTELLIGENCE SUMMARY

(Erase heading not required.)

Also
3d Cav Bde & Col

Hour, Date, Place	Summary of Events and Information	Remarks and references to Appendices
19th Nov. 1915. Fruges	R. R.F. Billets & Railhead unchanged. One draught horse transferred from H.Qrs. 9pe to 1st Royal Dragoons.	PJC
20th "	R. R.F. Billets & Railhead as for 19th	PJC
21st "	R. R.F. Billets & Railhead as for 20th. Instructions received to send 7,663 of fair. Sergt. Roberts to Base H.T. Depot. Application to A.D.S.T., Cav. Corps, for replacement of Sunbeam Car M.503 (Supply Officer 6th Cav. Bde.) which requires to too extensive overhaul for the Supply Column Workshops. 21. Cater. 2Lieut. granted 7 days leave from 23rd. Arrangements made	PJC

WAR DIARY
or
INTELLIGENCE SUMMARY
(Erase heading not required.)

Army Form C. 2118

Hour, Date, Place	Summary of Events and Information	Remarks and references to Appendices
21st Nov. continued	with O.C. Supply Column to send to A.A. motor cars for inspection once a month.	BM
22nd Nov. 1915 Lugar	R.F.A. Killed Railhead as of yesterday. First consignment of coal from Abreuy Mines due to arrive at Haisnes goal (railhead). Arrangements made for transport to be at station at fore. average time, 6th & 8th Cav Bde. were being transported by regtl. wagons trains for 7th Cav Bde. Supply Column by motor lorries. Consignments will be forty tons weekly on rail at Railhead ex Abreuy. Capt. C. Martin, Ammn Park 10 days leave from 25th Nov.	AW

WAR DIARY or INTELLIGENCE SUMMARY

Army Form C. 2118

Hour, Date, Place	Summary of Events and Information	Remarks and references to Appendices
23rd Nov. 15th Bruges	R.R.R. Killeets Railhead as for 22nd. Coal noted yesterday did not arrive. 3 G.S. Wagons detailed daily to cart truckwood at HEZECQUES forest.	AEU
24th "	R. R.R. Killeets Railhead as for 23rd. An extra 20 tons coal alloted to Div. from Bruay mines owing to difficulty of obtaining wood. ₮23612 W. Sadd. Sutton, Div. dr. 8th C.F.A. appointed Acting Sadd. Cpl. from 22.3.15.	AEU
25th "	R. R.R. Killeets Railhead as for 24th. One truck coal arrived & was collected by Supply Column. Estimated hours for Car Coys altered 12-2 from 4 m. Scheme submitted to S.O.3 E.a. for the purchase of wood from BOIS DE HOULLEFS at HESMOND.	KU

Army Form C. 2118

WAR DIARY
or
INTELLIGENCE SUMMARY

(Erase heading not required.)

HQrs. Bralow Wire A/C

Hour, Date, Place	Summary of Events and Information	Remarks and references to Appendices
26th Nov. 1915 Bruges	R.R.R. Billets unchanged. Racklean as for 25th. 1/31923 a/Cpl. Lawton, P.R. reverted to his permanent rank of Pr. transferred from H.Qrs. 6th Can. B.C. to H.Qrs. Bra Can Bee. A/C. 1/17967 Pr. Aitken, Pn. appointed acting Corpl. and transferred from H.Qrs. Bra Can Bee. Due A/C to H.Qrs. 6th Can Bee. Due for duty as Sept. N. Co. to regimental command duties.	SAL
27th Nov. Bruges	R.R.R. Billets Racklean as for 26th. O.C. Ba. Signal Sqrs. reports his Singer car M.1143 damaged to such an extent as to render replacement necessary. The car collided with tree through	SAL

Army Form C. 2118.

WAR DIARY
or
INTELLIGENCE SUMMARY

(Erase heading not required.)

Instructions regarding War Diaries and Intelligence Summaries are contained in F. S. Regs.; Part II. and the Staff Manual respectively. Title pages will be prepared in manuscript.

Hour, Date, Place	Summary of Events and Information	Remarks and references to Appendices
28th Nov '15 Bruges	shooting when they open threat.	
27th	R.R.C. Killed. Railhead as for acn 9 inst. Notification received from acn 9 inst, that the digging parties in 5th Corps area will be withdrawn on 1st December 1915. Supply Officers were accordingly informed to ration those belonging to their respective units as from 2nd Dec. The enemy in P12 afterwards. Complaint received from the Royal	SAC

Army Form C. 2118.

WAR DIARY
or
INTELLIGENCE SUMMARY

(Erase heading not required.)

Instructions regarding War Diaries and Intelligence Summaries are contained in F. S. Regs., Part II. and the Staff Manual respectively. Title pages will be prepared in manuscript.

Hour, Date, Place	Summary of Events and Information	Remarks and references to Appendices
28/11/15 (cont)	Dragoons though the alarm only as to rough treatment made indecences man delivery of mails to the digging party at Ouderdom. Instructions received that the only men who would be allowed to proceed on leave were those who had been in the country prior to 1st Jan. 19.15, who had not been granted leave. Returns in connection were called for from Alle. Units.	M.L.
29. Nov. '15 Supra.	R.R. billets Railhead as for 28. Amm. Park forward proceedings of Court of Enquiry re the Marquee	M.L.

WAR DIARY
or
INTELLIGENCE SUMMARY

(Erase heading not required.)

HQ 3rd Cav Div Cav

Army Form C. 2118

Hour, Date, Place	Summary of Events and Information	Remarks and references to Appendices
29ᵗʰ Nov. (cont.)	of their unit which caught fire at Zouges on 24ᵗʰ inst. owing to the low value of the lorry carrying them forced nl. The Court found that no one was to blame. Application was submitted by OC Ade to GOC 3ʳᵈ Cav Info to have the charge struck off charge. OC all inspected transport of MGvo. 7ᵗʰ Cav Bde, 2ⁿᵈ Life Guards & "A" Echelon, 7ᵗʰ Cav Field Ambulance at	1744
30	HUCQUILLERS. R.Q.F. Butler's Railhead OC all inspected transport of 1ⁿ Life Gds. fcia. Yro & 14ᵗʰ M.V.S. at VICQUINGHEM.	S/E Murray Molone OC Alb 3rd Cav Div

DEC-1915

H.Q. A.S.C. 3rd Cav. Dn.

Dec / Vol XIII

WAR DIARY

of

HEAD QUARTERS, 3rd CAVALRY DIVISIONAL A.S.C.

for

DECEMBER, 1915.

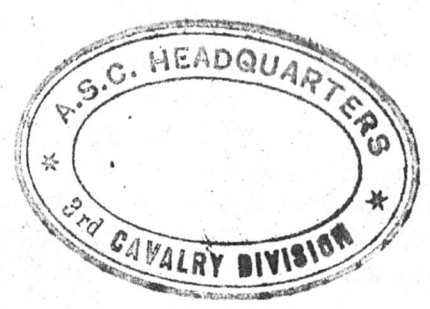

Army Form C. 2118.

H.Q. 2o Cav. Bde. A.S.C.

WAR DIARY
or
INTELLIGENCE SUMMARY
(Erase heading not required.)

Instructions regarding War Diaries and Intelligence Summaries are contained in F.S. Regs, Part II. and the Staff Manual respectively. Title pages will be prepared in manuscript.

Hour, Date, Place	Summary of Events and Information	Remarks and references to Appendices
1st Dec. 1915. FRUGES.	Rendezvous Billets Refilling Points & Railhead as for 31st. O.C. sub. reports Daimler Ambulance M.90.86 of 7th C.F.A. broken down with 2d speed gear wheels stripped. Instructions given by O.C. all for it to be towed into St Omer for repair. M.O.S.T. asked to supply another ambulance on loan. Amb. M.90.86 towed into St Omer Co.	SPL
2nd Dec. 1915. Fruges.	R.P.'s R.R. Railhead & Billets as for 1st. Two further motor ambulance casualties reported. H.O.M.T. asked to supply another on loan.	SPL
3rd Dec. 1915. Fruges.	R.P.'s R.R. Railhead & Billets as for 2nd. Supply Column ordered to move to MONTREUIL & park lorries on the Square.	MN

Army Form C. 2118.

WAR DIARY
or
INTELLIGENCE SUMMARY
(Erase heading not required.)

HQ 3rd Cav Div All

Hour, Date, Place	Summary of Events and Information	Remarks and references to Appendices
4th Dec. '15 Stripes	Billets being found in vicinity. R.R.C. Billets. Railhead as for 3rd. 1st Lt. S. Johnston S.O. 7th Cav Bde., 7 days leave to England 6 – 13.12.15.	Stil
5th Dec. '15 Stripes	R.R.C. Billets. Railhead as for 4th. Rendezvous for 7th Cav Bde. changes from PONT St MICHEL to MANNINGHEM as from 6th inst. December car M 952 reported from G.H.Q. 5.55 p.m. & was sent to Supply Officer 6th Cav Bde. to replace Sunbeam M 60 S. Supply Column moved to MONT TREVIL.	Stil

Army Form C. 2118.

WAR DIARY
or
INTELLIGENCE SUMMARY

(Erase heading not required.)

H.Q.rs. 2nd Can. Div. C. Ask.

Instructions regarding War Diaries and Intelligence Summaries are contained in F. S. Regs., Part II. and the Staff Manual respectively. Title pages will be prepared in manuscript.

Hour, Date, Place	Summary of Events and Information	Remarks and references to Appendices
6th Dec. 1915. Bruges.	R. R.R. Billets Railhead as for 5th	Nil
7th Dec. 1915. Bruges	R. R.R. billets. Railhead as for 6th. #346. S.S. Griffin att. as 6th C.F.A. appointed L/Cpl. from 5/12/15. a/Cpl. Petch, R. a/Cpl. from 16.10.15. 100th b. appointed a/Sergt. Complete establishment. Car No. 1790. broke down. Was taken into Workshops.	Nil

Army Form C. 2118.

WAR DIARY
or
INTELLIGENCE SUMMARY

HQrs 3o Cav. Bde l. A.E.

(Erase heading not required.)

Instructions regarding War Diaries and Intelligence
Summaries are contained in F.S. Regs., Part II.
and the Staff Manual respectively. Title pages
will be prepared in manuscript.

Hour, Date, Place	Summary of Events and Information	Remarks and references to Appendices
8th Dec. Bruges	Refilling Points & Billets unchanged. Railhead changed to MONTREUIL from to-day inclusive. Capt. C.J. Martin, Adj't & Lt. W.J. Luck R.A., 3a Cav. Div. Ammunition Park, admitted Hospital at St Omer. Application made to	AEL
9th Dec. Bruges.	R.R.P., Billets & Railhead as to 8th. Application made to A.D. of S.&T. for the replacement of car No h 1790, which requires to undergo repairs and overhaul.	SEL

Army Form C. 2118.

WAR DIARY
or
INTELLIGENCE SUMMARY
(Erase heading not required.)

H Qro 3rd Cav Bric Ade

Instructions regarding War Diaries and Intelligence Summaries are contained in F. S. Regs., Part II. and the Staff Manual respectively. Title pages will be prepared in manuscript.

Hour, Date, Place	Summary of Events and Information	Remarks and references to Appendices
10 Dec. 1915. Ypres	R. R.P. Weeks. Railhead as for 9th. Capt. Geo Davey granted 10 days leave of absence to England commencing 16th inst.	Sd/-
11th Dec 15. Ypres	R. R.P. Weeks. Railhead as to 10th. Received from G. H.Q. Napier Motor Ambulance No. 13979 to replace No. C9086. Also received Singer lightcar No. 96/14/142 to replace No. 114.3. 3rd Signal Sqn. Rations to Digging Party to be drawn from 2nd Cav Div. Railhead as from 13th.	Sd/-

1247 W 3299 200,000 (E) 8/14 J.B.C. & A. Forms/C. 2118/11.

Army Form C. 2118.

WAR DIARY
or
INTELLIGENCE SUMMARY
(Erase heading not required.)

HQrs 2nd Can. Div. Coy. A.S.C.

Hour, Date, Place	Summary of Events and Information	Remarks and references to Appendices
12th Dec. 1915.	R.R. Killed. Railhead unchanged. Ranges light car no. M1414 broke down between Bruges Radinghem with steering gear broken. Woladen Car no.790 evacuated to G.H.Q. for repairs. Lt. Col. W. Larser detailed to take over temporarily duties of So. Div. Supply from 13th inst. Capt. K.K. Moeser - leave to U.K. 7 days from 16.12.15.	Stu
13th Dec. 1915. Bruges	R., R.R. Killed. Railhead as for 12th. O.C. a/c suspected transport of 3rd Dragoon Guards. Notification received from A.D. of S.T. that coal loadings from Boulay will be temporarily reduced to 50%. Approval of Colonel i/c	Stu

Army Form C. 2118.

WAR DIARY
INTELLIGENCE SUMMARY
(Erase heading not required.)

HQrs. Below
Nil all

Hour, Date, Place	Summary of Events and Information	Remarks and references to Appendices
14th Dec. 1915. Sruges.	A.C. Section to M/T/s received in M/T/s 1/22170 at 6arr. Sergt. Newman & 1/21841 to book, & Railhead for 18 allow Corpl. Digging Party changed to WIZERNES (as Gen. Di. Railhead) R.R.F. Billets Railhead as for 13th. Orders received for the evacuation of Sunbeam Motor Ambulances A.979 and A.1115.	SU SU
15th Dec. 1915. Sruges.	R. R.R. Billets Railroads as for 14th. Sunbeam car A.1142 handed over to Workshops at St Omer. 4 E.R.S. lorries detached from Supply Column for temporary duty as Supply Officers Divisional Troops.	AU

1247 W³ 3299 200,000 (E) 8/14 J.B.C. & A. Forms/C. 2118/11.

WAR DIARY
or
INTELLIGENCE SUMMARY   1 Div. Ballow Adl

Army Form C. 2118.

(Erase heading not required.)

Hour, Date, Place	Summary of Events and Information	Remarks and references to Appendices
16th Dec. 1915. Fruges.	L.R.B. Billets Railheads as for 15th. W/2/033825 Pte Mitchell, A. & No. W/2/020572 Pte Garon, E. All attached 8th Bar. S.A. appointed paid Acting Corporals from 16.12.15. O.O. of S.T. arranges weekly meetings with O's C Cale. R.O's each Wednesday at 11 am at his office	
17th Dec. 1915. Fruges	L.R.B. Billets Railheads as for 16th. Rendezvous arranged as follows:- Div. Rendezvous - MONTREUIL @ 8.45 am 6th Ch. Fusrs. Bde. G.S. Dump @ 10 am 1st Brigade - MANNINGHEM x Roads @ 11 am 2nd " - AIX EN ISSART @ 9.45 am Div. Troops - FRUGES @ 11 am.	

Army Form C. 2118.

WAR DIARY
or
INTELLIGENCE SUMMARY
(Erase heading not required.)

Ha.Qrs. 2a Cav. Divl. All

Hour, Date, Place	Summary of Events and Information	Remarks and references to Appendices
17.12.15 (continued)	Horses of limb. subjected to Mallein test. Wolseley car K.268 in collision on 14th inst. at La Belle Croix X Roads. Report & application for replacement today submitted to AD of S.T. Cavalry Corps. Motor Ambulances A. 9791 & A. 11115 yesterday evacuated to GHQ.	MN
18.12.15.	R.R.F. Billets Railhead as fr 17⁰. Three loaders (Rev Forsdick, Howley & Flynn) arrived from B.H.L.D. Havre, to replace 3 leavers. Capt. Y.W. Davey leave 7 days proceeded on leave to England	MN

Army Form C. 2118.

WAR DIARY
or
INTELLIGENCE SUMMARY

NoDrs Bordon Owl Ale

(Erase heading not required.)

Instructions regarding War Diaries and Intelligence Summaries are contained in F. S. Regs., Part II. and the Staff Manual respectively. Title pages will be prepared in manuscript.

Hour, Date, Place	Summary of Events and Information	Remarks and references to Appendices
19.12.15. Bruges	R., R.Q., A.Q. Millers Railhead as for 18th. Pte Davis liked to B.M. P.D. Marie He Flynn to S.O. 7th Coy. up relief of Pte Stevens who is to go to R.A.T. Depot, Havre.	Nil
20.12.15. Bruges	R., R.Q. Millers Railhead as for 19th. Capt. Jas N. Bates proceeded on 14 days leave to U.K.	Nil
21.12.15. Bruges	R., R.Q., A.Q. Millers Railhead as for 20th. 2nd Cpl Rowe to Simpson, Ali attached 7th Car. Field Ambulance to Havre yesterday on transfer to New Armies.	

Army Form C. 2118.

WAR DIARY
or
INTELLIGENCE SUMMARY

(Erase heading not required.)

HQ 28 Divl 10th Atk

Hour, Date, Place	Summary of Events and Information	Remarks and references to Appendices
22.12.15 Krupa	R.R.F. Billets for 21st. Xmas leave as from 28.12.15. 4+4+11 Mls Plum Puddings distributed to Units today from Railhead. Divisional Reserve Coal Dump established at Krupa under care of S.O. Divl. Troops. Areas allotted for purchasing requisitioning of straw etc. In this connection all Ros. attended office of AQST at 6 pm.	ML

WAR DIARY
or
INTELLIGENCE SUMMARY
(Erase heading not required.)

Army Form C. 2118.

Instructions regarding War Diaries and Intelligence Summaries are contained in F. S. Regs., Part II. and the Staff Manual respectively. Title pages will be prepared in manuscript.

Hour, Date, Place	Summary of Events and Information	Remarks and references to Appendices
23.12.15	R. R.P. Relink & railhead as for 23rd. Motor Ambulances A. 15982 & A. 15983 replace A. 9791 & A. 1115 arrived & were handed over to A.D.M.S.	SPL
24.12.15	R. R.P. & Billet & Railhead as for 24th. Supply light car M. 17578 arrived to replace M. 14142	
25.12.15	R. R.P. Billet & Railhead as for 24th. Aux. Horse Transport Company ordered to rejoin Major on 27th inst.	SPL
26.12.15	R. R.P. Billet & Railhead as for 25th	SPL
27.12.15	R. R.P. Billet & Railhead as for 26th. Instructions received as to Dismounted Division to be concentrated in billets by evening of 28th	

Army Form C. 2118.

WAR DIARY
or
INTELLIGENCE SUMMARY

(Erase heading not required.)

Instructions regarding War Diaries and Intelligence Summaries are contained in F. S. Regs., Part II. and the Staff Manual respectively. Title pages will be prepared in manuscript.

Hour, Date, Place	Summary of Events and Information	Remarks and references to Appendices
27.12.15	Orders for 64 Bde Digging party to proceed to WALLONCAPELL cancelled. Auxiliary Horse Transport withdrawn from units.	MC
28.12.15	R. R.P. Buick & Railheads as for 24th. 2 Reinforcements received. Ration issued to units of dismounted divisions. 7th & 8th Brigade digging parties returned to Billet.	SL
29.12.15	R. R.P. Buick & Railhead as for 28th. Orders received that Railhead to be changed to BEUTIN. Iron rations for dismounted units completed.	MC

WAR DIARY
or
INTELLIGENCE SUMMARY

(Erase heading not required.)

Army Form C. 2118.

Hour, Date, Place	Summary of Events and Information	Remarks and references to Appendices
30.12.15	R.R.P. & Billets as for 29th. Railhead changes to BEUTIN. Orders received for 3 Cdo. Ammunition Park to proceed to BASRIEUX on 1st January. Capt. Preston - Lt. Riley & Lt. Trench proceed to CHOCQUES in connection with dismounted Sqn.	Nil
31.12.15	R. R.P. & Billets & Railhead as for 30th. Rations delivered by Aux H.T.Cy. to Batteries & Ammunition Col of Dismounted Move of 6th, 7th & 8th Bgde. I.D. held up till further orders.	Nil

3c

H.Q. 3rd Cav Div A.S.
Jan 1916.
Vol XIV

Army Form C. 2118.

WAR DIARY
or
INTELLIGENCE SUMMARY   HQrs 2nd Cav. Div. Ale

(Erase heading not required.)

Instructions regarding War Diaries and Intelligence Summaries are contained in F. S. Regs., Part II. and the Staff Manual respectively. Title pages will be prepared in manuscript.

Hour, Date, Place	Summary of Events and Information	Remarks and references to Appendices
1-1-16	R.R. Billets. Railhead as for 31.12.15. 3rd C.D. Am" Park proceeded to BASTRIEU. Orders received for Railhead to report to MONTREUIL.	Sd
2-1-16	R.R. Billets as for 1.1.16. Railhead changed to MONTREUIL	
3.1.16. Bruges	R. R.P. Billets & Railhead as for 2nd. Dismounted Brigade left MONTREUIL. Report received re accident to Napier Motor Ambulance A 15982 — recommended to A.D.S.T. that driver be charged £4, the cost of damage.	Sd

Army Form C. 2118.

WAR DIARY
or
INTELLIGENCE SUMMARY
(Erase heading not required.)

HdQrs 3rd Cav. Div. Ad...

Hour, Date, Place	Summary of Events and Information	Remarks and references to Appendices
4th Jan, 1916. Bruges	R. R.E. Billets - Railhead as for 3rd. Notification received that Temp. Capt. G.W. Davey on leave of absence, has been retained for duty in England. Temp Lt. Jn. Bathgate reported this day for duty vice Capt. Davey.	Nil
5th Jan '15. Bruges	R.R.E. Billets - Railhead as for 4th. Report received of accident to Napier Motor Ambulance A 15983 by runaway horses dashing into it near Bethune on 2nd inst - Radiator damaged - Indent submitted for new one.	Nil
6th Jan '15. Bruges	R.R.E. Billets - Railhead as for 5th Lieut. E.R.B. Davies appointed Supply Officer, Divisional Troops from D. Supply Column & Lieut N.A. Riley from R.O. 6th Cav Bde appointed Supply Officer Supply Column.	Nil

WAR DIARY
or
INTELLIGENCE SUMMARY

Army Form C. 2118.

Also
Zealous Point Ale

Hour, Date, Place	Summary of Events and Information	Remarks and references to Appendices
9½ Jan. 16. Bruges	A.R.R. Bills and Railhead as to 6th Approval received for the opening of Imprest Accounts by Capt. R. Roeder, S.O. 6th Cav. Bde. 2nd Lieut. C.D. Rotel, S.O. 6th Cav. Bde. 2nd Lieut. Mr. Bathgate to be retained with Divl. Shops for instruction in Supply Duties. S.O. 1st Cav. Bde. directed to send one Butcher to the 2nd Dismounted Brigade. Dismounted Troops. Also applied to A.D.S.T. for authority to send one man to learn the 3rd Dismounted Brigade. Notification received that the Q.S. Wagons of 1st & 3rd Reserve Parks may be used for transporting of supplies. Scheme to be submitted to D.A.Q.M.G. showing how it is proposed to utilize these.	M.C.

Army Form C. 2118.

WAR DIARY
or
INTELLIGENCE SUMMARY

(Erase heading not required.)

Hd Qrs. Bralau
Div All

Hour, Date, Place	Summary of Events and Information	Remarks and references to Appendices
8th Jan. 1915. Bruges	A. R.F. Sillele Railhead as to 1st Cavalry Notification from A.O.S.T. Corps stating that they may not be requisitioned under any circumstances. Copy of this letter sent to all S.O's. further comm. received from A.O.S.T. that straw may now be purchased in whole or present Cav Corps Area. Supply Officers were also informed of the contents of this letter. Approval (Ca. 1405/1/2) given to the purchase of wood by Bralau, on @ 20 fres per 1000 Kilos until such times as arrangements can be made to get it cheaper.	STC

WAR DIARY
INTELLIGENCE SUMMARY

(Erase heading not required.)

Army Form C. 2118.

HQ O. & 3rd Cav. Div. All

Hour, Date, Place	Summary of Events and Information	Remarks and references to Appendices
9th Jan. 16 Lupus	R.R.R. Killed. Railhead as for 8th. Instructions sent to O.C., 8th Cav. Bde. to negotiate for the purchase of trees at Lemps which had been used by horses. Hay ration temporarily reduced to 6 lbs per horse. 2 lbs per horse may be purchased. Notification from A.Q.& T. that no supplies may be now purchased in 1st Army Area previously allotted. J. Capt. Abbeville & J.J. & Colbert to report to O.C. A.V.S. Depot Abbeville, for duty overseas. To be relieved by Temp. Lieuts. Earle & Bellew. Lt. Earle reported & sent to 7th Cav. Bde.	P.C.

Army Form C. 2118.

WAR DIARY
or
INTELLIGENCE SUMMARY Hd Qrs 3rd Cav. Divl. Arty.
(Erase heading not required.)

Hour, Date, Place	Summary of Events and Information	Remarks and references to Appendices
10th Jan '16 Bruges	To R.R. Billets + Railhead as to 9th. Improved Hut tent scheme submitted to C.R.A. Only for utilizing horse transport of 1st + 3rd Reserve Parks. Capt A. B. W. Daniels left to Abbeville. Wire received from O.C. 2nd Res. Park, through Gen. H.Q. that L. Walker had applied for leave tendering it his transfer could be postponed until his return. Replied "no objection." Orders received for the transfer of Sergt. S. Co. Retch to 1st Army + to be relieved by L/ J. H. By J. Dunn. New lara ordered to 6th Cav. Bde. for duty as so.	AEC

WAR DIARY
or
INTELLIGENCE SUMMARY

Army Form C. 2118.

H. Qrs. 2nd Can. Cav. Bde.

Hour, Date, Place	Summary of Events and Information	Remarks and references to Appendices
13th Jan '16 Gouges	A. R.F. 16 illeg. Railhead as for 12th.	M.U.
14th "	R. R.E. Billets. Railhead as for 13th. O.C. Supply Col. reporting EMBRY as unavailable, S.O. 8th Can. Bde. informed in response to his application. May Ettre Yeo. remain at BOUBERS.	M.U.
"	R. R.F. Billets. Railhead at forenth 16th. Nt Can. Bde. dump arranged at HUCQUELIERS on & after 17th inst. Div. H. Qrs. proceed to join Mounted Gd. Division.	M.U.

Army Form C. 2118.

HQ 3rd Cav Div
Add

WAR DIARY
or
INTELLIGENCE SUMMARY

(Erase heading not required.)

Instructions regarding War Diaries and Intelligence Summaries are contained in F. S. Regs., Part II. and the Staff Manual respectively. Title pages will be prepared in manuscript.

Hour, Date, Place	Summary of Events and Information	Remarks and references to Appendices
15th Jan. '16 Sueges	R. R.P. Hills - Railhead as for 14th. L.y. McNaghten taken on strength as M.O. Div. Troops, vice T.J. Cotoah.	Nil.
16th Jan. '16 Sueges	R. R.P. Hills - Railhead as for 15th. One wagon + team detailed to R.H.Gds. for duty whilst Dismounted Divn. is up. Cor M1795 sent to temporary duty with J.O. Div. Troops, Dismounted Divn., to replace M1490, casualty.	Nil.
17th Jan. '16 Sueges	R. R.P. Hills - Railhead as for 16th.	Nil.

1247 W 3299 200,000 (E) 8/14 J.B.C. & A. Forms/C. 2118/11.

WAR DIARY
or
INTELLIGENCE SUMMARY

(Erase heading not required.)

Army Form C. 2118

Headqrs 3rd Cav. Divl. H.Q.

Place	Date	Hour	Summary of Events and Information	Remarks and references to Appendices
Burges	18.1.16.		R.R. Willets Railhead as for 17th. A.D.S.T. gives authority for use of Warren Queape Railway from MONTREUIL whenever trucks are available. O.C. Supply Column reports collision between Supply Column lorry & a Private French Car owned by M. Valet, the Surgeon of Compagne, on 15.1.16. near NEUVILLE. Reports forwarded to A.D.S.T. 16.1.16., when driver of French car to blame.	H.P.
Burges	19.1.16.		R. R.R. Willets Railhead as for 18th. Supply Officer 10th Cav. Bde. reports a collision between Wolseley car M.5/75 & a French car 17624 near MARESQUEZ Station Wolseley Station on 16.1.16.	H.P.

Army Form C. 2118

WAR DIARY
or
INTELLIGENCE SUMMARY

(Erase heading not required.)

Hd Qrs 3rd Can. Div¹. Art

Instructions regarding War Diaries and Intelligence Summaries are contained in F.S. Regs., Part II. and the Staff Manual respectively. Title Pages will be prepared in manuscript.

Place	Date	Hour	Summary of Events and Information	Remarks and references to Appendices
FRUGES.	20th Jan 16		R. R.E. Billets Railhead as for 19th. 1/Col. A.E. Amey proceeded to England on 10 days leave. Provisional programme of dates for fortnightly examination of sole cases sent to A.D.S.T. Car 141796 broke down at BETHUNE with broken hub shell.	HP
FRUGES.	21st Jan 16		R. R.E. Billets Railhead as for 20th. A/Cpl. Sanford, R.C. 8th Can.Hos. appointed Acting Sergeant with pay. Report to A.D.S.T. on serious shortage in weight of hay delivered to Royal Horse Guards.	HP HP

1875 Wt. W591/826 1,000,000 4/15 J.B.C. & A. A.D.S.S./Forms/C. 2118.

Army Form C. 2118

WAR DIARY
or
INTELLIGENCE SUMMARY
(Erase heading not required.)

Hd.Qrs. 3rd Can. Div. Ale

Instructions regarding War Diaries and Intelligence Summaries are contained in F.S. Regs., Part II. and the Staff Manual respectively. Title Pages will be prepared in manuscript.

Place	Date	Hour	Summary of Events and Information	Remarks and references to Appendices
FRUGES.	22/1/16		R. R.P. Billets Railhead as for 21st. Branch of Expeditionary Force Canteen opened at MARSNLA, arrangements being made to pass supply units through the Supply Column. Acting on instructions of A.D. of S.&T. Cavalry Corps, Supply Officers were directed by S.O. to have all potatoes in their respective areas, requisitioning being resorted to if necessary.	H.T.
do -	23/1/16		R. R.P. Billets Railhead as for 22nd reported by O. from MANINGHEM - Pt St MICHEL Daimler car to Hdll road badly cracked, Supply Column sent out and towed car into Workshops.	H.T.

Army Form C. 2118

WAR DIARY
or
INTELLIGENCE SUMMARY
Head Quarters
3rd Cav. Div., A.D.
(Erase heading not required.)

Place	Date	Hour	Summary of Events and Information	Remarks and references to Appendices
FRUGES.	24/1/16		R. R.R. Billets. Railhead as for 23rd. Received report on accident to motor car Daimler 111 forwarded same to A.D.S.T. As driver is in hospital full report cannot yet be obtained. Temp. Lieut. C. G. R. WELLER A.D. reported this evening for duty as O.C. 3rd Cav. Div. Aux. H.T.C. Report received through O.C. 8th Cav.Bde. of Medical Officer, Royal Horse Guards of several cases of food poisoning in that Unit caused through the men consuming "Kewril" Tinned Butter. Immediately reported the matter to A.D.S.T. wacked for instructions.	H.P.
— do —	25/1/16		R. R.R. Billets. Railhead as for 24th. Instructions received from A.D.S.T. to stop all issues of Kewril Butter until further notice & to forward sample tin. Transmitted these directions	H.P.

Army Form C. 2118

WAR DIARY
or
INTELLIGENCE SUMMARY

(Erase heading not required.)

HQrs. 3rd Cav. Div. A.S.C.

Place	Date	Hour	Summary of Events and Information	Remarks and references to Appendices
FRUGES	26.1.16		directions to Supply Officers to Cart supplies to A.D.S. R.R. Sheds. Railhead as for 25th. Exchange of duties ordered between Temp. Lieut. G.F. EARLE, Ass. Transport Officer, 1st Cav. Bde., and 2/Lieut (S.R.) S.H. COX, A.S.C., Reqmtl. Officer, 2nd Cav. Div. Reported to A.D.S. by wire case of requisitioning by French Army at EMORY.	H.P.
do.	27.1.16		R. Rlys. Welleh. Railhead as for 26th. Instructed A. Supply Column, to collect from Dismounted Division, motor cars No.576 & No.490 both of which had broken down. 2600 Iron Rations drawn at DESVRES from No.1 Reserve Park to replace a similar number to be consumed on 29th instant. 2/Lieut. Lit. Cox. Reported for duty.	H.P.

Army Form C. 2118

WAR DIARY
or
INTELLIGENCE SUMMARY

Hd. Qrs. 3rd Cav. Divl. Amm. Coll.

(Erase heading not required.)

Instructions regarding War Diaries and Intelligence Summaries are contained in F. S. Regs., Part II. and the Staff Manual respectively. Title Pages will be prepared in manuscript.

Place	Date	Hour	Summary of Events and Information	Remarks and references to Appendices
FRUGES	28-1-16		R., R.P., Billets. Railhead as for 27th. Reported to A.D.S.T. several cases of purchasing & requisitioning in 8th Cav. Div. area by the French. 2/Lt. Price from Supply Column to 8th Cav. Bde. for temporary duty as Supply Officer.	A.P.
-do-	29-1-16		R., R.P., Billets. Railhead as for 28th. Capt. P. Koch, Supply Officer, 8th Cav. Bde., admitted hospital.	A.P.
-do-	30-1-16		R., R.P., Billets. Railhead as for 29th. Result of reconnaissance of supplies in 8th Cav. Bde. forwarded to A.D.S.T.	A.P.

WAR DIARY
or
INTELLIGENCE SUMMARY

Head Quarters
3rd Can. Div. Art.

Army Form C. 2118

Place	Date	Hour	Summary of Events and Information	Remarks and references to Appendices
FRUGES.	31.1.16		R. R.R. Willets Railhead as for 30th	

S.H. Lumsden
Lieut. Colonel
Commanding Head Quarters
3rd Cavalry Divisional Art.

Feb 1916

WAR DIARY
or
INTELLIGENCE SUMMARY

(Erase heading not required.)

Army Form C. 2118

Head Quarters 3rd Cav. Div. Ad.

Instructions regarding War Diaries and Intelligence Summaries are contained in F. S. Regs., Part II and the Staff Manual respectively. Title Pages will be prepared in manuscript.

Place	Date	Hour	Summary of Events and Information	Remarks and references to Appendices
FRUGES.	1.2.16		R. R.E. Willis Railhead as for 31st.	See
-"-	2.2.16		R. R.E. Billets Railhead as for 1st. Orders received for Capt. & Adjt half wages to proceed for duty with 2 GHQ Amn Park to be relieved by Temp. Lieut. R. C. Lyle.	See
-"-	3.2.16		R. R.E. Willis Railhead as for 2nd. Divl H.Qrs returned from Dismounted Division.	See
-"-	4.2.16		R. R.E. Billets Railhead as for 3rd. Triple echelon system of lorries for transporting supplies from Railhead to come into force from 10th inst.	See

Army Form C. 2118

WAR DIARY
or
INTELLIGENCE SUMMARY

(Erase heading not required.)

Head Qrs
3rd Cav. Div. A.S.C.

Instructions regarding War Diaries and Intelligence Summaries are contained in F. S. Regs., Part II. and the Staff Manual respectively. Title Pages will be prepared in manuscript.

Place	Date	Hour	Summary of Events and Information	Remarks and references to Appendices
FRUGES	5.2.16		Rendezvous, Refilling Points, Billets. Railhead Railhead as for 14th. Temp. 2/Lt. C.R. Fyle reported for duty from No 3 Reserve Park for duty as Adjutant HQrs 3rd Cav. Div. A.S.C. Proposal received this A.M.S.T. to transferring E.A.W. Mule Supply Column. Information received of return to Dismounted Divn on 10th inst.	M26
FRUGES	6.2.16		R.R.P. Railhead + Billets as for 5th. Temp. Captain J.W. Bates left the post for duty with No 2 C.H.O. Ammunition Park. Requisitioning Officers to do all purchasing for Brigades etc from 8th inst. war. A.A.Q. only supplies to ADST what this order he holds over until return of his Divn.	PH

WAR DIARY
or
INTELLIGENCE SUMMARY

(Erase heading not required.)

Army Form C. 2118

Head Qrs
3rd Can. Inv. Bde.

Place	Date	Hour	Summary of Events and Information	Remarks and references to Appendices
FRUGES	7.2.16		L. R.Q. Billets. Railhead as for 6th.	Ptl
FRUGES	8.2.16		L. R.Q. Billets. Railhead as for 7th. Leave of J. Coates extended to 14th inst. Notification received that Dismounted Brigade will return on 11th instant. Supply Officers directed to secure all available hay, straw and vegetables in their respective areas. Purchasing of all supplies in Ros. deferred until after return of Divnl Divn.	Ptl

Army Form C. 2118

WAR DIARY
or
INTELLIGENCE SUMMARY
(Erase heading not required.)

Hd. Qu. 2d Cavalry Divisional A.C.

Instructions regarding War Diaries and Intelligence Summaries are contained in F.S. Regs., Part II. and the Staff Manual respectively. Title Pages will be prepared in manuscript.

Place	Date	Hour	Summary of Events and Information	Remarks and references to Appendices
Fruges	Aug 9.	2.16	R. R. Meets Railhead as for 8th.	OK
Fruges	10.	2.10.	Bills Railhead as for 9th. Adv. Rendezvous at Brigade Refilling Points. Refilling Points — Div. C. Troops FRUGES, 6th Cav Bde BEAURAINVILLE, (1st Dragoons FRUGES) 9th Cav. Bde. HUCQUELIERS — 8th Cav. Bde. AIX-EN-ISSART. Times — 9am Fruges 10 a.m.	KR
Fruges	11.	2.16	R. R. Bill's Railhead as for 10th. Report sent to D.Q.S. of all hay straw potatoes & which Supply Officers were able to secure. Report to A.A. & Q.M.G. on difficulty of feeding bayonets into Div. Area in event of hay ration being permanently reduced.	KR

1875 Wt. W593/826 1,000,000 4/15 J.B.C. & A. A.D.S.S./Forms/C. 2118.

WAR DIARY
or
INTELLIGENCE SUMMARY

Army Form C. 2118

HqQrs 3rd Cav. Divl. A.S.C.

(Erase heading not required.)

Place	Date	Hour	Summary of Events and Information	Remarks and references to Appendices
Lugies	12.2.16		R., R.E. Billets + Railhead as for 11th. Dismounted Brigade, less Artillery, returned last night. Arranged with R.O.T. for future weekly supply of 60 tons coal for Div. Two Field Ambulances evacuated to G.H.Q.	Nil
"	13.2.16		R., R.E. Billets + Railhead as for 12th.	Nil
"	14.2.16		R., R.E. Billets + Railhead as for 13th.	Nil

Army Form C. 2118

WAR DIARY
or
INTELLIGENCE SUMMARY

(Erase heading not required.)

Headqrs. 2o Cav. Div. Afr.

Place	Date	Hour	Summary of Events and Information	Remarks and references to Appendices
Lucques	15.	2.16	R., R.E., Billets, Railhead as for 14th. A.D. Rly. asked to supply 30 men to assist in wood cutting at BOIS D'HEZECQUES. N.O.S.T. wires that the 4 Motor Ambulances earmarked on 12th should be brought back, as rails/cab are now available.	Phl
Lucques	16.	2.16	R., R.E., Billets, Railhead as for 15th.	Phl

WAR DIARY
or
INTELLIGENCE SUMMARY

Head Qrs.
3rd Cav. Div. A.S.C.

(Erase heading not required.)

Army Form C. 2118

Place	Date	Hour	Summary of Events and Information	Remarks and references to Appendices
Sarges	17.2.16		R.R.P. Billets & Railhead as for 16th. 30 O.R. of 3rd Sikh Squadron detailed for wood cutting at Bois d'Hesecques. Two Kapok Ambulances brought back from G.H.Q. 8 Carts applied for extension leave under 21st inst.	Nil
Sarges	18.2.16		R. R.R. Billets & Railhead as for 19th. Received from A.H.Q. Hd.Q. Scheme of the O.M.Q. for supply of hay, straw & potatoes from local resources & suggested to him that depots be established at each of the present Brigade H.Qrs. R.H.A. to return to permanent billets on morning of 23rd inst. H.Q.S.T. intimate that he will order 3000 lbs Meals & Bran daily from Sars.	Nil

Army Form C. 2118

WAR DIARY
or
INTELLIGENCE SUMMARY
2nd Cav Div C ASC

(Erase heading not required.)

Place	Date	Hour	Summary of Events and Information	Remarks and references to Appendices
Lucques	19.2.16		R. R.F. Billets Railhead as for 18th. Iron Rations in Barges No 57 & H8 at HARDRECQUES to be turned over, reviewed in lieu of ordinary rations.	SR1
Lucques	20.2.16		R. R.F. Billets & Railhead as for 19th. Cav. Corps issue Circular with the object of preventing wastage of supplies.	RR1

Army Form C. 2118

WAR DIARY
or
INTELLIGENCE SUMMARY Hd Qu.
(Erase heading not required.) 3rd Cav. Div. Ade

Instructions regarding War Diaries and Intelligence Summaries are contained in F. S. Regs., Part II. and the Staff Manual respectively. Title Pages will be prepared in manuscript.

Place	Date	Hour	Summary of Events and Information	Remarks and references to Appendices
Bruges	21.9.16		R.R.Q. Billets Railhead as for 20th. 340/2007 Actig Corpl. Bigley, F. Cav. A.P. Corder appointed acting sergeant with pay. Arrangements made to deliver rations for R.H. direct to billets on 23rd inst. Motor ambulance broke down at Torcy on way from Bosroms to 3rd Cav Div. (Amb Park sent out to bring which to Bruges.	Nil
Bruges	22.9.16		R. R.Q. Billets Railhead as for 21st. Arranged that the 2 rations from barges at Bairecques be drawn on Thursday following by units in lieu of ordinary rations on Saturday next. Notified Supply Officers that R.H.A. Batteries would be attached to Divisional Troops for supplies commencing for consumption 25th instant.	Nil

WAR DIARY
or
INTELLIGENCE SUMMARY

Headqrs. 3rd Can. Divl. Alc.

Army Form C. 2118

Place	Date	Hour	Summary of Events and Information	Remarks and references to Appendices
FRUGES	23.2.16		R., R.E. details & Railhead as for 22nd. R.H.A. arrived rations delivered to their billets. Took up with A.A.only question of deficiencies of horses on G.S. limbered wagons. Digging Party to proceed on 29th (about 400 all ranks) to be billeted at LYNDE. 2nd Can. Div. to be responsible for feeding. Decided that the rations Oats from Calais will be drawn but not issued till further orders.	MA
Lynde	24.2.16		R., R.E. Billets & Railhead as for 23rd. Batteries, R.H.A., draw rations from Fruges. Instructions received from Q. to detail Transport Officer to take 8 vehicles to ST OMER Depot on 28th in connection with Digging Party. 9th Can. 7th C.S. detailed to supply Column directed to abolish Reserve Rations & all inspected transport of Divl. Hdqrs.	MA

WAR DIARY or INTELLIGENCE SUMMARY

Army Form C. 2118

Heading: Hesdigneul / 2nd Car. Div. L. of C.

Place	Date	Hour	Summary of Events and Information	Remarks and references to Appendices
Hesdigneul	25.2.16		R. R.f. Gillete / Railhead o.c. for Div. Notified Nos 7" M. that 9 Cox. will take Marches of Bergues Estly to ESQUEROES where it will be billeted. The Troops to C. will rendezvous at 60UT de la MILLE at 11.30 a.m on 26". Brigades / Field Sqn. notified accordingly. Arranged to meet at FRESSIN Bonduct to Div. Nos on 27" inst. the Machine Gun Squadron transport (M.G.S.) Bagn. & Batn. Carts to take (See). Wire received from A.S.C. that Supply Train assuming Railhead on Sunday will be short of meat breadstuffs Tea, Sugar took Saturday that Div. Ration / Oats wherewithal he from Bayeux should be issued accordingly. Leave of 9 O/rates extended to 29.2.16. Director of Supply Col. to send Rations & Ammn Column direct to COUPELLE VIEILLE.	M.C. M.C.

WAR DIARY
or
INTELLIGENCE SUMMARY

Army Form C. 2118

(Erase heading not required.)

No. 3w
3a OD ASC

Place	Date	Hour	Summary of Events and Information	Remarks and references to Appendices
Bruges	26.2.16		R.E. Billets Railhead as for 25th. Orders received for Capt. C.E. FARRAN, 3a Cn. Supply Column, to report to the Director of Railways at G.H.Q. for duty. Temp. Lieut. W.R. Steed A.S.C. posted to Supply Column. This latter Officer reported for duty yesterday 25th inst. Furnished to A.D.S. & T. 3Cn. statement of journeys to and from MONTREUIL - BEURAINVILLE done by Column lorries — this in connection with complaint by French Authorities. Court of Inquiry held to investigate circumstances of damage to Gr. Mtr. M.T.815. Court estimated damage at £100. Considered driver was not to blame.	Ftd
Bruges	27.2.16		Billets Railhead as for 26th. Owing to thaw, important supplies were diverted from lorries as follows :— Dirt Troops – 4/7th Royal Dragoons	Ftd

1875 Wt. W593/826 1,000,000 4/15 T.R.C. & A. A.D.S.S./Forms/C. 2118.

WAR DIARY
or
INTELLIGENCE SUMMARY

Army Form C. 2118

1a Oh
2a Cav Div l ADC

Place	Date	Hour	Summary of Events and Information	Remarks and references to Appendices
(Continued)	27.2.16		at FRUGES - 6th Cav Bde, hos 1st RA at BEURBRAINVILLE, 7th Cav Bde at BERNIVILLES and 8th Cav Bde at BRIMEUX. From these dumps supplies were taken to billets by Horse Transport. Owing to late arrival of the detachment of 10th Reserve Park, 1st Cav Bde rations had necessarily to be taken by the lorries to HUCQUELLIERS, the usual dumping place. The Digging Party which was to have proceeded to LYNDE on 29th inst. was today postponed until further orders owing to the inclement weather.	Nil
Fruges	28.2.16		R Billets + Railhead as for 27th. Brigade Dumps as in force yesterday continued. Received complaint from G.O.C. 7th Cav Bde on late arrival of rations at HUCQUELLIERS. Arrangements then made to have lorries at BERNIVILLES at 7.30 each morning so as to ensure the Horse Transport reaching HUCQUELLIERS by 12.30 pm the scheduled time.	Nil

WAR DIARY
or
INTELLIGENCE SUMMARY

Army Form C. 2118

(Erase heading not required.)

Ra Dio
Bo Cav. Div.

Place	Date	Hour	Summary of Events and Information	Remarks and references to Appendices
	28/2/16	contind	Orders given to Brigade Supply Officers at 8.15pm to suspend all forward purchasing until further orders. Court of Inquiry held to investigate circumstances of damage to Gov. Motor Car No. 17578 in charge of Sgt Signal Sqn. O. Supply Col. yesterday reported that rails have recently arrived too late to be taken out on Supply Columns — Report passed to A.A.Q.M.G.	WA
Bruges	29.2.16		R. R.C. Billets + Railhead as for 28th. Major L.O. Peebles, D.O. proceeded to H.Q. Cavalry Corps for temporary duty with A.D.V.S.	STL

S.H. Miming, Lieut. Colonel,
Comdg. 3rd Cavalry Div. ACE

Army Form C. 2118

WAR DIARY
or
INTELLIGENCE SUMMARY
(Erase heading not required.)

No. Dr
3rd Can Div' Arty

Instructions regarding War Diaries and Intelligence Summaries are contained in F. S. Regs., Part II. and the Staff Manual respectively. Title Pages will be prepared in manuscript.

Place	Date	Hour	Summary of Events and Information	Remarks and references to Appendices
Bruges	1.3.16		Rendezvous, Refilling Points, Billets & Railhead as for 29t.	Nil
" "	2.3.16		R.V., R.P., Billets & Railhead as for 1st. Received intimation of the prohibition of the use of certain roads during thaw. Ordinary system of delivery supplies will therefore could not be run tomorrow. Supply Column was informed accordingly. Division will probably change billeting area with 1st Can Div. on 6th inst. Digging Party cancelled.	Nil

Army Form C. 2118

WAR DIARY
or
INTELLIGENCE SUMMARY
(Erase heading not required.)

Ag Oro
Salar Owl ADL

Place	Date	Hour	Summary of Events and Information	Remarks and references to Appendices
Druges	3.3.16		Rendezvous - Refilling Points as usual. Hilles Railhead unchanged. Officially informed at 7 pm that the Division will not move more. Major Peebles returned from H.Q. Cavalry Corps.	AH
Druges	4.3.16		R.R. Billets - Railhead as for 3d. Informed by H.Q.T. that the two Brigades of 1st Cav. Dn. now being fed from 3a Cav. Dn. Railhead will be fed from 1st Cav Dn Railhead from & including 6th inst. All agreements for all forward purchases were sent to A.D. of S.T., Cavalry Corps, yesterday. Received authority from ADC in C. to evacuate from Supply Column, Vauxhall car No 810.	HI

Instructions regarding War Diaries and Intelligence Summaries are contained in F.S. Regs., Part II. and the Staff Manual respectively. Title Pages will be prepared in manuscript.

1875 Wt. W593/826 1,000,000 4/15 J.B.C. & A. A.D.S.S./Forms/C. 2118.

Army Form C. 2118

WAR DIARY
or
INTELLIGENCE SUMMARY

(Erase heading not required.)

Army HQ
3rd Cav. Div. A.D.S.

Place	Date	Hour	Summary of Events and Information	Remarks and references to Appendices.
Bruges	5.3.16		R., R.E., Billets & Railhead as for 4th.	ff.
Bruges	6.3.16		A., R.E., Billets & Railhead as for 5th. 3rd Cavalry Division becomes part of G.H.Q. Troops. Applied to A.A. & Q.M.G. for relief for Capt. J.K. Roeder who was admitted Hospital on 29th Jan. 1916	ff.
Bruges	7.3.16		A., R.E., Billets & Railhead as for 6th. Received thro' Ammn. Park claim (865.15 frcs) of M.E. PRUVOT of Fourches en Campagne for damage to his car by one of Ammn. Park. lorries by collision on 19.12.15. Claim recd. to A.A. & Q.M.G.	ff.

WAR DIARY
or
INTELLIGENCE SUMMARY

Army Form C. 2118

#9 3rd Div. Divl. A.D.C.

Place	Date	Hour	Summary of Events and Information	Remarks and references to Appendices
Bruges	8.3.16		R., R.E. Billets & Railhead as for 7th. Major Prescott-Roberts D.A.D. of S.T., G.H.Q., called & discussed points in connection with new administration. Lt. A.E. Johnston applies for service in A.D.C. with Infantry Divn. His application forwarded to A.A.Q. 3rd Divl.	HP
Bruges	9.3.16		R., R.E. Billets & Railhead as for 8th. Lieut. Colonel A.E. Dunning proceeded on 7 days special leave of absence. O.C. Supply Column reports on bad state of roads between Montreuil. Suggests reversion to "thaw" arrangement.	HP

Army Form C. 2118.

WAR DIARY
or
INTELLIGENCE SUMMARY

N⁰ Gro
3d Cav. Div. Art

(Erase heading not required.)

Hour, Date, Place	Summary of Events and Information	Remarks and references to Appendices
Bruges. 10.3.16	R, R.Q. Billets, Railhead as for 9ᵗʰ. Reported to D.A.D. of S.T. 9 M.O. cases of men arriving from Scaer with their own Rations loose, i.e., greasy portions wrapped in newspaper.	H.P.
Bruges 11.3.16	R, R.Q. Billets, Railhead as for 10ᵗʰ.	H.P.
Bruges. 12.3.16	R, R.Q. Billets, Railhead as for 11ᵗʰ. Supply Column reports a collision between S/6 lorry 7301 & R.E. Car M8457 at Montreuil on 10.3.16. Damage to lorry £6. Driver of lorry considered not to blame.	H.P.

War Diary
H.Qn
2nd Cav. Div¹ Adm. Col.

Fruges	10.3.16	R. Billets Railhead as for 12th. R.R. unchanged except for 1st Cav. Bde. supplies for which S.A.A. were dumped at BERNIEULLES & conveyed to FRUQUELIERS by Horse Transport. This arrangement necessary owing to bad state of roads. HP
Fruges	11.3.16	R. + R.R. Billets + Railhead as for 13th. auth/3920 Lt Summers, A.O.C. details surplus to establishment of Divl H.Q. sent to Supply Column. HP

WAR DIARY
or
INTELLIGENCE SUMMARY

Head Qrs. 3rd Cav. Div. A.D.C.

Army Form C. 2118

Place	Date	Hour	Summary of Events and Information	Remarks and references to Appendices
FRUGES	15/3/16		R. R.F. Billets Railhead as for 14th. Notification from D.A.D.g.S & S., G.H.Q., that on and after 17th inst., the 6th & 9th Labour Battalions, R.E., are to be detached from 3rd Cavalry Division Railhead. G.S. forwards details of Divisional School of Instruction to be established at TRAMECOURT — necessary arrangements for rations made.	H.P.
FRUGES	16/3/16		R. R.F. Billets, Railhead as for 15th.	H.P.
FRUGES	17/3/16		R. R.F. Billets, Railhead as for 16th. Water Cart from H.Q. A.D.C. to TRAMECOURT on loan to the Divisional School. Reported to A.D.Q. M.G. the impossibility of hiring civilian horses to pull brushwood at HEZECOURT & asked him to arrange fatigue party.	H.P.

Army Form C. 2118

WAR DIARY
or,
INTELLIGENCE SUMMARY
(Erase heading not required.)

Headqrs.
3rd Cav. Div. A.S.O.

Place	Date	Hour	Summary of Events and Information	Remarks and references to Appendices
Lurges	18.3.16		R. R.P. Billets Railhead as for 17th. Rations delivered to Divisional School at Framecourt by lorry. Rations delivered to 6th & 9th Labour Battalions, R.E. in accordance with instructions received on 15th inst.	H.P.
Lurges	19.3.16		R. R.P. Billets Railhead as for 18th. Received yesterday Daimler Car No. 9016 in place of Daimler Car Notification received thro' A.A.Q.M.G. that all vehicles of Supply Column are to be thoroughly overhauled, one section at a time. Report sent within as now approaching completion	P.L.

Army Form C. 2118

WAR DIARY
or
INTELLIGENCE SUMMARY

Head Qrs. 3rd Cav. Div. A.D.S.

(Erase heading not required.)

Instructions regarding War Diaries and Intelligence Summaries are contained in F.S. Regs, Part II. and the Staff Manual respectively. Title Pages will be prepared in manuscript.

Place	Date	Hour	Summary of Events and Information	Remarks and references to Appendices
Fruges	20.3.16		R. R. Billets Railhead as for 19th	Nil
Fruges	21.3.16		R. R. Billets Railhead as for 20th. Received information of move of Supply Column to BEURAINVILLE. D. of T. sees information regarding Renault car said to have been issued to L. Cadier on 9.11.14	Nil
Fruges	22.3.16		R. R. Billets Railhead as for 21st. Supply Column move to BEURAINVILLE. Railhead remains at MONTREUIL. M.O. 6 Cav. Bde. reports case of reinforcements of 3rd Dragoon Gds. handing over their haversack rations to the Police at Railhead. Instructions given for the return to O.H.Q. of field Syr. lorry.	Nil

Army Form C. 2118

WAR DIARY
or
INTELLIGENCE SUMMARY   HQrs 3rd Cav Divisle
(Erase heading not required.)

Instructions regarding War Diaries and Intelligence Summaries are contained in F. S. Regs., Part II. and the Staff Manual respectively. Title Pages will be prepared in manuscript.

Place	Date	Hour	Summary of Events and Information	Remarks and references to Appendices
FRUGES	23.3.16		R. R.R. Bullets - Railhead as for 22D. Supply Columns Billets at BEURAINVILLE. 2/Lt R.C. Lyle recommended for appointment to Adjutant Divl. M/of S on enquiries to M/2/01907 Re A Skipper, Supply Col., sent to Col/c Adl Section Rhse.	PCL
FRUGES	24.3.16		R. R.R. Bullets - Railhead as for 23rd Lorry attached 3rd Field Squadron sent to G.H.Q. T.S. Co. Received discharge documents of M/M023 S/S G. of Stark, handed them to A. Supply Col. to deal with.	WCL
FRUGES	25.3.16		R. R.R. Bullets - Railhead as for 24th 1/22170 L/Cpl. Newman L. attd H.Q. 3CD. appointed paid Acting Lan. Staff Sergt to date 23/11/15. Two claims (26 & 20 fcs) against supply Col. at MONTREUIL	CCL

1875 Wt. W503/826 1,000,000 4/15 J.B.C. & A. A.D.S.S./Forms/C. 2118.

Army Form C. 2118

WAR DIARY
or
INTELLIGENCE SUMMARY

(Erase heading not required.)

Instructions regarding War Diaries and Intelligence Summaries are contained in F. S. Regs., Part II. and the Staff Manual respectively. Title Pages will be prepared in manuscript.

Place	Date	Hour	Summary of Events and Information	Remarks and references to Appendices
Fruges	26.3.16		Moved to Adv. J.H.Q. R., R.S., Billets Railhead as Fr. 25th.	Sy
Fruges	27.3.16		R.H.Q. Billets Railhead as Fr. 26th Moseley Car M 539 working to Establishment of H.Q. 3 Car Dn. sent to 30 Car Supply Eleven Lorries Vauxhall M 1810.	MS
Fruges	28.3.16		R.H.Q. Billets Railhead as Fr. 27th Temp. Lieut. B.A. Emby, R.E. reported for duty vice Temp. Capt. C.D. Roche, R.E. posted to England. O.C. Adv. inspected transport of 6th Cav. Bde.	MS
Fruges	29.3.16		R.H.Q. Billets Railhead as Fr. 28th Court of Enquiry in collision between Eleven Lorry & R.F.C. Car.	MS

1875 Wt. W 593/826 1,000,000 4/15 T.R.C. & A. A.D.S.S./Forms/C. 2118.

Army Form C. 2118

WAR DIARY
or,
INTELLIGENCE SUMMARY
(Erase heading not required.)

HQrs 3rd Cav Div ADS

Place	Date	Hour	Summary of Events and Information	Remarks and references to Appendices
Surges	30. 3. 16		R.R.P. Billets Railhead as for 29th. O.C. ADS inspected transport of 8th Cav Bde.	
Surges	31. 3. 16		R.R.P. Billets Railhead as for 30th.	

St Murney
Lieut. Colonel
O.C. H.Qrs 3rd Cavalry Div. ADS

Army Form C. 2118.

WAR DIARY
or
INTELLIGENCE SUMMARY.
(Erase heading not required.)

Army: 3rd Cavalry Div. A.S.C.

April 1916

Vol 17

Place	Date	Hour	Summary of Events and Information	Remarks and references to Appendices
FRUGES.	1.4.16		Rendezvous. Refilling Points. Railhead & Billets as before.	
"	2.4.16		R., R.P., Railhead and Billets as for 1st. Directed by "Q" to take steps to abolish of A.T. Unit, personnel vehicles of which (less 1 car, 1 lorry and 3 drivers) are to be absorbed by Supply Column	
"	3.4.16		R., R.P., Railhead & Billets as for 2nd. "Q" directed Supply Column to send an Officer each week to Railhead to meet reinforcements.	
"	4.4.16		R., R.P., Railhead & Billets as for 3rd.	
"	5.4.16		R., R.P., Railhead & Billets as for 4th.	
"	6.4.16		R., R.P., Railhead & Billets as for 5th. Motor car & 30 cwt lorry of J.A.W.R. evacuated to C.H.Q.	
"	7.4.16		R., R.P., Railhead & Billets as for 6th. Rum issue to Divn. ceased. Dump of 7th Cav. Fd. charges to MANNINGHEM. This will release Horse Transport of 10th Reserve Park & will take effect from 11th inst.	
"	8.4.16		R., R.P., Railhead & Billets as for 7th.	
"	9.4.16		R., R.P., Railhead & Billets as for 8th. Canadian Cavalry Brigade to arrive CRECY EN PONTHIEU on G.L stationed b.10"	

Army Form C. 2118.

WAR DIARY
or
INTELLIGENCE SUMMARY.

(Erase heading not required.)

HQrs. 3rd Cavalry Div. A.b.C.

Instructions regarding War Diaries and Intelligence Summaries are contained in F. S. Regs., Part II. and the Staff Manual respectively. Title pages will be prepared in manuscript.

Place	Date	Hour	Summary of Events and Information	Remarks and references to Appendices
FRUGES	9.4.16 (cont)		Move of Temp. Lieut. S.F.S. JOHNSTON to 35th Divl. Train ordered. To be relieved by Temp. Lieut. A. BAYLY.	
"	10.4.16		R, R.P: Billets – Railhead as for 9th. Three days' supply of coal, wood + potatoes delivered to Canadian Cavalry.	
"	11.4.16		R, R.P: Billets – Railhead as for 10th – Temp. Lt. A. Bayly reported for duty and sent to Supply Column for instruction in M.T. work – * Supplies for 1st Cav. Bde. taken by M.T. direct to MANNINGHEM.	
"	12.4.16		R, R.P: Billets – Railhead as for 11th. Received instructions from D.A.D.S.T. that O.C. a/b., 3rd Cav. Div., is to admindle Canadian Cavalry Brigade as regards A.b.C. Duties. On the authority of D. of J. 7598/4 of 8.4.16, the following motor vehicles were sent to D.D.T. (Northern), St Omer, on reduction of establishment :– From HQ. 3rd Cav. Div:– Daimler car M 9016. De Dion lorry 7211	

WAR DIARY
INTELLIGENCE SUMMARY.
(Erase heading not required.)

Army Form C. 2118.

Hdrs, 3rd Cavalry Divl. A.S.C.

Place	Date	Hour	Summary of Events and Information	Remarks and references to Appendices
FRUGES.	13.4.16		From HDrs. Divl. A.S.C., Sunbeam Car M 1795 " " " Wolseley Car M. 575. 3rd Cav. Divl. Supply Col. Sunbeam Car M. 755 " " " Wolseley Car M. 559. One other car, Wolseley M.1796, also to be sent to D.D.T.(N.) is in shops and will not be transferred for a few days.	
-"-	14.4.16		R.R. Billets. Railhead as for 12th. R.R., R.P., Billets. Railhead as for 13th. Submitted to A.A.& Q.M.G. a scheme whereby, with a railhead at MARESQUEL, supplies could be delivered to units by a single echelon of Supply Column. O.C. C.A.D. Canadian Troops called.	
-"-	15.4.16		R.R., R.P., Billets. Railhead as for 14th. Court of Inquiry convened for 11 am 18.4.16, Ammn. Park Office, to investigate circumstances of collision between Napier Motor Ambulance A.9393 of 6th C.D.A., & Supply Column lorry 5185 near LEBIEZ on 10th instant.	

Army Form C. 2118.

WAR DIARY
or
INTELLIGENCE SUMMARY.
(Erase heading not required.)

NRI 3rd Cavalry Div. A.S.C

Instructions regarding War Diaries and Intelligence Summaries are contained in F.S. Regs., Part II. and the Staff Manual respectively. Title pages will be prepared in manuscript.

Place	Date	Hour	Summary of Events and Information	Remarks and references to Appendices
FRDGES	16.4.16		R., R.F. Billets. Railhead as for 15th. Received authority from D.A.D.S.T. G.H.Q. (336.114.4.16) to continue purchasing potatoes. Training camp to be opened at CUCQ. Arranged lorries and H.T. for transport of stores from ETAPLES.	
-"-	17.4.16		R., R.F. Billets. Railhead as for 16th. Authority received for Supply Col. to draw 10,000 rounds S.A.A. for practice purposes and to open range at BEAURAINVILLE. W.3535 to D.A.D.O.S. covering loss of 114,400 lbs of oats through faulty packing of sacks.	
-"-	18.4.16		R., R.F. Billets & Railhead as for 17th. 3rd Field Amb. reported men suffering with boils, caused by an insufficiency of green vegetables. Replied their green vegetables are practically impossible to obtain & that prices are exorbitant. Received from A.A.-Q.M.G. details of arrangements to be made in case of a forward move. Supply Officer of Canadian Cavalry Brigade reports about 60 tons of straw at BLANGY & authority to draw. This was referred to G.H.Q.	
-"-	19.4.16		R., R.F. Billets. Railhead as for 18th. Orders received yesterday for Major G.H. Archibald. 3rd Cavalry Supply Column to proceed to England & report to Director of Supplies & Transport, War Office.	

T2134. Wt. W708—776. 500000. 4/15. Sir J.C. & S.

Army Form C. 2118.

WAR DIARY
or
INTELLIGENCE SUMMARY.
(Erase heading not required.)

WO 3rd Cavalry Div. Ad.

Instructions regarding War Diaries and Intelligence Summaries are contained in F. S. Regs., Part II. and the Staff Manual respectively. Title pages will be prepared in manuscript.

Place	Date	Hour	Summary of Events and Information	Remarks and references to Appendices
FRUGES	20.4.16.		R, R.P., Billets + Railhead as for 19th. Major Q.W. Archibald left for England. Vet. S.T.J. Johnstone left to join 36th Divisional Train, Capt E.S. Coke over duties of Supply Officer 7th Cav Bde., 7/Lt. R.C.Emby three of Requisitioning Officer.	
"	21.4.16.		R, R.P., Billets + Railhead as for 20th. Cav Sgn. + Cyclist Coy. of 19th Divn. to be attached to 3rd Cav Div for training. Rations for consumption on 23rd arranged.	
"	22.4.16.		R, R.P., Billets + Railhead as for 21st. Orders received for Capt. S.H. Bentley to proceed to the Sr. J. School of Instruction, at Cmer. Dump for "C" Battery, R.H.A., changed to TRESSIN, with effect from tomorrow. Temp/Lt.-Col. Pz. Mitant A.S.C. reported from Boulogne, vice Capt. Bentley.	
"	23.4.16.		R, R.P., Billets + Railhead as for 22nd. Capt. (T Major) L.O.A. DUNPHY, A.S.C. posted from 6th Divisional Supply Column to 3rd Cavalry Divisional Supply Column, vice Major Archibald.	

Army Form C. 2118.

WAR DIARY
or
INTELLIGENCE SUMMARY.

(Erase heading not required.)

HQrs. 3rd Cavalry Div. Ade

Instructions regarding War Diaries and Intelligence Summaries are contained in F. S. Regs., Part II. and the Staff Manual respectively. Title pages will be prepared in manuscript.

Place	Date	Hour	Summary of Events and Information	Remarks and references to Appendices
FRUGES	24.4.16		R, R.S., Billets & Railhead as for 23rd. Railhead to be changed to BEURAINVILLE — first drawing on Thursday, 27th inst.	
" "	25.4.16		R, R.S., Billets & Railhead as for 24th. Capt. S.R. Bentby, S.O. & C.B., yesterday left for St Omer. New supply dumps to come into force with change of Railhead. New dumps arranged & letter circulated to S.O.'s & Bdes. Major Dunphy reported for duty as C.C. Supply Col.	
" "	26.4.16		R, R.S., Billets & Railhead as for 25th.	
" "	27.4.16		R, R.S., Billets as for 26th. Railhead Beauvainville.	
" "	28.4.16		R, R.S., Billets & Railhead as for 27th.	
" "	29.4.16		R, R.S., Billets & Railhead as for 28th.	

Army Form C. 2118.

WAR DIARY
or
INTELLIGENCE SUMMARY.
(Erase heading not required.)

HQrs. 3rd Cavalry Divl. Ade

Instructions regarding War Diaries and Intelligence Summaries are contained in F. S. Regs., Part II. and the Staff Manual respectively. Title pages will be prepared in manuscript.

Place	Date	Hour	Summary of Events and Information	Remarks and references to Appendices
FRUGES	30-4-16		R., R.R., Billets & Railhead as for 29th. Issued instructions re supply arrangements for impending move of Divn to ST RIQUIER area. Forwarded to A.A. & Q.M.G. the report of supply column Workshop Officer on neglected state of cars Nr 14857. (H.Qrs. of Cav Bde.)	

Certified true copy

St Mursey Lieut. Colonel.
Comdg. H.Qrs. 3rd Cavalry Divl. Ade.

Army Form C. 2118

WAR DIARY
or
INTELLIGENCE SUMMARY

H.Qrs. 3rd Cav. Divl. Amb.

May 1916

Vol X/18

Place	Date	Hour	Summary of Events and Information	Remarks and references to Appendices
Bruges	1st May '16		Rendezvous, Rejoining Points, Billets, Railhead as for 30".	H.P.
Bruges	2.5.16		R.R.R. Billets, Railhead as for 1st. Acting O.C. Amb visited Canadian Cavalry Brigade.	H.P.
Bruges	3.5.16		R.R.R. Billets, Railhead as for 2nd. Informed by 'Q' that Ans No. 1. Co. is to be held during Brunnen for water carrying purposes & a Reserve Res. the former to carry 2 days rations and Drains for 3rd Cav. Div. Capt. W.O. Campbell 3rd Can. Amb. ordered by wire on 30". ult. to report to D.S.T. War Office, 1st B.J.R. the Battn. returned on 1st. Vier Capt Caughtrees.	H.P.
Bruges	4.5.16		R.R.R. Billets, Railhead as for 3rd.	
Bruges	5.5.16		R.R.R. Billets, Railhead as for 4th.	H.P.

Army Form C. 2118

WAR DIARY
or
INTELLIGENCE SUMMARY
(Erase heading not required.)

HQrs 2n Cav Bde Ade

Instructions regarding War Diaries and Intelligence Summaries are contained in F. S. Regs, Part II. and the Staff Manual respectively. Title Pages will be prepared in manuscript.

Place	Date	Hour	Summary of Events and Information	Remarks and references to Appendices
Bruges	6.5.16		R., R.F. Billets + Railhead as for 5th. Lt./V.D. Riley, S.O. Supply Col., took over duties of R.t.o. 2n Cav. Div. Railhead in the temporary absence of Capt Campion.	HQ
Bruges	7.5.16		R. R.F. Billets + Railhead as for 6th. Canadian Cav. Bde. ordered to go to S.Regins training area on 22nd instead of returning to Divisn. wagon to 3rd R.F.A. camp.	Std
Bruges	8.5.16		R. R.F. Billets + Railhead as for 7th.	
Bruges	9.5.16		R. R.F. Billets + Railhead as for 8th. Order received for Division to move to S.Regins training area on 15th inst. all R.O.H.t. R.F. wagons delivered.	Std
Bruges	10.5.16		R. R.F. Billets + Railhead as for 9th.	Std
Bruges	11.5.16		R. R.F. Billets + Railhead as for 10th.	Std

Army Form C. 2118

WAR DIARY
or
INTELLIGENCE SUMMARY
(Erase heading not required.)

Instructions regarding War Diaries and Intelligence Summaries are contained in F. S. Regs., Part II. and the Staff Manual respectively. Title Pages will be prepared in manuscript.

Place	Date	Hour	Summary of Events and Information	Remarks and references to Appendices
Fruges	12.5.16		R.R.P. Billets & Railhead as for 11th Inst.	Appx
Fruges	13.5.16	7th	"A" Echelon moves to New Training Area. Dumps for supplies at GAVRON ST. MARTIN 10.00 a.m. B." R.R. Billets Railhead as for 11.00	Appx
Fruges	14.5.16		Divisional training before closed down. S.Q. R.R. Railhead as for 13th Lieut E.R.B.Farrer, Lt/Col O'Malley, Lt Allen, Winterbro, Edwards, Pearce, & De Andrews proceed to ST RIQUIER. RENDEZVOUS for "A" Echelon.	Appx
Fruges	15.5.16		"A" Echelon move to new training area also Dist Head Qrs, Auxiliary Horse Transport move from CUCQ to ROYON & Neighb., "B" Echelon draws rations direct from Railhead also Econ Sec, remainder of 8th Brigade & the 7th Brigade to dump as a Brigade (another supplement sent) at AIX-EN-ISSART and HUCQUELIERS, Dist Hosp. at FRUGES. Fourteen move to Macmoore Area.	Appx
Fruges	16.5.16		Supply Column delivering rations direct to Billets for "B" Echelon. R.R.P. Billets as for 10th	Appx
Fruges	17.5.16		R.R.P. as for 16th	Appx

WAR DIARY
or
INTELLIGENCE SUMMARY

Army Form C. 2118

A.Dio. 3rd Cav. Div. Ade

Place	Date	Hour	Summary of Events and Information	Remarks and references to Appendices
Bruges	18.5.16		R. R.R. Killus Railhead as for 17".	Mil
Bruges	19.5.16		R. R.R. Killus Railhead as for 18".	Mil
Bruges	20.5.16		R. R.R. Killus Railhead as for 19".	Mil
Bruges	21.5.16		R. R.R. Killus Railhead as for 20".	Mil
Bruges	22.5.16		R.R.R. Killus Railhead as for 21".	Mil
Bruges	23.5.16		R.R.R. Billus Railhead as for 22nd. Field Cashier directed to take his car with D.P.O.S. (A.Q.Mr.Gs Instructions) Field Sqn to remain as Ve Brigade under 3rd Div.	Mil

Army Form C. 2118

WAR DIARY
or
INTELLIGENCE SUMMARY
(Erase heading not required.)

Instructions regarding War Diaries and Intelligence Summaries are contained in F.S. Regs., Part II. and the Staff Manual respectively. Title Pages will be prepared in manuscript.

Place	Date	Hour	Summary of Events and Information	Remarks and references to Appendices
Fruges	24.5.16		Railhead + Billets as for 23rd. 3rd Dn: Gots 16th Rfl. S. move to MERLIMONT. 2nd Life Guards + 1st Rfl. S. go to Hurlemont Plage tomorrow for training. Roy: Dragoons to go from Fruges to Frévent on Saturday. 7th Lgt. Armoured Car Battery are billeted at Fregent.	Md
Fruges	25.5.16		R.R. Billets + Railhead as for 24th. 2 A/T. wagons attached to North Somerset Yeomanry to assist in drawing rations.	Md
Fruges	26.5.16		R.R.S. Billets + Railhead as for 25th. Reports hospital. Yesterday cases of Officers kits arriving at Railhead unsealed & also explosives being sent.	Md
Fruges	27.5.16		R. R.R. Billets + Railhead as for 26th.	Md
Fruges	28.5.16		R. R.S. Billets + Railhead as for 27th. 3rd Cav. Div: Reserve Park joins 29th will be billeted at LA LOGE.	Md

WAR DIARY
or,
INTELLIGENCE SUMMARY

(Erase heading not required.)

Army Form C. 2118

HdQrs.
3rd Cav. Divl. Ab

Place	Date	Hour	Summary of Events and Information	Remarks and references to Appendices
FRUGES	29.5.16		R., R.E., Billets, Railhead as for 29th	M
Sarges	30.5.16		R., R.E., Billets, Railhead as for 29th. 3rd Cavalry Reserve Park billetted for convenience in GHQ Troops area at LA HOGE but comes under 3rd Cavalry Division for discipline. Supplies for the Park will be drawn from G.H.Q. 2nd Echelon Railhead (Telegram R.17 of Reserve Army 'Q' to 3rd Cavalry Division 'Q' 29.5.16). Drew the attention of AAQMG to the necessity of all motor cars in Division being taken into shops for ten days for thorough overhaul.	M
Sarges	31.5.16		R., R.E., Billets, Railhead as for 30th. Remainder of 6' Cav. Bre moved down to the Coast.	GM

S.W. Murray, Lieut. Colonel
Comdg. HdQrs. 3rd Cav. Divl. Ab

WAR DIARY

INTELLIGENCE SUMMARY.
(Erase heading not required.)

Army Form C. 2118.

Ladyio
3rd Cav. Div. Amm. Col.

June 1916

VOL 19

Place	Date	Hour	Summary of Events and Information	Remarks and references to Appendices
FRUGES	1.6.16		R.R.R. Billets & Railhead unchanged. Received approval of G.O.C. Reg to proceed with overhauling of Divl. motor cars. Capt. & Major H.A.C. GARDNER posted to O.C. 3rd C.D. Supply Col vice Capt. & Major Dunphy (invalided).	S&L
FRUGES	2.6.16		R.R.R. Billets & Railhead unchanged. Instructed OC Supply Col to carefully check all receipt trains of petrol owing to constant shortages reported by that unit. Major Gardner reported for duty.	S&L
FRUGES	3.6.16		R.R.R. Billets & Railhead. as for 2nd.	S&L
FRUGES	4.6.16		R.R.R. Billets & Railhead as for 3rd. Received decision of O.R.O. that 3rd C.D. Reserve Park may be used for supply purposes. Both GHQ Troops & 3rd Cav. Div. have use of wagons of this Park but each must inform the other when she vehicles are being used.	10&L
FRUGES	5.6.16		R.R.R. Billets & Railhead as for 4th.	12&L M&L
FRUGES	6.6.16		R.R.R. Billets & Railhead as for 5th.	M&L
FRUGES	7.6.16		R.R.R. Billets & Railhead as for 6th.	M&L
FRUGES	8.6.16		R.R.R. Billets & Railhead as for 7th. Arrangements made for supplies to troops during the two days	N&L

WAR DIARY
or
INTELLIGENCE SUMMARY.

Headquarters, 3rd Cavalry Divl. A.S.C.

(Erase heading not required.)

Army Form C. 2118.

Place	Date	Hour	Summary of Events and Information	Remarks and references to Appendices
FRUGES	9.6.16		Manoeuvres commencing 14th inst. R.R.R. Bill's Railhead as for 9th inst.	Nil
"	10.6.16		R.R.R. Bill's Railhead as for 9th inst. B.Q. am. held on R.E. Latimer, Ade. Sala. Sr. Ammunition Park in office O.C. Cav.	Nil
"	11.6.16		5 Metham Fair. British forces from Havre. R.R.R. Mills Railhead as for 10th.	Nil
"	12.6.16		R.R.R. Mills Railhead as for 11th.	Nil
"	13.6.16		-do- Manoeuvres cancelled. W.O. Riva complained of flinty nature of oat sacks — heard his complaint to D.A.D.S.T., G.H.Q. to see if anything could be done.	Nil
"	14.6.16		R.R.R. Mills Railhead as for 13th.	
"	15.6.16		-do- Reported to A.A.Q.M.G. complete plans of new routine of Corps Allotp. Supply Column for transmission to War Office.	Nil
"	16.6.16		inclosures of partition of Q.S. Limbered wagons. R.R.R. Mills Railhead as for 15th.	

Army Form C. 2118.

WAR DIARY
or
INTELLIGENCE SUMMARY.
(Erase heading not required.)

Headqrs.
3rd Cavalry Divisional A.S.C.

Instructions regarding War Diaries and Intelligence Summaries are contained in F.S. Regs., Part II. and the Staff Manual respectively. Title pages will be prepared in manuscript.

Place	Date	Hour	Summary of Events and Information	Remarks and references to Appendices
FRUGES	17.6.16		R., R.R. Billets Railhead as for 16th	
"	18.6.16		— " —	
"	19.6.16		— " — In view of impending move, Supply Column instructed to deliver rations on 21.6.1 to Units Permanent billets.	
"	20.6.16		R., R.R. Billets Railhead as to 19th. Owing to difficulties experienced in fitting Lewis Gun trucks & weapons of 3rd Cav. Divn. Amn. "H.T. Co. (now receipt of are fitting &c) the whole Company will proceed tomorrow to Calais, Horse Transport Depot at ABBEVILLE where arrangements is to be given to stay at LE BOISLE night of 21.6.16 and arrive at Abbeville on 22nd. Company rationed up to and for 23rd. Detachment of Coy at CUCQ Camp will proceed to Abbeville direct. Applied to D.A.D.S., G.H.Q. for permission to evacuate 3 unserviceable lorries of the Supply Column.	

Army Form C. 2118.

WAR DIARY
or
INTELLIGENCE SUMMARY.
(Erase heading not required.)

H.Qrs. 3rd Cav. Div. Ade.

Place	Date	Hour	Summary of Events and Information	Remarks and references to Appendices
FRUGES	21.6.16		R., R.E., Sigs. Railhead as for 20th. 3rd Cav. Div. Auxiliary Horse Transport Coy. Strength 112 all ranks, 179 horses and 38 vehicles left for ABBEVILLE at 2pm on arrival.	MEL
FRUGES	22.6.16		R., R.E., Sigs. Railhead as for 21st. 304 Coy R.A.S.C. Supply Col. Surplus. 58097 Cpl. Bax to arrived from base 14TR and sent to H.Q. 8th Cav. Bde. as Requisitioning N.C.O. Yesterday received orders for Capt. T. Major W. Peebles to report to D.D.S.T., Third Army, for duty as D.A.D. of Supplies. Genl. Major G.I. Carver reported last night in relief. Wired to D.D.S.T., 3rd Army, that Major Peebles will report on Saturday morning.	MEL
FRUGES	23.6.16		R., R.E., Sigs. Railhead as for 22nd.	MEL
FRUGES	24.6.16		R., R.E., Sigs. Railhead as for 23rd. H.Qrs. 3rd Cav. Div. Ade. left FRUGES 7 pm. 2IC 6.16 H. received by march route via HESDIN to FONTAINE SUR MAYE arriving there about 3.30 am 25th.	MEL

Army Form C. 2118.

WAR DIARY
or
INTELLIGENCE SUMMARY.
(Erase heading not required.)

Headqrs.
3rd Cav. Div. A.& Q.

Place	Date	Hour	Summary of Events and Information	Remarks and references to Appendices
FONTAINE S/MAYE	25.6.16		Left FONTAINE S/MAYE at 8pm and arrived at DOMART EN PONTHIEU at 3 am 26th. Rendezvous 2pm at 1pm 2 kms. East of COULONVILLERS. Refilling points in vicinity of billets.	S.E.L
DOMART EN PONTHIEU	26.6.16		Left DOMART EN PONTHIEU at 7.30 pm & proceeded by march route via AMIENS to LE NEUVILLE near CORBIE arriving 6.30 am. Office at LE NEUVILLE — BONNAY road. Company bivouacked in fields on LE NEUVILLE — BONNAY road. Refilling point in vicinity of morning billets — Railhead CAYEUX.	S.E.L
LE NEUVILLE	27.6.16		Railhead MERICOURT. Refilling Points on LE NEUVILLE — BONNAY road. Remained in LE NEUVILLE.	S.E.L
-,,-	28.6.16		R.,R.R. Billets Railhead as for 27th.	M.I.
-,,-	29.6.16		R.,R.R. Billets Railhead as for 28th. M/2/018467 Cpl. Grainge, G.T. reported from Remy Kent to Supply Column.	M.I.
-,,-	30.6.16		R.R.R. Billets Railhead as for 29th.	M.I.

S.E.Murray. Lieut. Colonel.
Comdg. HQrs. 3rd Cavalry Divl. A.C.

Army Form C. 2118.

WAR DIARY
or
INTELLIGENCE SUMMARY.

(Erase heading not required.)

H.Qrs,
3rd Cavalry Divisional A.S.C.

July 1916

WC 20

Place	Date	Hour	Summary of Events and Information	Remarks and references to Appendices
LA NEUVILLE (SOMME)	1st July 1916		Rendezvous LA NEUVILLE - BORAY Road. Refilling Point rendezvous placed on same Road. Railhead MERICOURT L'ABBÉ. Office billets of H.Qr Adc. Rue de République. LA NEUVILLE, Company barracked in LA NEUVILLE - BORAY Road.	Nil
LA NEUVILLE	2nd July 1916		R, RP, Billets, Bivouac & Railhead as for 1st.	Nil
-"-	3rd July 1916		- do -	Nil
-"-	4th July 1916		H.Q.Ors Divl Ade left LA NEUVILLE at 7am. Preceded by march route to HALLENCOURT (S.E. of ABBEVILLE) arriving there 9.30 p.m. same day. Rendezvous HANDGEST - Refilling Points - Div. Troops HALLENCOURT, 6th CavBde at MERELESSART, 7th CavBde. at WANEL & 8th BDE. at BAILLEUL. Railhead remained at MERICOURT.	Nil
HALLENCOURT (SOMME)	5th July 1916		Rendezvous, Nil - Refilling Points as yesterday, also billets as occupied yesterday at HALLENCOURT. Railhead changed to LONGPRÉ - Supply Column moved to AIRAINES.	Nil
-"-	6th July 1916		RP, Billets Railhead as for 5th. Orders received to be in readiness to move at 1½ hrs notice from tomorrow.	Nil

Army Form C. 2118.

WAR DIARY
or
INTELLIGENCE SUMMARY.
(Erase heading not required.)

Hd Qrs 3rd Cavalry Div. A.A.

Place	Date	Hour	Summary of Events and Information	Remarks and references to Appendices
HALLENCOURT (SOMME)	7th July '16		Refueling Points, Billets, Railhead as for 6th. Orders received cancelling 1½ hour notice to be ready to move.	Nil
—"—	8th July '16		Refueling Points, Billets and Railhead as for 7th. Received orders at 12.30 a.m. that Division should be prepared at 1 hour's notice again to the neighbourhood of QUERRIEUX. Left HALLENCOURT at 1.15 pm and proceeded by march route to DAOURS, arriving there 1.30 am on 9th. Supplies for this dumped at new Billets & Hrs.	SEL
DAOURS (SOMME)	9th July '16		Company on arrival billeted at entrance to village. Railhead MERICOURT. Refueling Point - 6th Cav Bde. at VENUX — 7th (VAUX) Cav. Bde. at LA NEUVILLE. 8th Cav Bde. at BONNAY, Divisional troops at DAOURS. Moved to field just outside village of DAOURS on right bank of the river SOMME where railway crosses the river and bivouaced.	Nil
DAOURS	10th July '16		Railhead MELTON. Refilling Points as on 9th. Bivouac as 9th. Supply Column S.S. detached to Supply Column	Nil
—"—	11th July '16		Railhead, Refilling Points as as usual Bivouac Nil

Army Form C. 2118.

WAR DIARY
or
INTELLIGENCE SUMMARY.
(Erase heading not required.)

H.Qu. 3rd Cavalry Div. A.L.

Instructions regarding War Diaries and Intelligence Summaries are contained in F. S. Regs., Part II. and the Staff Manual respectively. Title pages will be prepared in manuscript.

Place	Date	Hour	Summary of Events and Information	Remarks and references to Appendices
DAOURS	11th July 16		Railhead MELTON. Rendezvous list — Refilling Points: Div. troops at DAOURS - 6th Cav Reg VAUX, 7th Cav Bde BONNAY, 8th Cav Bde CORBIE. The 1st & 2nd Life Gds at SENLIS, received breakfast only for 12th July, the remainder of the rations being descended at CORBIE, where they return on morning of 12th.	PTW
" "	12th July 16		Railhead MELTON. Refilling Points: Div. troops 6th Cav Bde. VAUX, 7th CORBIE, 8th BONNAY, Div. troops DAOURS, loading at Railhead was delayed by 4th Army at 3.30 am but the train did not arrive until 6 am. Rations were loaded according to 'A' & 'B' Echelons, Heavy section of C.F.A's loaded with Div. troops 'A' also 13th & 14th Hussars. Returns 20th Vet. S. loaded with Div. troops 18th. Mobile sections transferred from Ammunition Column to Each Battery. Three transfers in effect the last mentioned will not take effect until the Divs. required.	PTW
" "	13th July 16		Railhead, Refilling Points and accommodation unchanged.	PTW
" "	14th July 16		Railhead, Refilling Points, accommodation as for 13th. Half hours' notice to move suspended during night to be resumed 5 am tomorrow.	PTW

Army Form C. 2118.

WAR DIARY
or
INTELLIGENCE SUMMARY.
(Erase heading not required.)

3rd Cavalry Divl. Adc.

Place	Date	Hour	Summary of Events and Information	Remarks and references to Appendices
D.NOURS.	15th July 16		Railhead, Refilling Points & accommodation as yesterday.	Ref.
-"-	16th July 16		Railhead, R.P. & accommodation as for 15th.	Ref.
-"-	17th July 16		— do —	Ref.
-"-	18th July 16		— do —	Ref.
-"-	19th		— do —	Ref.
-"-	19th		Railhead & accommodation as for 18th. Refilling Points the same except that of 7th Cav. Bde. at LA NEUVILLE instead of VAUX	Ref.
-"-	20th -"-		Railhead, Refilling Points and accommodation as for 19th.	Ref.
-"-	21st -"-		-"-	Ref.
-"-	22nd -"-		-"-	Ref.
-"-	23rd -"-		-"-	Ref.
-"-	24th -"-		-"-	Ref.
-"-	25th -"-		-"-	Ref.
-"-	26th -"-		-"-	Ref.
-"-	27th -"-		Railhead and accommodation as to 26th. Refilling Points as follows, unchanged. A working party from 7th Cav. Bde. went to BOIS DE HENNECOURT on 25th instant and then returns with	Ref.

Army Form C. 2118.

WAR DIARY
or
INTELLIGENCE SUMMARY.
(Erase heading not required.)

HQrs.
3rd Cav. Div. A.I.S.

Place	Date	Hour	Summary of Events and Information	Remarks and references to Appendices
DAOURS	28th July /16		sent to them there. Working parties from 6th & 8th Cavalry Brigades have been near BÉCOURT since 25th. Their rations are dumped at VIVIER MILL. Another party from 7th Cav. Bde. working for III Corps has its rations dumped at the same place. Railhead Refilling Point, Railhead & accommodation as for 27th.	Nil
	29th	— " —	One day's reserve rations for men and horses handed over to the forages at CORBIE. A detachment of 3rd Sucks Squadron is with the working parties of 6th & 8th Cavalry Brigades mentioned yesterday.	Nil
" "	30th	— " —	No change in Railhead, Refilling points or accommodation. Railhead Refilling Points accommodation as for 29th. All working parties to be withdrawn tomorrow and Division will move westwards on 1st August.	Nil
" "	31st	— " —	Railhead Refilling Point, accommodation as for 30th. Working parties except that at CONTAY, were withdrawn today & arranged, were rations from usual Bde dumps	Nil

St. Wynne, Lt. Colonel
Comdg. HQ. 3rd Cavalry Divisional Arty.

Army Form C. 2118.

WAR DIARY
or
INTELLIGENCE SUMMARY.

3rd Cavalry Divisional A.S.C.

August 1916

Place	Date	Hour	Summary of Events and Information	Remarks and references to Appendices
DAOURS (SOMME)	1st August 16		HQrs 3rd Cavalry Divn. A.S.C. left DAOURS at 9am and proceeded by march route via AMIENS, to LE QUESNOY (SOMME) arriving there 3pm same day. Railhead for today — MERICOURT. Rendezvous — CROUY. Refilling Points were as follows:— 6th Cav. Bde. — MESGES r.. 7th Cav. Bde. — CAVILLON r.. 8th Cav. Bde. — HANGEST r.. Divisional Troops LE QUESNOY.	S/L
LE QUESNOY (SOMME)	2nd "		Left LE QUESNOY at 9am and proceeded by road to ST RIQUIER which place was reached at 2pm. Railhead for today — ST RIQUIER. Rendezvous at ST RIQUIER. Refilling Points:— Divisional Troops at YVRENCH. 6th Cav. Bde. at CROUS. 7th Cav. Bde. at ST RIQUIER. 8th Cav. Bde. at DRUCAT.	S/L
ST RIQUIER	3rd "		Remained at ST RIQUIER all day. Railhead, Rendezvous and Refilling Points as yesterday.	S/L
ST RIQUIER	4th "		HQrs 3rd Cav. Divl. A.S.C. left ST RIQUIER at 10 am. proceeded by road to LIGESCOURT, arriving there 2.30 pm. Railhead — ST RIQUIER. Rendezvous for Divisional Troops remained at ST RIQUIER, that for 6th & 7th Cdn. at VRON. & 8th Cd. at LIGESCOURT. (cont.)	S/L

Army Form C. 2118.

WAR DIARY
or
INTELLIGENCE SUMMARY

(Erase heading not required.)

H.Qrs. 3rd Cavalry Divisional A.S.C.

Place	Date	Hour	Summary of Events and Information	Remarks and references to Appendices
Ht. Aug. (cont.)			Refilling Points for this day as follows:- Divisional troops at LIGESCOURT. 8th Cav. Bde. at DOURIEZ. 6th Cav. Bde. MAINTENAY. 7th Cav. Bde. SAULCHOY.	S.R.U.
LIGESCOURT	5th Aug./16		Left LIGESCOURT at 8 am and proceeded by march route to FRUGES (via C.) arriving there about 3.30 pm. Railhead returned to BEAURAINVILLE. No rendezvous. Refilling Points at old billets, ie. except 8th Cav Bde in AUCHY area. H.Qrs. Adv. received files on FRUGES - CREQUY road.	Nil
FRUGES	6th Aug/16		Railhead, Refilling Points & accommodation are as per 5th.	Nil
"	7th "		" " "	Nil
			7. Cpl. Blanchard, F.W. admitted hospital. T.10860 6981 Badger, N.S.G. arrived from Base A.S.C. Depot. proceeded to 6th Cavalry Field Ambulance on 8th.	Nil
"	8th "		Railhead, Refilling Points & accommodation as for 7th.	Nil
"	9th "		Railhead, Refilling Points & accommodation as for 8th.	Nil

Army Form C. 2118.

WAR DIARY
or
INTELLIGENCE SUMMARY.
(Erase heading not required.)

Head qrs. 3rd Cav. Div. A.D.S.

Instructions regarding War Diaries and Intelligence Summaries are contained in F. S. Regs., Part II. and the Staff Manual respectively. Title pages will be prepared in manuscript.

Place	Date	Hour	Summary of Events and Information	Remarks and references to Appendices
FRUGES	10th Aug '16		Railhead Refilling Points reaccomodation as for 9th — 6th Cavalry Brigade, conveying yesterday drew their supplies direct from Railhead by horse transport. T/586 Wheeler Corporal Elliott. A. A.S.C. arrived from Base Horse Transport Depot and was admitted to hospital in evening.	AW
"	11th Aug '16		Railhead Refilling Points and accomodation as for 10th. Notification received from Div. H.Qrs. that as a temporary measure, D.A.D. of S. + T. G.H.Q. Troops, will supervise supply arrangements of 3rd Cavalry Division.	S.W.
"	12th Aug '16		Railhead Refilling Points and accomodation as for 11th. T/4/058026 Act'g Wheeler Corporal BYRNE, P. to 4th Can. 6. Ambulance.	AW
"	13th Aug '16		Railhead Refilling Points & accomodation as for 12th. 2/124 Driver Blake. G. admitted hospital suffering from effects of horse kick on face.	AW
"	14th Aug '16		Railhead. Refilling Points & accomodation as for 13th. Programme issued for new supply arrangements with a	AW

Army Form C. 2118.

WAR DIARY
or
INTELLIGENCE SUMMARY.

Morgan,
3rd Cav. Div. A.S.C.

(Erase heading not required.)

Place	Date	Hour	Summary of Events and Information	Remarks and references to Appendices
FRUGES.	15th Aug 16		Railhead at HESDIN which commenced tomorrow. Railhead HESDIN. Following arrangements for carriage of supplies came into force — 6th Cav. Bde. continued as before. 7th Cav. Bde. to ERGNY from MONTREUIL by light railway. Cav. Hdqrs. (less 10th Hussars, H.Q. Sqn & Q. Batt.) by lorry to a Brigade Dump at BLANGY, thence to billets by Regtl. transport. 10th Hussars & Kilgour Sqn & "Q" Battery drawing direct from HESDIN Railhead by Regimental transport. Divisional troops (less Reserve Park & Supply Column) are conveyed by light railway from Montreuil to FRUGES. Supply Column draw at HESDIN and Reserve Park BEAURAINVILLE. Q6. All indented transport of 8th Cavalry Brigade.	Nil Nil
"	16th Aug 16		Railhead HESDIN. Supply arrangements same as in force yesterday except that in the case of 1st Royal Dragoons & Kilgour Squadron & C.R.H.A. the Reserve Park wagons conveyed supplies from railhead to a dump at the x roads	Nil

WAR DIARY or INTELLIGENCE SUMMARY.

Army Form C. 2118.

H.Q.
3rd Cav. Div. A.C.

Place	Date	Hour	Summary of Events and Information	Remarks and references to Appendices
	16th Aug. continued		North of W in R. WAMIN on main HESDIN-FRUGES road (ref 1/100,000.), thence by Regimental transport to billets. 1/3865 Whelr. Corpl. Elliott returned from 26 Gen. Hosp. Étaples.	Nil
Wt FRUGES	17th Aug/16.		Railhead, supply arrangements and accommodation as yesterday.	Nil
-"-	18th Aug/16		No change in Railhead or supply arrangements. Accommodation as of yesterday. G.O.C. commented upon inadequate punishments meted out to many offenders in 3rd Cavalry Division Reserve Park. Directed the O.C. Park to read extract from G.O.C's remarks on parade to host them to all men to read. He is also to forward 80869 Pte Irvine at each week. 1/23865 Corpl. Blanchard, R.H. rejoined from hospital. Lieut. A/Capt. Luce, R.F.A., 3rd Cav. Div. Ammunition Park, joined 3.5 p.m. Division for duty.	Nil
-"-	19th Aug		No change in accommodation, railhead or supply arrangements.	Nil
-"-	20th Aug/16		Accommodation, railhead + supply arrangements as on 19th.	Nil

Army Form C. 2118.

WAR DIARY
or
INTELLIGENCE SUMMARY
(Erase heading not required.)

Hdqrs.
3rd Cavalry Div. A.V.

Instructions regarding War Diaries and Intelligence Summaries are contained in F. S. Regs., Part II. and the Staff Manual respectively. Title pages will be prepared in manuscript.

Place	Date	Hour	Summary of Events and Information	Remarks and references to Appendices
FRUGES	21st Aug '16		Accommodation, railhead and supply arrangements as for 20th.	Nil
" "	22nd Aug '16		" " " "	Nil
			O.C. A.D.C. inspected the transport of the 7th Cavalry Bde.	Nil
" "	23rd Aug '16		Accommodation, railhead and supply arrangements as for 22nd.	Nil
" "	24th Aug '16		Accommodation, railhead and supply arrangements as for 23rd.	Nil
		7/26	Lt. Col. Luff D.S.O. arrived from Base A.V. Depôt.	
" "	25th Aug '16		Accommodation, railhead and supply arrangements as for 24th.	Nil
		7/2224	O.C. Clarke G. reported from Hospital	
" "	26th Aug '16		Accommodation, railhead and supply arrangements as for 25th.	Nil
			1 Lieut. A.J. Pearce A.V.C. posted from 3rd Divisional Train to 3rd Cavalry Divisional AD., in anticipation of the move of Temp. Lieut. A.M.S. Dunn R.O. 6th Cav. Bde.	
" "	27th Aug '16		Accommodation, railhead and supply arrangements as for 26th.	Nil
			D.A.D.S.T. G.H.Q. arranged that 3rd Can. Div. should take over the Bois de Gardmont for fuel supply. Forwarded to H.Q. a proposal to use limbers of Regts for carting thos wood. Cartage

Army Form C. 2118.

WAR DIARY or INTELLIGENCE SUMMARY.

(Erase heading not required.)

A.Dr: 3rd Cav. Div: Adm

Place	Date	Hour	Summary of Events and Information	Remarks and references to Appendices
FRUGES	28 Aug 16		will start on 30th inst. Accommodation railhead and supply arrangements as for 27th. 1 Capt. E.O. Bax Adm. Transport Officer 6th Cavalry Brigade was admitted to Duchess of Westminster Hospital on 18th inst. suffering from dislocation of shoulder. Owing to shortage of pool cars called upon the supply Column & Ammunition Park to supply me cars each to the pool as a temporary measure. Application of Lieut. N. Coates Supply Column for Transfer to R.A. refused on the ground that he is an N.T. Officer.	Nil
"	29 Aug 16		Accommodation, railhead and supply arrangements as for 28th.	Nil
"	30 Aug 16		Accommodation railhead and supply arrangements as for 29th. Drawing of wood from Bois de Gohament postponed until 1st Prox. 2nd Lieut. M. Pearce reported for duty vice 2nd Lieut. N. W. J. DUUS. Temp Lieut N. W. J. DUUS, Adm. R.o. 6th Car Bde, tried by General Court Martial at Maisin, FRUGES.	Nil

Army Form C. 2118.

WAR DIARY
or
INTELLIGENCE SUMMARY.
(Erase heading not required.)

Hd Qrs 3rd Cavalry Divl. Alt

Instructions regarding War Diaries and Intelligence Summaries are contained in F. S. Regs., Part II. and the Staff Manual respectively. Title pages will be prepared in manuscript.

Place	Date	Hour	Summary of Events and Information	Remarks and references to Appendices
FRUGES	31st Aug 1916		Accommodation reached and supply arrangements as for 30th. Supplies to Royal Dragoons, 6th Machine Gun squadron & E Baton RHA to be dumped at 9.45 am from tomorrow, inclusive instead of 8.45 am as at present. Drawing of wood from Bois de Gosnaywood to start tomorrow.	SEE

S.H. Murray Lieut Colonel
Cmdg Hd Qrs 3rd Cavalry Divisional Alt
31st August 1916

Confidential

AA-Q.M.G.
3rd Cav. Div.

Herewith War Diary
of H.Q. 3rd Cav. Divisional
A.S.C. for the month of
September 1916.

S.E. Cumming
Lt. Colonel
1.10.16.   OC ASC 3rd Cav Div

Army Form C. 2118.

No 22
HQrs. 3rd Cavalry Div. A&Q

WAR DIARY
or
INTELLIGENCE-SUMMARY.
(Erase heading not required.)

Instructions regarding War Diaries and Intelligence Summaries are contained in F.S. Regs., Part II. and the Staff Manual respectively. Title pages will be prepared in manuscript.

Place	Date	Hour	Summary of Events and Information	Remarks and references to Appendices
FRUGES.	1st Sept '16		Accommodation, railhead and supply arrangements as for yesterday.	Nil
"	2nd Sept '16		Accommodation, railhead and supply arrangements as for 1st.	Stu
"	3rd Sept '16		Accommodation railhead and supply arrangements as for 2nd. Applied to Division Col. for loan of 8 G.S. Wagons and 4th men to assist in moving a quantity of brushwood from Hesdigneul Wood.	Stu
"	4 Sept '16		Accommodation, railhead and supply arrangements as for 3rd. Considered it advisable to make certain changes in supply officers clerical staff and so ordered the following moves:- 5/23754 S/Sergt. G.I. Reading from 6th Cav. Bde. to H.Q. A.S.C. SS/11155 Pte. G.D. O'Malley from A.S.C. HQrs to 6th Cav. Bde. 5/SH456 A/Sergt. R.C. Lambert from 8th Cav. Bde. to 6th Cav. Bde. SS/935 Pte. B.J. Grant from 6th Cav. Bde. to 8th Cav. Bde. D.A.S.T. GHQ asked for a guard for store dumps at BLANGY. This was referred to A and Q. rely.	Nil

Army Form C. 2118.

WAR DIARY
or
INTELLIGENCE SUMMARY.
(Erase heading not required.)

3rd Cavalry Divisional A.D.C.

Place	Date	Hour	Summary of Events and Information	Remarks and references to Appendices
FRUGES	5th Sept. 1916		Accommodation, railhead and supply arrangements as for 4th	Nil
	6 - " -		- do -	Nil
	7 - " -		- do -	Nil
	8 - " -		- do -	Nil
	9 - " -		Division to move from present billeting area on 10th inst. Accommodation, railhead and supply arrangements as for 7th	Nil
	10 - " -	9 a.m.	HQrs. A.D.C. left FRUGES at 9.30 a.m. and proceeded by march route via HESDIN to DOMPIERRE on the AUTHIE RIVER. Arrived at DOMPIERRE at 4 p.m. and bivouaced. Railhead remained at HESDIN. Refilling points as follow:- Divisional Supply FRUGES (for details reverse blind) and DOMPIERRE. 1st Cav. Bde. Authie R. area. 7th Cav. Bde. and 8th Cav. Bde. same area. Supply Column remained at HESDIN. Ammunition Park at FRUGES and Reserve Park at GUISY.	See }
See } Apx
DOMPIERRE	11th Sept. 16		The Unit left DOMPIERRE at 1 p.m. and proceeded by road to GUESCHART arriving there 3.30 p.m. On arrival found accommodation	Nil

WAR DIARY or INTELLIGENCE SUMMARY

Army Form C. 2118.

3rd Cavalry Divisional Ad.

Place	Date	Hour	Summary of Events and Information	Remarks and references to Appendices
			In Chateau there. Railhead ST RIQUIER. Refilling Points as follow:- Divl. troops @ MAISON PONTHIEU, 6 Cav Bde at ST RIQUIER etc 7th Cav. Bde at ST RIQUIER etc and 8th Cav Bde same. Ammunition Park moved from Surges to GUESCHART	Md.
12th Sept 16. GUESCHART.			Adv Ad. left GUESCHART at 9 am proceeded by road to BELLOY SUR SOMME arriving there 3.30 p.m. Railhead remained at ST RIQUIER. Refilling Points:- Divl troops BELLOY sur SOMME, 6th Cav. Bde. LA CHAUSSÉE, 7th Cav. Bde. BOURDON 8th Cav Bde ST SAUVEUR. Temp. Lieut. A Smith Adc posted from 1 to 2 Reserve Park vice Temp. Capt. E.W. Barr (invalided).	Md
13th Sept. BELLOY			BELLOY sur SOMME all day. Adc Hopkinson the new Adc Hopkinson - Railhead at VIGNACOURT. Remained at Refilling Points as yesterday.	Md.
14.6 Sept BELLOY			H.Q.Ad. left BELLOY sur SOMME at 9 am proceeded by	

Army Form C. 2118.

WAR DIARY
or
INTELLIGENCE SUMMARY.
(Erase heading not required.)

H.Qrs. 3rd Cavalry Div. A.S.C.

Place	Date	Hour	Summary of Events and Information	Remarks and references to Appendices
			road to DAOURS. Railhead CORBIE. Refilling Points in area around Daours. 3rd Cavalry Divisional Auxiliary H.T. Co opened Division after handing over late wagons to 10th Reserve Park in exchange for G.S. wagons not to fitted Aux H.T. Co to be used in future for carriage of ammunition & the company loaded up with ammunition this evening. Regiments & "A" Echelons of Brigades to leave tomorrow for BONNAY & LA NEUVILLE areas. "B" Echelons remaining at DAOURS.	Nil
DAOURS	15th Apr. 16		Removing ten wagons of aux H.T. Co. required Company, arrived camp. Attempt, filled up with ammunition. Sent to Lieut. B.F. Emby, Ro, 7th Car. Sch, admitted to New Zealand Hospital Amiens. Railhead ALBERT. Refilling Points at Units' billets and camping grounds.	Nil

Army Form C. 2118.

WAR DIARY
or
INTELLIGENCE SUMMARY.
(Erase heading not required.)

H. Qrs. 3rd Cavalry Divl. A.S.C.

Instructions regarding War Diaries and Intelligence Summaries are contained in F. S. Regs., Part II. and the Staff Manual respectively. Title pages will be prepared in manuscript.

Place	Date	Hour	Summary of Events and Information	Remarks and references to Appendices
DAOURS	16th Sept. 16		Railhead ALBERT. Refilling points in vicinity of billets and camping grounds. Temp. Lce. Lieut. J.C. SMITH A.S.C. arrived from No. 2 Reserve Park for duty as Brigade Transport Officer, 8th Cavalry Bde. vice Temp. Capt. E.W. BAKER (invalided). Arrangements made for drawing rations of "B" Echelon in bulk from CORBIE Brigade Reserve Park. A.Q.M.G. proceeding Transport.	Nil
DAOURS	17th Sept. 16		Railhead ALBERT. Fighting troops returned to Daours when Received letter from L. General Earl of Cavan, Commanding XIV Corps, appreciating the work performed by the 3rd Cavalry Divl. Auxiliary M.T. Co. whilst attached to the XIV Corps for water carrying.	Nil
DAOURS	18th Sept. 16		Railhead VECQUEMONT. Refilling points in vicinity of billets and camping grounds.	Nil
DAOURS	19th Sept. 16		Railhead FRECHEN COURT. Refilling Points as yesterday.	Nil
DAOURS	20th Sept. 16		Railhead VECQUEMONT. Refilling Points as yesterday.	Nil

Army Form C. 2118.

H.Q.rs
3rd Cavalry Divl. Art.

WAR DIARY
or
INTELLIGENCE SUMMARY.
(Erase heading not required.)

Place	Date	Hour	Summary of Events and Information	Remarks and references to Appendices
	20th Sept (continued)		Temp. Capt. R. CLIBBORN left 6th Cavalry Brigade on transfer to 12th Bn. Northumberland Fusiliers. Temp. Lieut FAUX posted in relief. Two parties of Amn.H.T.Co. returned to H.Q. Park at Mericourt.	Nil
DAOURS	21st Sept 16.		Railhead FRECHEN COURT. Refilling Points as yesterday. The Division is to move westwards tomorrow	Nil
DAOURS	22nd Sept 16		H.Qrs Adv. left DAOURS. arrived at LE QUESNOY (Somme). Temp. Lee Lieut. P. FAUX arrived from 1st Army Auxiliary (Horse) Co. for duty as Transport Officer. 6th Cav. Bar. was temp. Capt. R. CLIBBORN. Railhead FRECHEN COURT. Refilling Points in vicinity of troops' billets.	Nil
LE QUESNOY	23rd Sept 16		Railhead AUXI-LE-CHATEAU. Refilling Points in vicinity of billets. H.Qrs Adv. left LE QUESNOY at 6am. proceeded by road to FROHEN LE GRANDE (about 7 km S.E. AUXI-LE-CHATEAU) —	Nil
FROHEN LE GRAND DE	24th Sept		Railhead HESDIN – Refilling points in vicinity of billets. Unit left FROHEN at 8 am & proceeded to	Nil

Army Form C. 2118.

WAR DIARY
or
INTELLIGENCE SUMMARY.
(Erase heading not required.)

Instructions regarding War Diaries and Intelligence Summaries are contained in F. S. Regs., Part II. and the Staff Manual respectively. Title pages will be prepared in manuscript.

Place	Date	Hour	Summary of Events and Information	Remarks and references to Appendices
CAPELLE	25^t Sept 16		CAPELLE (S.H. HESDIN) Railhead HESDIN by boat. Refilling points in vicinity of troops billets. H.Q.s also moved to Chateau at N.E. E of TORTEFONTAINE (100.000 Abbeville 14)	Nil
TORTEFONTAINE	26 Sept		Railhead and Refilling Points as yesterday. Exchange of duties between Lieut. W.T. Stead, Supply Officer, Supply Col., and Lieut. E.P.W. Stewart, Supply Officer, W^{6th} Coy A.S.C. took place yesterday.	Nil
"	27^t Sept 16		Railhead Refilling Points as yesterday. Lieut. Sec. Lieut. B.H. Emby rejoined from Hospital on 18^t instant.	Nil
"	28 Sept		Railhead and Refilling Points as yesterday.	Nil
"	29 Sept		Railhead and Refilling Points unchanged.	Nil
"	30^t Sept 16		Railhead Refilling Points as yesterday.	Nil

S.E. Mumery Lieut Colonel
Comdg. H.Q. 3rd Cav. Divl. Sup. Col.

Confidential

MEMORANDUM.

31st October 1916

From O.C. A.A. 3rd Cav. Div.

To A.A. & Q.M.G. 3rd Cav. Div.

Herewith War Diary of H.Qrs. 3rd Cavalry Div. A.A. for the month of October 1916.

R.E. Lyle
Lieut. & Adjt.
for O.C. A.A. 3rd Cav. Div.

Army Form C. 2118.

A.S.C.
Q'Quarters
3rd Cavalry Div. A.S.

WAR DIARY
or
INTELLIGENCE SUMMARY.
(Erase heading not required.)

Vol 23

Place	Date	Hour	Summary of Events and Information	Remarks and references to Appendices
FORTEFONTAINE	1st Oct 15		Railhead HESDIN - Refilling Points in vicinity of Willie.	Nil
-do-	2d "		-do-	Nil
			Sent the Lieut. A.M.I. DVVS, surplus to establishment of No. 3 & Cav. Div. A.S.C. sent to report to OC No 2. Regulating Depot. A.S.C. at ABBEVILLE.	Nil
-do-	3rd Oct		Railhead and refilling points as yesterday	Nil
-do-	4th Oct		Railhead and refilling points as yesterday	Nil
-do-	5th Oct		Railhead and refilling points as on 4th	Nil
-do-	6th Oct		Railhead and refilling points as for 5th. Took up question of the supply of Reinforcements to units of the Division as several cases, more demand but on B213's by units direct were long outstanding. Today received a reply from D.A.Q. suggesting that when available, they would be supplied by HQ 1st Cav Div Ade but as spare men are very seldom available with HQ we, this suggestion does not help us much. Propose that an consolidated demand on B213 on base for reserves	Nil

T2134. Wt. W708-776. 50C000. 4/15. Sir J. C. & S.

Army Form C. 2118.

WAR DIARY
or
INTELLIGENCE SUMMARY.
(Erase heading not required.)

H.Qrs. 3rd Cav. Div. A.S.C.

Place	Date	Hour	Summary of Events and Information	Remarks and references to Appendices
			awaiting complete 3rd whole Div. A.S.C. and distribute reinforcements to units as they arrive	See
TORTEFONTAINE	7. Oct.16		Railhead and refilling points as for 6th Oct.	Md
-"-	8. Oct.16		Railhead and refilling points as for 7th.	Md
-"-	9. Oct.16		Second anniversary of arrival of Company overseas. Railhead and refilling points as for 8th.	Md
-"-	10th -"-		Railhead and refilling points as for 9th.	Md
-"-	11th -"-		Railhead and refilling points as for 10th.	Md
-"-	12th -"-		Railhead and refilling points as for 11th. O.C. A.S.C. with A.D.S.T. Cavalry Corps, inspected the transport of 7th Cavalry Brigade	
			Major H.A.C. Gardner Commanding 3rd Cav. Div. Supply Column, vacated to the Duchess of Westminster's Hospital, Le Touquet, yesterday, 11th instant.	Md
-"-	13th -"-		Railhead and refilling points as for yesterday	Md
-"-	14th -"-		Railhead and refilling points as for 13th.	Md

Army Form C. 2118.

WAR DIARY
or
INTELLIGENCE SUMMARY.
(Erase heading not required.)

Headquarters
3rd Cavalry Divisional A.S.C.

Instructions regarding War Diaries and Intelligence Summaries are contained in F. S. Regs., Part II. and the Staff Manual respectively. Title pages will be prepared in manuscript.

Place	Date	Hour	Summary of Events and Information	Remarks and references to Appendices
½ mile S. of last E. in TORTE-FONTAINE (sheet 1/100,000)	15th Oct		Railhead refilling points as for 17th.	
— " —	16th		Railhead refilling points as for 15th. Lt.Colonel M.E. Cuming, 86 A.S.C. proceeded on special leave to England. Major Corser acting O.C. A.S.C.	Per
— " —	17th Oct.		Railhead and refilling points as for 16th.	Per
— " —	18th Oct		Divl. HQrs, including HQrs A.S.C. to move to WAILLY on Thursday, 19th inst. Railhead & refilling points as for 17th.	Per
— " —	19th Oct.		Divl. HQrs, including HQrs A.S.C. arrived at WAILLY. HQ A.S.C. billeted at last house in WAILLY on Left of MONTREUIL ABBEVILLE road, in direction of MONTREUIL. Railhead as for yesterday, refilling points in vicinity of units' billets	Per
WAILLY	20 Oct		Railhead refilling points as yesterday	"
— " —	21st Oct		Railhead refilling points as yesterday. Capt. G.R.B. Farrer, 1/4/07302 Pte Watson & 1 driver horse left for duty with DDST Third Army. Fourth Sqn. RHA, left Division with rations for 22nd	Per

T2134. Wt. W708—776. 50C000. 4/15. Sir J. C. & S.

Army Form C. 2118.

WAR DIARY
or
INTELLIGENCE SUMMARY.
(Erase heading not required.)

HQ No. 3rd Cavalry Divisional A.S.C.

Instructions regarding War Diaries and Intelligence Summaries are contained in F.S. Regs., Part II. and the Staff Manual respectively. Title pages will be prepared in manuscript.

Place	Date	Hour	Summary of Events and Information	Remarks and references to Appendices
	1916.			
WAILLY	22nd Oct.		Railheads and refilling points as for 21st. Temp. Capt. A.R. Riley arrived from A.B. Base Depot have for duty vice Temp. Capt. R.P.S. Garner.	Ree
"	23rd Oct		Railheads and refilling points as for 22nd.	Ree
"	24th Oct		Railheads and refilling points as for 23rd.	Ree
"	25th Oct.		Railheads and refilling points as for 24th.	Ree
"	26th Oct.		Railheads and refilling points as for 25th. Arrangements made for the release of several M.T. drivers who are employed on other than transport work.	Ree
"	27th Oct		Railhead and refilling points as for 26th.	Ree
"	28th Oct.		Railhead and refilling points as for 27th.	Ree
"	29th Oct		Railhead and refilling points as for 28th. The magneto stolen from Wolseley car No 1799 entering A.B. Mess	Ree
"	30th Oct		Railheads and refilling points as for 29th.	Ree
"	31st Oct		Railheads and refilling points as for 30th.	Ree

R.C. Lyle Lieut Col.
for O.C. H.Qs. 3rd Cavalry Divisional A.S.C.

Army Form C. 2118.

WAR DIARY
or
INTELLIGENCE SUMMARY.
(Erase heading not required.)

November 1916

HQ 3rd Cavalry Divisional Tn.

Vol 24

Place	Date	Hour	Summary of Events and Information	Remarks and references to Appendices
WAILLY	6th Nov.		Railheads & refilling points as for 5th. Lieut. Colpr. C.J. TINDELL-GREEN A.D.S. arrived from Adv. Base Depot for duty with H.Q. 3rd Cav. Div. Adv. via Lieut. Capt. A.R. RILEY, is to return to 25th Divisional Train.	NIL
WAILLY	7th Nov.		Railheads & refilling points as for 6th. Lieut. Capt. A.R. RILEY left for 25th Divisional Train. Lieut. Capt. N.D. RILEY, 3rd Cav. Div. Supply Column, left for duty with 50 Railhead, Expd. Army. Lieut. Lee Jeun. C. STEVENS, Adc. from 3rd Cav. Div. Reserve Park to M.T. School of Instrn.	NIL
WAILLY	8th Nov.		Railheads & refilling points as for 7th.	NIL
WAILLY	9th Nov.		Railhead & refilling points as for 8th.	NIL
WAILLY	10th Nov.		Railheads & refilling points as for 9th. Applied for casualty of H.Q. Con. Tn. the Drival of Nov/1913b 2nd C. Driver T.50/23616 Pte G.J. Petrie, took of 3rd C.D. Supply Col. Rect. for 7 horses attached to 19th Div Supply Column & feed & tie Rifles horses of 3rd C.D. Supply Col, attached to 3rd Cav. Div, returned to unit.	NIL

Army Form C. 2118.

WAR DIARY
or
INTELLIGENCE SUMMARY.

(Erase heading not required.)

HQrs. 3rd Cavalry Divisional A.S.C.

Instructions regarding War Diaries and Intelligence Summaries are contained in F.S. Regs., Part II. and the Staff Manual respectively. Title pages will be prepared in manuscript.

Place	Date	Hour	Summary of Events and Information	Remarks and references to Appendices
WAILLY	11th Nov. 1915		Railheads and refilling points as for 10th. Trial of Pte Brown — Return fixed for 10.30 am 13th inst. at Supply Col. HQrs. Court of Enquiry to assemble at ADC. HQrs. 10 am. 13th inst. to investigate circumstances under which Supn Car. M.17257 was damaged on 3.10.15.—	PTL
-"-	12th Nov		Railheads and refilling points as for 11th.	PTL
-"-	13th Nov		7.8th Cav. Bde. Railhead to change tomorrow from BEAURAINVILLE to MARESQUEL. Div. HQrs. 6th Cav. Bde. remain at MONTREUIL. Railhead for Div. troops & 6th Cav. Bde. at MONTREUIL, for 7. 8th Cav. Bde. at MARESQUEL.	PTL
-"-	14th Nov.		Court of Enquiry held as mentioned on 11th. 3rd Cav. Div. Reserve Park the retained in Forward Area under Fourth Army — 30 wagons of 2nd Indian Cavalry Divisional Reserve Park to be attached to 3rd Cav. Div. for carriage of supplies so that the Supply Column may be laid up for the winter months. Railheads and Refilling Points as in was yesterday.	
-"-	15th Nov.		Railheads and Refilling Points as for 14th.	PTL

2353 Wt. W2544/1454 700,000 5/15 D.D. & L.   A.D.S.S./Forms/C. 2118.

Army Form C. 2118.

WAR DIARY
or
INTELLIGENCE SUMMARY.
(Erase heading not required.)

H.Qu. 3rd Canadian Div. Ad...

Place	Date	Hour	Summary of Events and Information	Remarks and references to Appendices
	1916			
WAILLY	16th Nov		Ordinary Issue re-commenced. Railheads and refilling points as for 15th. On instructions of A.D.S.T., Cavalry Corps, arrived 3rd Can. Ammunition Park to send half their workshop transport to Cavalry Corps Ws'hops. Supply Column to temporary duty. Ordered three Can. H.T. wagons thereto also. G.S. to temporary duty.	A.U.
WAILLY	17th Nov.		Railheads and refilling points as for 16th. Move of Lieut. Capt. R. Kirsch, 3rd Can. Amn. Park, ordered to H.Q. Co. Ltd. attached H.Q. XI Ac. Heavy Artillery - Relief by Lieut. & W.O. Prescott.	A.U.
WAILLY	18th Nov.		Railheads and refilling points as for 17th. Pioneer Battalions (Brit. Can. Pioneers (New) formed from 7th & 8th Can. Bns. Strength each 851 all ranks, to go up on 20th inst. Will be attached to IV & V Corps - lorries to be detached from Division to feed these troops. Arrangements with D.A.D.S.T. 2/19 Corps to supply 50 lbs ? oats possible, grain to each battalion, their being taken up with other requirements being met from new railhead.	A.U.

2353 Wt. W2544/I454 700,000 5/15 D.D. & L. A.D.S.S./Forms/C. 2118.

WAR DIARY
or
INTELLIGENCE SUMMARY.

(Erase heading not required.)

Army Form C. 2118.

M.Ges. 3rd Cavalry Div. A.L.

Place	Date	Hour	Summary of Events and Information	Remarks and references to Appendices
WAILLY	May 19th	hrs.	Railheads and refilling points as for 18th. Arrangements made to ration 7th Reserve Batt. up to 22nd. Sup. up to including 21st. 1st Batt. leaves HESDIN & am on 21st & the 8th Div. leaves MARESQUEL & am tomorrow 20th inst.	MW
WAILLY	20th	hrs.	Railheads and refilling points as for 19th. Move of Lieut. J.C. Smith A.R. D.T.O. 6th Cav. Bde. ordered to 60th Divl. Train. Temp. Capt. G.W. Baker ordered in relief.	MW
WAILLY	21st	hrs	Railheads and refilling points as for 20th. Lt. J.C. Smith left for 60th Divisional Train. Information received of return to Division of H.Q. Staff. These will be fed from Rail Car Coy Railhead 25th inst.	MW
WAILLY	2.25	hrs.	Railheads + refilling points as for 21st. Temp. Capt. E.W. BAKER joined for duty as D.T.O. 6th Cavalry Brigade. Car N.1576 broke down outside MONTREUIL on way back from BOULOGNE & was towed into Supply Column workshops.	MW
WAILLY	2.3rd	hrs.	Railheads + refilling points as for 22nd	MW

Army Form C. 2118.

WAR DIARY
or
INTELLIGENCE SUMMARY.

(Erase heading not required.)

Headqrs. 3rd Cavalry Div. A.S.C.

Place	Date	Hour	Summary of Events and Information	Remarks and references to Appendices
(cont)	23rd Nov. 1915		Sec. Lieut. A.H. BORTON ordered from Supply Column to No 5 G.H.Q. Ammn Park. Relief by Temp. Lieut. F.R. HODGSON. Temp. Lieut. R.H. STEVENS ordered from 3rd Cav. Ammn. Park to 15th Siege Battery. Relief by Temp. Sec. Lieut. L.H. FRANCIS.	MEC
WAILLY	24th Nov.		Railheads and refilling points as for 23rd.	Nil
WAILLY	25th Nov.		Railheads and refilling points as for 24th. Ammunition S.S. Co. moved to St IENOEUX from BEAURAINVILLE. Ordered further Ammunition S.S. Co. to be detached to Regimentals. Numbers are detailed the whole of the transport of the Coy. would be detached with the exception of two wagons for H.Sec of Coy. These wagons under Lieut.	Nil
WAILLY	26th Nov.		Railheads and refilling points as for 25th.	Nil
WAILLY	27th Nov.		Railheads and refilling points as for 26th. Applied for authority to leave a detachment of Supply Column facing Div. Supplies through MONTREUIL on their way to Railhead on account of bad state of road at present used.	Nil
WAILLY	28th Nov.		Railheads and refilling points as for 27th.	Nil

WAR DIARY or INTELLIGENCE SUMMARY.

(Erase heading not required.)

Army Form C. 2118.

December 1916 H.Q. 3rd Cavalry Divisional HQ

Place	Date	Hour	Summary of Events and Information	Remarks and references to Appendices
WALLY	1st Dec 1916		Railheads and refilling points as for yesterday.	MEC
-"-	2nd Dec		Railhead and refilling points as for 1st.	MEC
-"-	3rd Dec		Railhead and refilling points as for 2nd.	MEC
-"-	4th Dec		Arrangements made for drawing rations by horse transport in the event of a thaw Roads are closed to M.T. Railheads and refilling points as for 3rd.	MEC
-"-	5th Dec		Yesterdays sent out motors in 6 wagons to be attached to 6th Cav. Bde. and 6 wagons to 7th Cav. Bde. for carriage of hay for use in the event of a thaw. Railheads and refilling points as for 4th.	MEC
-"-	6th Dec		1st S.H. Co, B.T.O. 7th Cav Bde. granted an extension of leave on medical grounds until further orders. Yesterday admitted 29 names of N.C.Os. men of Supply Column + 2 names of N.C.Os. 17 Co. for transfer to the Heavy Branch, Machine Gun Corp. Railheads and refilling points as for 5th. Ordered one wagon from	MEC

Army Form C. 2118.

WAR DIARY
or
INTELLIGENCE SUMMARY.
(Erase heading not required.)

H.Qrs. 3rd Cavalry Div. A.C.

Place	Date	Hour	Summary of Events and Information	Remarks and references to Appendices
WAILLY	1916 29th Nov 30th Nov.		Railhead and refilling points as for 28th. Railhead and refilling points as for 29th. Detachment of 6th Cav. Bn. Reserve Park arrived Wadendour. Marching in strength 1 Offr. 92 O.R. 13 P. animals & 30 wagons.	

J E Cumming
Colonel
Comdg. HQrs. 3rd Cavalry Divl. A.C.

Army Form C. 2118.

WAR DIARY
or
INTELLIGENCE SUMMARY.

(Erase heading not required.)

HQrs 3. Cavalry Divl Adt

Instructions regarding War Diaries and Intelligence Summaries are contained in F. S. Regs, Part II and the Staff Manual respectively. Title pages will be prepared in manuscript.

Place	Date	Hour	Summary of Events and Information	Remarks and references to Appendices
NAILLY	7th Dec.		One Reserve Pair to each Brigade in replacement of one wagon sent by each Brigade to the R.H.A. Battery as a sup. wagon. Railheads Repilling points as yesterday. Detailed 12 wagons of 3rd Can. Div. Res. Park to proceed to CAMPIGNEULLES - LES - PETITS. Will be rationed there by Commissaries.	M.I.
"	8th Dec.		Railheads and Repilling points as yesterday. Received information from Q of a possible inspection of the 5th Cav. Div. Reserve Park Detachment by the G.O.C. Commander. Instructed the O.C. Ans. M.T. Co. to submit indents to replace all unserviceable & deficient clothing and equipment.	M.I.
"	9th Dec.		Railheads and Repilling points as yesterday. T/23865 Cpl. A. Blanchard appointed Acting Sergeant (unpaid) to complete new establishment with effect from 3.12.16.	M.I.
"	10th Dec.		Railheads and Repilling points as yesterday.	M.I.

Army Form C. 2118.

WAR DIARY
or
INTELLIGENCE SUMMARY.
(Erase heading not required.)

H.Qrs. 3rd Cavalry Div. A.L.

Instructions regarding War Diaries and Intelligence Summaries are contained in F. S. Regs., Part II. and the Staff Manual respectively. Title pages will be prepared in manuscript.

Place	Date	Hour	Summary of Events and Information	Remarks and references to Appendices
	1916			
WAILLY	11th Dec		Railheads and refilling points as for 10th. 6th Rouen Battalion to relieve 8th Rouen Battalion on 20th instant. 399 all ranks of 1st Rouen Batt. relieved by similar number of 7th Cav. 6th & 8th Cav. Bdes. to exchange billeting areas about 22nd inst.	M.
"	12th Dec		Railheads and refilling points as for 11th. Arrangements made in hateaux for Rouen battalion relief up.	M. M. M.
"	13th Dec		Railheads and refilling points as for 12th.	M.
"	14th Dec		Railheads and refilling points as for 13th.	M.
"	15th Dec		Railheads and refilling points as for 14th. Divisional Headquarters to move to TREPIED (with S.L. Staffs) on Sunday 17th instant.	M.
"	16th Dec		Railheads and refilling points as for 15th.	M.
"	17th Dec		Divisional Headquarters, including 3rd Ox. Own ede moved to TREPIED. Railheads + refilling points as for 16th except to Divisional H.Qtrs who dumped at CUCQ	M.
TREPIED	18th Dec		Railheads refilling points as for 17th.	M.

Army Form C. 2118.

WAR DIARY
or
INTELLIGENCE SUMMARY.

(Erase heading not required.)

Instructions regarding War Diaries and Intelligence Summaries are contained in F.S. Regs., Part II. and the Staff Manual respectively. Title pages will be prepared in manuscript.

N.O.u.
3rd Cavalry Divisional A.S.C.

Place	Date	Hour	Summary of Events and Information	Remarks and references to Appendices
TREPIED	1916 19th Dec		Railheads and refilling points as for 18th.	M.C.
-"-	20th Dec		Refilling points and Railheads as for 19th. A.D.S.T. in Conference that were in Brehove to Inchange 2 h. 30 wt Drew horses of Supply Co. for Details. 4 Stowers as the later become available in now is doing our carrying capacity up to that of other Divisions.	M.C.
-"-	21st Dec		Railheads and refilling points as for 20th. With the approval of A.D.S.T., instructed 96 Canadr.a Staff with Workshop the Daimler Bus attached for Issue of Spare Thro' which is in bad condition and leaves with team 21 days.	M.C.
-"-	22nd Dec		Railheads as for 21st. b. 1.8. Cavalry Brigades changed billeting area. Received instructions for Supply Column and Ammn. Park. Received instructions that straw will come up from Base in lieu of forage ration.	M.C.
-"-	23rd Dec		Railheads and refilling points as for 22nd.	M.C.

Army Form C. 2118.

WAR DIARY
or
INTELLIGENCE SUMMARY
(Erase heading not required.)

Hd Qrs. 3rd Cavalry Div. C. All.

Place	Date	Hour	Summary of Events and Information	Remarks and references to Appendices
	1916			
TREPIED	24th Dec		Railheads and refilling points as for 23rd.	
			Received Quartermaster General's approval to hire of Government lorries by civilians.	
"	25th Dec		Railheads and refilling points as for 24th	
"	26 Dec		Railheads and refilling points as for 25th.	
			OC Supply Column complains that two lorries attached to 17 Corps for feeding Flower Sect. are not receiving proper attention. Directed him to send Officer to inspect the lorries and report further.	Med
"	27th Dec		Railheads and refilling points as for 26th.	Med
			2/210 Lt. S. Davidson ADC at HQ Claude remanded by O2 etc for trial by GGC on charge of Drunk on line of march.	
"	28 Dec		Railheads and refilling points as for 27th.	Med
"	29th Dec		Railheads and refilling points as for 28th.	Med
"	30 Dec		Railheads and refilling points as for 29th	Med
"	31st Dec		Railheads and refilling points as for 30th.	Med
			Capt Weller 3rd C. Am HTC ordered to hot School of Instr. Relief by Capt 14th Hussars Ind.	
			Commanding HQrs 1st Squadron 3rd Cavalry Div. C. All.	

WAR DIARY
or
INTELLIGENCE SUMMARY.

Army Form C. 2118.

No. 8u.   Vol 26

3rd Cavalry Divisional A.C.

Place	Date	Hour	Summary of Events and Information	Remarks and references to Appendices
	1917			
TREPIED	1st Jan		Railheads and Refilling Points as for yesterday.	Nil
"	2nd Jan		Capt. W. Buckley joined 3rd Car. Div. Ambar. Sec. Co. 50th A.C.	Nil
"	3rd Jan		Railheads and Refilling Points as for 1st. Railheads and Refilling Points as for 2nd. 2/5210 Lt Davidson, d. A.L., A.H. M.O 6th Car. Sec. died on A.C. on a sharp attack of pneumonia and acquitted.	Nil
"	4th Jan		Railheads and Refilling Points as for 3rd. 1 Capt. W.G.R. Weller left 3rd Car. Am. Ambulary W.C. to join the N.T. School of Instruction.	Nil
"	5th Jan		Railheads and Refilling Points as for 4th. Relief of 7th Pioneer Battalion to be carried out on 6th inst and two following days. Details of lorries to be arranged between Staff Capt. 1 O.C. Supply Column.	Nil
"	6th Jan		Railheads and Refilling Points as for 5th. Rations & baleS taken to the Park le Chevaux below at 4.45 m.g. & 2 days 16 magazine of HAYES for the above. This was known.	Nil

Army Form C. 2118.

WAR DIARY
or
INTELLIGENCE SUMMARY.

(Erase heading not required.)

H.Q.
2ⁿᵈ Cavalry Div. Ade.

Place	Date	Hour	Summary of Events and Information	Remarks and references to Appendices
			the det. of 5 Cav. Div. Reserve Park at CAMPIGNEULLES LES PETITES. Owing to difficulty of effecting transport returns, 2DSR. Cavalry Corps suggests the formation of a central wheelers shop in each Brigade, withdrawing the wheelup and shoe-smith from the Cavalry Field Ambulance for this purpose.	
TREPIED	7 Jan 1917		Railheads and Refilling Points as for 6ᵗʰ. Reference the central wheelers shop scheme suggestion received from Cavalry Corps, Ordnance that the wheelers shop should be a Divisional one. This is considered in any case taken in Beauvoir-wabbé, the heavy the most suitable part of the area.	A/1
TREPIED	8 Jan 1917		Railheads and Refilling Points as for 7ᵗʰ. Court of Inquiry held on 6ᵗʰ sent to establish the alleged absence of No. 29123 D/r G Clarke. Railheads and Refilling Points as for 8ᵗʰ.	A/2.
TREPIED	9 Jan 1917 10 Jan 1917		Railheads and Refilling Points as for 9ᵗʰ.	A/3 A/4

Army Form C. 2118.

WAR DIARY
or
INTELLIGENCE SUMMARY.
(Erase heading not required.)

H.Qrs. 3rd Cavalry Div. Ade

Instructions regarding War Diaries and Intelligence Summaries are contained in F. S. Regs., Part II. and the Staff Manual respectively. Title pages will be prepared in manuscript.

Place	Date	Hour	Summary of Events and Information	Remarks and references to Appendices
TREPIED	1917.			
	11th Jan		Railheads and Refilling Points as for 10th	Nil
-"-	12th Jan		Railheads and Refilling Points as for 11th. A.M. visits the BEAURAINVILLE area to select a site for Divisional Wheelers Shop and selects CONTES as the place wherein to establish this shop.	Nil
-"-	13th Jan		Railhead for 8th Car. Bde, Div Troops Refilling point as for 12th. Railhead for 6th & 7th Car Brdes at BEAURAINVILLE instead of MARESQUEL. Supply Column Detachment feeding 8 Car Bde & Div Troops Moved from CUCQ to PIRON ST YANST. Reported K.M.H.Q. that the devious situation of the hay supply only 6 lbs per horse arriving at Railhead and the total resources will be totally exhausted by the 15th January.	N.A.
-"-	14th Jan		Railheads and Refilling points as for 13th	Nil
-"-	15th Jan		Railheads and Refilling points as for 14th	Nil
-"-	16th Jan		Railheads and refilling points as for 15th. Submitted to A and Q.M.G. a report together the retention by H.Q. A.D.C	Nil

2353 Wt. W2544/1454 700,000 5/15 D. D. & L. A.D.S.S./Forms/C. 2118.

Army Form C. 2118.

WAR DIARY
or
INTELLIGENCE SUMMARY
(Erase heading not required.)

HQrs. 3rd Cavalry Divl. Ad.

Place	Date	Hour	Summary of Events and Information	Remarks and references to Appendices
TREPIED	17th Jan		of a water cart & G.S. wagon in lieu of cart now return to the provisional establishment.	
"	18th Jan		Railheads and refilling points as for 16th instant.	
			Railheads and refilling points as for 17th. Reports to A.D.S.T. by O.C. as to the completion of repairs & drawn from 7.30 a.m. and for instruction as to the disposal of Sup & Gro 1696.	Pel
			Cav Ho793, Divl HQ Posl, evacuated noncombatants Divl HQ established as received by I Lorries, 1 Wheeler Corpl, 6 Drivers	
"	19th Jan		Railheads and refilling points as for 18th	Pel
"	20th Jan		Railheads and refilling points as for 19th. Received telephone instructions from A.A. & Q.M.G. ordering the move of 3rd Cav Supply Column from HESDIN to BEAURAINVILLE.	Pel
"	21st Jan		Railheads and refilling points as for 20th.	Pel
"	22nd Jan		Railheads and refilling points as at 21st	Pel
"	23rd Jan		Railheads and refilling points as for 22nd. Supply Column completed move to Beaurainville nr Aux HG	Pel

Army Form C. 2118.

WAR DIARY
or
INTELLIGENCE SUMMARY.

W.O₉ 2ⁿᵈ Cavalry Divᶥ A.S.C.

(Erase heading not required.)

Instructions regarding War Diaries and Intelligence Summaries are contained in F. S. Regs., Part II. and the Staff Manual respectively. Title pages will be prepared in manuscript.

Place	Date	Hour	Summary of Events and Information	Remarks and references to Appendices
	1917			
TREPIED	24ᵗʰ Jan		to LESPINOY. Railheads and refilling points as for 23ʳᵈ. Reported to A.D.S.T. Corbin, a casualty to Triumph motor cycle No 953 Ld. 7ᵗʰ Signal Troop damaged on 24.12.16. by a R.O.C. car skidding into it.	R.S.
"	25ᵗʰ Jan		Railheads and refilling points as for 24ᵗʰ.	R.S.
"	26ᵗʰ Jan		Railheads and refilling points as for 25ᵗʰ. A.D.S.T. Carton's wired for a report on the number of motor casualties to M.T. vehicles and 3ʳᵈ Cav. Div. A. commenting on the number of casualties called for a report as to who is to blame.	R.S.
"	27ᵗʰ Jan		Railheads and refilling points as for 26ᵗʰ. Wired to A.D.S.T. Carton's particulars of M.T. pool casualties. These are in the Supply Column - 14 Daimler CC lorries (cylinder heads), 1 Daimler TR/30, 3 Thorford 650 and 3 4-ton Denno lorries (radiators) and in the 1ˢᵗ ⅔ Am Battery, 2 Daimler CC lorries (one radiator & front heads) and the front heads of a Daimler ¾ lorry.	R.S.

WAR DIARY or INTELLIGENCE SUMMARY.

Army Form C. 2118.

3rd Cav. Div. A.D.

Place	Date	Hour	Summary of Events and Information	Remarks and references to Appendices
(cont)	1917 27th Jan.		Leave suspended owing to congestion on French Railways. Went A.A.Q.M.G. to provide a N.C.O. for the Rest Billet which has been established at Beauvainville for leave parties.	R.C.
TREPIED	28th Jan		Railheads and refilling points as for 27th. Passed to O.C. Supply Column detailed drawings of the scheme for heating motor ambulances by means of pipes led from the exhaust and directed him to proceed with the work. Leave to places in France suspended.	R.C.
"	29th Jan.		Railhead and refilling hours as for 28th. In reply to an application of 22nd inst. to exchange the forage carts of Cav. G. Carts for G.S. Limbered wagons, A.D.S. Sup. raised the general question of the utility of these carts. Replied that there were several other forage carts in the Division and that it would be a good thing if we could have them all as they yet for G.S. Limbered wagons. Forage carts are found to be clumsy, of uneven draught, and altogether unpractical.	R.C.

Army Form C. 2118.

WAR DIARY
or
INTELLIGENCE SUMMARY.
(Erase heading not required.)

W. Oss.
3rd Cavalry Divl. Arty.

Instructions regarding War Diaries and Intelligence Summaries are contained in F. S. Regs., Part II. and the Staff Manual respectively. Title pages will be prepared in manuscript.

Place	Date	Hour	Summary of Events and Information	Remarks and references to Appendices
	1917.			
TREPIED	30th Jan.		Railheads and refilling points as for 29th. Forwarded to A.A.Q.M.G. a nominal roll of R.A. personnel serving with the Ammn. Park considered suitable for transfer to Battery or Column. Leave to places in France re-opened.	R.C.
-do-	31st Jan		Railheads and refilling points as for 30th. Received circular letter, noting the displeasure of the A.C.G. Cavalry Corps, on the number of casualties to H.T. Vehicles caused by frost. Owing to the stoppage of leave trains, today we started a scheme to convey the daily leave party to BOULOGNE by G.S. wagons. The party was collected at TREPIED & Nest Ville being established and taken in 2 G.S. wagons by road to NEUFCHATEL, thence, with fresh drivers and horses hurriedly billeted there, to BOULOGNE. After setting down the forward party, returning party was picked up and brought back.	R.C.

R.C. Lyle
Lieut Adjutant
for OC MOss. 3rd Cavalry Divl. Arty.

WAR DIARY
or
INTELLIGENCE SUMMARY.

(Erase heading not required.)

Army Form C. 2118.

Vol 2 H
HQrs 3rd Cavalry Div. A.D.S.

Place	Date	Hour	Summary of Events and Information	Remarks and references to Appendices
TREPIED	1st Feb	19/17	Railheads and refilling points as for yesterday except for 7 & 8 the R.P. which were 7 & 8 Cav. Bdes. changed over.	See
"	2nd "		Railheads and refilling points as for 1st.	See
"	3rd "		Railheads and refilling points as for 2nd. Called to hand report from Supply Column on frost casualties.	See
"	4th "		Railheads and refilling points as for 3rd. Frost casualty report :- Lorries off road last report - 11, three put on road - the now put on road - 12, Now off road - nil. Cars off road - 2 - Ambulances off road 2.	See
"	5th "		Railheads and refilling points as for 4th. Frost casualty report :- Lorries off road last report - 12, three put on road - nil, Now off road - 12. Cars off road 2, Ambulances off road 2.	See

WAR DIARY
or
INTELLIGENCE SUMMARY.
(Erase heading not required.)

Army Form C. 2118.

Place	Date	Hour	Summary of Events and Information	Remarks and references to Appendices
TREPIED	6th Feb.		Railheads and Refilling points as for 5th. Frost Casualty Report:- Lorries off Road last report - 12 - Since put on Road - Nil - Now off Road - 12 - Cars off Road - 2 - Ambulances off Road - 2	M.
TREPIED	7th "		Railheads and Refilling Points as for 5th. Frost Casualty Report:- Lorries off Road last report - 12 - Since put on Road - Nil - Now off Road - 12 - Cars off Road - 2 - Ambulances off Road - 2	M.
TREPIED	8th "		Railheads and Refilling Points as for 7th. Frost Casualty Report: Lorries off road last report - 12 - Since put on road - Nil - Now off road - 12 - Cars off road - 2 - Ambulances - 2 - Since put on road - 1 Car - Now off road - 1 Car - 2 Ambulances	M.

WAR DIARY or INTELLIGENCE SUMMARY.

Army Form C. 2118.

(Erase heading not required.)

Instructions regarding War Diaries and Intelligence Summaries are contained in F.S. Regs., Part II. and the Staff Manual respectively. Title pages will be prepared in manuscript.

Place	Date	Hour	Summary of Events and Information	Remarks and references to Appendices
TREPIED	9 Feb.		Railheads and Refilling points as for 8th. Post Casualty report:- Lorry off road last report – 12 – Since put on road – Nil – Remaining off road – 12. Car/road Park report – 1 – Ambulance – 2 – Since put on road – 1 Ambulance. Still off road – 1 Car – 1 Ambulance.	Nil
TREPIED	10 Feb.		Railheads and Refilling points as for 9th. Post Casualty report:- Off road last report – 1 Car – 1 Ambulance. Since put on road – 4 Lorries. Remaining off road – 8 Lorries – 1 Car – 1 Ambulance.	Nil
TREPIED	11 Feb.		Railheads and Refilling points as for 10th. Post Casualty report:- Off road last report – 8 Lorries – 1 Car – 1 Ambulance & 1 Car – 1 Ambulance. Since put on road – Nil –	Nil

Army Form C. 2118.

WAR DIARY
or
INTELLIGENCE SUMMARY.
(Erase heading not required.)

Instructions regarding War Diaries and Intelligence Summaries are contained in F. S. Regs., Part II. and the Staff Manual respectively. Title pages will be prepared in manuscript.

Place	Date	Hour	Summary of Events and Information	Remarks and references to Appendices
TREPIED	12 Feb		Remaining off road — 8 lorries — 1 car — 1 ambulance Railhead and Refilling points as for 11th Frost Casualty report off road — 8 lorries	MEC
			— 1 car — 1 ambulance Sick put on road — Nil — Remaining off road — 8 lorries — 1 car — 1 ambulance	MEC
TREPIED	13 Feb.		Seven P.B. men reported for duty. Railheads and Refilling points as for 12th Frost Casualty report as for 12th	MEC
TREPIED	14th Feb.		Railheads and Refilling points as for 13th Frost Casualty report — off road last report — lorries — cars — 1 Ambulance — 1. (ADST No. T 536/10)	MEC
			1 Bus returned to Bus Park, ST. VALERY — Put on Road — Nil — Remaining off road — 7 lorries — 1 Car. 1 ambulance	
TREPIED	15 Feb		Railheads and Refilling points as for 14th	

Army Form C. 2118.

WAR DIARY
or
INTELLIGENCE SUMMARY.
(Erase heading not required.)

M.T. 3rd Cav. Div. A.S.C.

Instructions regarding War Diaries and Intelligence Summaries are contained in F. S. Regs., Part II. and the Staff Manual respectively. Title pages will be prepared in manuscript.

Place	Date	Hour	Summary of Events and Information	Remarks and references to Appendices
TREPIED	16th Feb.		Frost Casualty report – Off road last report – Lorries 7 – Cars – 13 – Ambulances 1 – Sick put on Road – Nil – Remaining off road – Lorries – 7 – Cars – 1 – Ambulance. –1–	Nil
"	17th Feb.		Railheads and Refilling points as for 15th. Frost Casualty Report as for 15th	Nil
"	18th Feb.		Railheads and refilling points as for 16th. Frost Casualty Report as for yesterday.	Nil
"	18th Feb.		Railheads and refilling points as for 17th. Frost Casualty Report as for 17th.	Nil
"	19th Feb.		Railheads and refilling points as for 18th. Frost Casualty Report as for 18th. Temp. Lieut. A.Y. CAMPBELL joined 3rd Cavalry Supply Column, vice Temp. Lieut. E.S.M. STEWART who is to join the M.T. School of instruction 14 days from date.	Nil

Army Form C. 2118.

WAR DIARY
or
INTELLIGENCE SUMMARY.
(Erase heading not required.)

3rd Cavalry Divl. A.d.S.

Place	Date	Hour	Summary of Events and Information	Remarks and references to Appendices
	1917			
TRE PIED	20th Feb.		Railheads and Refilling Points as for 19th. Frost Casualty Report unchanged.	Nil
"	21st "		Railheads and Refilling Points as for 20th. Frost Casualty Report as for 20th.	Nil
"	22nd "		Railheads and Refilling Points as for 21st. Frost Casualty Report as for 21st. Instructed O.C. Supply Column Ammn Park to commence a Class of Instruction for M.T. men. The course to include instruction in technical construction of various types of vehicles, care and cleaning of same, frost precautions, extracts from O. & F.S. Circulars and Routine Orders and any information likely to be useful to men who may be detached with supply lorries.	Nil
"	23rd "		Railheads and Refilling Points as for 22nd. Frost Casualty Report as for 22nd. Applied to A.A.Q.M.G. for assembly of F.G. C.M. for trial of Pte. McMAHON, A.S.C., attached 3rd Cavalry Ammn. Park.	Nil

Army Form C. 2118.

WAR DIARY
or
INTELLIGENCE SUMMARY.

3rd Cavalry Divisional Art

(Erase heading not required.)

Place	Date	Hour	Summary of Events and Information	Remarks and references to Appendices
(cont)	1917 23rd Feb.		The Division apply for the return of 6th & 8th Machine Gun Sqns on or about 1st March. Railheads and Refilling Points as for 23rd	Nil
TREPIED	24th Feb.		Front Casualty Report as for 23rd. Railheads and Refilling Points as for 24th. Front Casualty Report as for 24th.	Nil
-"-	25th Feb.		Capt. C. J. Tindell-Green, Supply Officer Divisional Troops admitted to the Duchess of Westminster Hospital. Tonight the Classes of Instruction mentioned on 22nd inst. commence tomorrow 26th instant. Four troops attached to the Division ordered by M.S.S.T., Cav. Corps, to return to the Bno Park.	Nil
-"-	26th Feb.		Railheads and Refilling Points as for 25th. Front Casualty Report as for 25th. The two troops at Divisional School to remain till further orders. The R.H.A. Batteries with Armies to return to the Division	Nil

Army Form C. 2118.

WAR DIARY
or
INTELLIGENCE SUMMARY.
(Erase heading not required.)

WDs. 3rd Cavalry Divl. Ade.

Place	Date	Hour	Summary of Events and Information	Remarks and references to Appendices
TREPIED	27th Feb.		Between March 1st and March 7th. Railheads and Refilling Points as for 26th.	F.S.
"	28th Feb.		Great Casualty Report as for 26th. Railheads and Refilling Points as for 27th. Great Casualty Report as for 27th. Called for returns from A.C. Units showing number of men in the Division who could be replaced by men of lower categories and thus be released to fighting units.	F.S.

S. McCurvey
Lt. Colonel
Commanding WDs 3rd Cavalry Divl. Ade.

Army Form C. 2118.

WAR DIARY
or
INTELLIGENCE SUMMARY.

W.Orr.
3rd Cavalry Divisional A.S.C.

Vol 2 ⚡

(Erase heading not required.)

Place	Date	Hour	Summary of Events and Information	Remarks and references to Appendices
TREPIED	1917. 1st March		Railheads and Refilling Points unchanged. Front Casualty Report as for yesterday. Capt. C.F. Tindell-Green, S.O. Div. Troops, discharged hospital.	W.O.C.
„	2nd Mar.		Railheads and Refilling Points as for 1st. Front Casualty Report as for 1st. Lieut. E.J.M. Stewart, S.O. Supply Col. to M.T. School of Instruction (A)	W.O.C.
„	3rd Mar		Railheads and Refilling Points as for 2nd. Front Casualty Report as for 2nd. Four lorries returned to Bus Park at ST YAKERY-SUR-SOMME. Our M.T.O. moved to St. BERTOUX. One G.S. wagon, two light draught horses and one driver of St. Ou. A.C. evacuated to Advanced M.T. Depot, ABBEVILLE.	W.O.C.
„	4th Mar		Railheads and Refilling Points as for 3rd. Front Casualty Report as for 3rd. Reported to "Q" on the condition of the horses of A.H.Q. Reserve Park.	W.O.
„	5th Mar.		Railheads and Refilling Points as for 4th.	W.O.

WAR DIARY
or
INTELLIGENCE SUMMARY

Army Form C. 2118.

H.Qrs. 3rd Cavalry Divisional A.S.C.

Place	Date	Hour	Summary of Events and Information	Remarks and references to Appendices
(cont)	1917 5th Mar		Stock Casualty Report as for 4th. Lt M.Mahon 3rd Cav Res Park attached 3rd Cav Ammn Park sentenced by F.G.C.M. to 56 days F.P. No. 2 for stealing. Reported to "Q" the case of an officer driving a lorry on which he was a passenger, over a route different to that allotted. Div. Routine Order subsequently published prohibiting this interference with men in charge of lorries.	Nil.
TREPIED	6th Mar		Railheads and Refilling Points as for 5th. Stock Casualty Report the same. Reported to A.A. & S.T. Cavalry Corps and to M.A.-Q.M.G., on the economy of man power, with special reference to the A.S.C. personnel employed with the Division. My recommendations as to the replacement of the present men by others of lower categories were:- (i) That the supply personnel of Brigades and Divisional troops remain Category "A" men, all others being replaced by Category "B" men. (ii) That 25% of H.J. & Category "B" for employment with	Nil.

Army Form C. 2118.

WAR DIARY
or
INTELLIGENCE SUMMARY.
(Erase heading not required.)

H.Qrs.
3rd Cavalry Divisional A.C.

Place	Date	Hour	Summary of Events and Information	Remarks and references to Appendices
	1917.			
			"A". Fahelow, others to be B(i)-(ii).	
			(iii) That 50% of Supply Column M.T. Drivers, drivers of motor ambulances and divisional cars and motor cyclists remain Category "A", all others being replaced by Category "B" providing these latter are sufficiently skilled.	
RAPAREWO.	3rd.		T.1932 A/Whl. Corpl. Trueman A. reported for duty from 3rd Divisional Train. Mos.1. Cav. Corps. notifies in response to our query, that No G.S. wagon shown for a Mobile Veterinary Section in War Establishments Pt. VII as "Train transport" should not be held for the Sections attached to Cav. Divs.	M.D.
TREPIED.	7th. Mar.		Railheads and Refilling Points as for 6th. Ghost Cavalry Report the same. Made arrangements for the gunners of Light Armoured Battery to attend at Ammn. Park to receive instruction in motor driving. The instruction, which will be merely elementary, will commence on 14th. inst., five men being taken at one time.	M.D.
TREPIED.	8th. March.		Railheads and Refilling Points as for 7th. Ghost Cavalry Report the same. Major H.G. PEACHEY, A.S.C. assumed command of 3rd Cavalry Division Reserve	

Army Form C. 2118.

WAR DIARY
or
INTELLIGENCE SUMMARY.

(Erase heading not required.)

H.Qrs. 3rd Cavalry Divisional A.C.

Place	Date	Hour	Summary of Events and Information	Remarks and references to Appendices
	1917		Park nil.	
			Arranged for the horse of Lieut. S.T. Cav. Div. Reserve Park to be put through the Divisional Horse Dip on Monday 12th instant.	M.1
TREPIED	9th March		Railheads and Refilling Points as for 8th inst. Casualty position unchanged. Submitted to Base Records the names of 2 N.C.O. & 4 W.O. N.C.Os & men who are recommended for appointment to higher rank.	M.1
TREPIED	10th March		Railheads and Refilling Points as for 9th inst. Casualty position unchanged. Directed O.C. Amn. S.S.C. to parade on 12th inst., all horses which can be produced for casting.	M.1
TREPIED	11th March		Railheads and Refilling Points as for 10th inst. Casualty Report unchanged. Complaint received from A.S.M. of length of time demands to A.O. reinforcements for 1st 2.D.S.A. have been outstanding. We have applied for these since January but no A.T. reinforcements have been received for the Division since 12th December 1916. Sunbeam Car M1490 was damaged on 6th inst. by being run into by an Army Lorry. Reports on this case forwarded to D. Damage to	M.1

Army Form C. 2118.

WAR DIARY
or
INTELLIGENCE SUMMARY.

(Erase heading not required.)

N.O.n.
3rd Cavalry Divisional A.C.

Instructions regarding War Diaries and Intelligence Summaries are contained in F. S. Regs., Part II. and the Staff Manual respectively. Title pages will be prepared in manuscript.

Place	Date	Hour	Summary of Events and Information	Remarks and references to Appendices
	1917			
TREPIED	12th March		car estimated at about £5. It is proposed to again convert the Auxiliary M.T. Co. into an ammunition-carrying column. Railheads and refilling points as for 11th.	Rec.
-"-	13th March		Temp. Lieut. W.R. STEED. S.O. to O/C. AS admitted to hospital on 8th inst. Temp. Lieut. B.A. BOWES joined 3rd Cav. Supply Column today. 1st Cast Casualty Report as for 12th.	Rec.
-"-	14th March		Railheads and Refilling Points as for 12th. 1st Cast Casualty Report as for 13th.	Rec.
-"-	15th March		Railheads and Refilling Points as for 13th. Temp. Capt. A.H. Bolton joined 3rd Cav. Div. Reserve Park. 1st Cast Casualties as for 14th.	Rec.
-"-	16th March		Railheads and Refilling Points as for 14th. 6th & 8th Can. Pioneer Bns. rejoined Division. 1st Cast Casualty Report as for yesterday.	Rec.
-"-	17th March		M.Gn. A.C. to be fitted with Box Respirators on 2nd Proximo. Railheads and Refilling Points as for 15th. 1st Cast Casualty Report as for 16th.	Rec.
-"-	18th March		Railheads and Refilling Points as for 16th. 1st Cast Casualty Report as for 17th.	Rec.
-"-	19th March		Railheads and Refilling Points as for 17th. 1st Cast Casualty Report unchanged. 1st Cast Casualty Report as for 18th.	Rec.

Army Form C. 2118.

WAR DIARY
or
INTELLIGENCE SUMMARY.
(Erase heading not required.)

5th Cavalry Divisional A.C.

Place	Date	Hour	Summary of Events and Information	Remarks and references to Appendices
	1917			
TRÉPIED	20th March		Railheads and Refilling Points as for 19th. Frost Casualty Report as for 19th. Ordered Supply Col. Ammunition Column to draw new water tank trailers from 5th Aux. Petrol Co. Abbeville.	Pe.
-"-	21st March		Railheads and Refilling Points as for 20th. Frost Casualty Report as for 20th. Temp. Lieut. R.W.R. Halliday joined 3rd Cav. Div. Supply Column as Supply Officer. Det. 5th Cav. Div. Reserve Park marched to rejoin their unit, marching to BUIRE-AU-SEC today, thence to FONTAINE-SUR-MAYE. Received from O.S. particulars of a scheme to recharge the accumulators of Aldis lamps, used for signalling by Capt. Callow, by the Supply Column.	Rec.
-"-	22nd March		Railheads and Refilling Points as for 21st. Frost Casualty Report as for 21st.	Rec.
-"-	23rd March		Railheads and Refilling Points as for 22nd. Frost Casualty Reports as for 22nd. Submitted to A.D.S.T. a fresh report on the number of able men who can be released for fighting services.	R.C.L.
-"-	24th March		Railheads and Refilling Points as for 23rd. Frost Casualty Reports as for 23rd. Forwarded to "Q" proposals for the allotment of Aux. M.J. Co. wagons as Sup. wagons.	R.C.L.
-"-	25th March		Railheads and Refilling Points as for 24th. Frost Casualty Report awaited.	

Army Form C. 2118.

WAR DIARY
or
INTELLIGENCE SUMMARY.

(Erase heading not required.)

H.Qrs. 3rd Cavalry Div'l. A.d.C.

Place	Date	Hour	Summary of Events and Information	Remarks and references to Appendices
TREPIED	1917 26th March		Railheads and Refilling Points as for 25th. Sgt. Foot Casualty Report unchanged. Temp. Lieut. H.R. STEED discharged hospital.	Nil
" "	27th March		Railheads and Refilling Points as for 26th. Sgt. Casualty Report as for 26th. Temp. Lieut. J.T. WATSON joined vice Temp. Capt. J.B. TREND (posted to U.K.) and was posted to 8th Cav. Bde. Temp. Lieut. H.G. MORRISON joined vice J. Lt. P. FAUX (officer of strength 27.3.17 on proceeding on leave to South Africa).	Nil
" "	28th March		Railheads and Refilling Points as for yesterday, 53 limbers from 10th Reserve Park to join Division for carriage of gas rations.	Nil
" "	29th March		Railheads and Refilling Points as for 28th.	Nil
" "	30th March		Railheads and Refilling Points as for 29th.	Nil
" "	31st March		Railheads and Refilling Points as for 30th. Lieut. (T. Capt.) C.J. Martin, N.C, ordered from 5th Cav. Ambulance to "S" Corps Amm. Sn. Relief by Temp. Major J.M. Edwards.	Nil

S.C. Murray
Lt. Colonel
Comdg. H.Qrs. 3rd Cavalry Div'l. A.d.C.

WAR DIARY or INTELLIGENCE SUMMARY

Army Form C. 2118.

Vol 29

HDW. 1st Cavalry Divisional Arty.

Place	Date	Hour	Summary of Events and Information	Remarks and references to Appendices
TREPIED	1917 1st April	-	Railheads MONTREUIL and BEAURAINVILLE. Refilling Points in Brigade areas.	Nil
"	2nd	-	Railheads and Refilling Points as 1st. Capt. J. B. TREND, 2.O, 8th Cav. Bde. to ENGLAND with a view to transfer to Royal Artillery.	Nil
"	3rd	-	Orders issued to Auxiliary H.T.C. to send out wagons to units tomorrow to convey horse rugs to FREVENT area when the Division moves. Railheads and Refilling Points as for 2nd.	Nil
"	4th	-	Railheads and Refilling Points as for 3rd. Division to move to a concentration area tomorrow.	Nil
"	5th	-	With Railheads and Refilling Points as for 4th. HQrs Arty. left TREPIED at 10 am & proceeded by march route to HESDIN. Supply Col. moved there 3 p.m.	Nil
MARESQUEL	6th	-	MARESQUEL arriving there 3 p.m. Railhead BOUQUEMAISON. 40 mules sent from LE BOISLE to BEAURAINVILLE to replace others unfit to work with the 53 Limbers detached for duty with the Division from 10th Reserve Park.	Nil
"	7th	-	Railhead BOUQUEMAISON. Ammn Park & Brigaderie 1 m. N. of FREVENT.	Nil

Army Form C. 2118.

WAR DIARY
or
INTELLIGENCE SUMMARY.
3rd Cavalry Divisional Ad....

(Erase heading not required.)

Instructions regarding War Diaries and Intelligence Summaries are contained in F. S. Regs., Part II. and the Staff Manual respectively. Title pages will be prepared in manuscript.

Place	Date	Hour	Summary of Events and Information	Remarks and references to Appendices
	7th April (cont)		HQrs A.B. proceeded by road from MARESQUEL to MONCHEL, 9 miles S.E. of HESDIN. Auxiliary M.T.C. & Det: 10th Reserve Park left billets at ST DENOEUX and proceeded to MONCHEL. Gap rations loaded.	Nil
MONCHEL	8th April		Railhead BOUQUEMAISON. "B" Echelon of Division divisionalized and came under the orders of Cav. HQrs. & "A" Echelon of Division moved to GOUY-en-ARTOIS. "B" Echelon moved from MONCHEL and concentrated at BOUBERS-sur-CANCHE - with "B" Echelon were Auxiliary M.T.C. & Cavalry Corps Bridging Park. Owing to congestion of village, applied for and obtained permission to use LIGNY-sur-CANCHE, where Corps Bridging Park moved next morning.	Nil
		10ct	10th Reserve Park moved to BARLY.	
BOUBERS-sur-CANCHE	9th April		Railhead BOUQUEMAISON. "B" Echelon remained at BOUBERS. "A" Echelon & DUISANS	Nil
"	10ct		Railhead BOUQUEMAISON.	Nil
			"B" Echelon, including Auxiliary M.T.C. and Corps Bridging Park, proceeded by march route to ETREE-WAMIN.	Nil

Army Form C. 2118.

WAR DIARY
or
INTELLIGENCE SUMMARY. H.Qrs. 3rd Cavalry Divisional A.C.
(Erase heading not required.)

Instructions regarding War Diaries and Intelligence Summaries are contained in F.S. Regs., Part II and the Staff Manual respectively. Title pages will be prepared in manuscript.

Place	Date	Hour	Summary of Events and Information	Remarks and references to Appendices
ETREE-WAMIN	11th April		Railhead BOUQUEMAISON. "B" Echelon remained at ETREE-WAMIN. 10H remounts received and remained with "B" Echelon. 1 Major J.H. BLUNDELL, A.V.C., arrived yesterday to assume command of 3rd Cavalry Ammunition Park, vice Capt. C.J. MARTIN, M.C., ordered to "S" Corps Amn. Park. Auxiliary H.T. Co. moved to FOSSEUX.	Nil
ETREE-WAMIN	12th April		Railhead BOUQUEMAISON. "B" Echelon proceeded to and joined up with the Division at GOUY-EN-ARTOIS, on the Division coming out of action – Cavalry Corps Bridging Park remained at ETREE-WAMIN.	Nil
GOUY-EN-ARTOIS	13th April		Railhead BOUQUEMAISON. Division remained in area of GOUY-EN-ARTOIS. Capt. C.J. MARTIN, M.C., 3rd Can. Amn Park to "S" Corps Amn. Pk on 12th inst.	Nil
GOUY-EN-ARTOIS	14th April		Railhead BOUQUEMAISON.	Nil
GOUY-EN-ARTOIS	15th April		Railhead BOUQUEMAISON. Amm. Park withdrew part of ammunition from Aux. H.T. consequent upon	Nil

2353 Wt. W2344/1454 700,000 5/15 D.D.&L. A.D.S.S./Forms/C. 2118.

Army Form C. 2118.

WAR DIARY
or
INTELLIGENCE SUMMARY.

H.Qrs. 3rd Cavalry Divisional Arty.

(Erase heading not required.)

Instructions regarding War Diaries and Intelligence Summaries are contained in F. S. Regs., Part II. and the Staff Manual respectively. Title pages will be prepared in manuscript.

Place	Date	Hour	Summary of Events and Information	Remarks and references to Appendices
GOUY-EN-ARTOIS	16th April		An arrangement to lighten the loads carried. Railhead BOUQUEMAISON. Division moved to the area of FROHEN-LE-GRANDE. HQrs. Att. billeted at WAVANS, 2½ m. S.E. of AUXI-LE-CHATEAU.	Nil
WAVANS	17th April		Railhead BOUQUEMAISON. Division remained in same area.	Nil
WAVANS	18th April		Railhead BOUQUEMAISON. 2 L.D. horses of Aux. H.T. lost by Dismounted Battalion.	Nil
WAVANS	19th April		Railhead BOUQUEMAISON. Division moved to LIGESCOURT area. HQrs. Att. with Auxiliary H.T.Co. and Ammn. Park, billeted at REGNAUVILLE. Supply between BEAURAINVILLE and Oct. 10th Reserve Park at ESTRÉES-LES-CRÉCY. Divl. Troops Supply Dump, together with supply details, located at LIGESCOURT.	Nil
REGNAUVILLE	20th April		Railhead BEAURAINVILLE. 900 remounts advised to be at No. Base Remount Depot, ECHINGHEN.	Nil
REGNAUVILLE	21st April		Railhead BEAURAINVILLE. Orders issued for the distribution of Aux. H.T. wagons amongst	

Army Form C. 2118.

WAR DIARY
or
INTELLIGENCE SUMMARY. *H.Q.* 3rd Cavalry Divl. Arte.
(Erase heading not required.)

Instructions regarding War Diaries and Intelligence Summaries are contained in F. S. Regs., Part II. and the Staff Manual respectively. Title pages will be prepared in manuscript.

Place	Date	Hour	Summary of Events and Information	Remarks and references to Appendices
	1917			
	22nd April		units of the Division — These will be withdrawn in the event of a move. 30 mules advised for Det. 10th Reserve Park.	Met. Met.
REGNAUVILLE			Railhead BEAURAINVILLE. Arrangements made for receiving down parties to ECHINGHEN to collect remounts.	Met. Met.
"	23rd April		Railhead as for 22nd.	Met.
"	24th April		Railhead and Refilling points as for yesterday	Met.
"	25th April		Railhead and Refilling points as for yesterday	Met.
"	26th April		Railhead and Refilling points as for yesterday. 1 admitted to our transport	Met.
"	27th April		Railhead and Refilling points as for yesterday. 1 R.O. Div troops admitted No 24 General Hospital	Met.
"	28th April		Lieut. H. Bothgate R.O. Div troops admitted No 24 General Hospital	Met.
"			Railhead and Refilling points as for yesterday. 06 All expected transport of 6 Cavalry Brigade	Met.
"	29th April		Railhead Refilling points as for yesterday.	Met.
"	30 April		Railhead Refilling points as for yesterday	Met.

J.C. Twining/ Colonel
06 11 Dec 3rd Cavalry Divl. Arte.

Army Form C. 2118.

WAR DIARY
or
INTELLIGENCE SUMMARY.

(Erase heading not required.)

Army Cavalry Divisional A.V.S. Vol 30

Place	Date	Hour	Summary of Events and Information	Remarks and references to Appendices
	1917.			
REGNIÈVILLE	1st May		Railhead BEAURAINVILLE. Refilling points in Regards area. Approval of D.A.D.S. received to the scheme in the survey which Staff view lists by Cav. A.V. Co. until all my horses with no future operation.	
"	2nd May		Railhead as A.V.	
			1st All Mechant Transport of M Cavalry Brigade	
"	3rd May		Railhead as for 2nd	
"	4th May		Railhead as for 3rd	
			Insp. Au. Bridges No. Det. Horse Mobilizes Hospital	
"	5th May		Railhead as for 4th	
			Detailed 15 Cullises to "10" Reserve Park to assist with animals	
			at CRECY - EN - PONTHIEU.	
"	6th May		Railhead as for 5th	
			Percentage of spare draught animals enabled from 10% to 5%	
"	7th May		Railhead as for 6th	
			Reports from Veterinary Officers Cav. Div. reports of anim...	

Army Form C. 2118.

WAR DIARY
or
INTELLIGENCE SUMMARY.

(Erase heading not required.)

HQrs. 3rd Cavalry Div. Arty.

Instructions regarding War Diaries and Intelligence Summaries are contained in F. S. Regs., Part II. and the Staff Manual respectively. Title pages will be prepared in manuscript.

Place	Date	Hour	Summary of Events and Information	Remarks and references to Appendices
	1917			
			accident on the Bailey - Rang au Thero road on 6 inst resulting in the death of a woman -	M.O.
REGNAUVILLE	8 May		Railhead BEAURAINVILLE. Applied to Div. HQrs. for a ruling as to what transport in the Division the OC Arty is actually responsible for. Some doubt exists as to whether the transport of Artillery and the Machine Gun Squadron come under his control.	P.S.L
REGNAUVILLE	9 May		Railhead BEAURAINVILLE.	P.S.L
REGNAUVILLE	10 May		Railhead BEAURAINVILLE. Arranged for the testing of 54 tradesmen of the division in supply column and Ammunition Park Workshops. Instructor Amman Park to fill up with I.A.A.	P.S.L
REGNAUVILLE	11 May		Railhead BEAURAINVILLE. Temp. Lee. Lieut. R. DARBY A.B. joined 3rd Cav. Supply Col. vice Lieut. Capt. M.R. TOOMEY posted to command of No. 40 Ammunition Sub. Park.	M.O.

2353 Wt. W2544/1454 700,000 5/15 D.D.&L. A.D.S.S./Forms/C. 2118.

Army Form C. 2118.

WAR DIARY
or
INTELLIGENCE SUMMARY.

(Erase heading not required.)

3rd Cavalry Div. A.D.S.

Place	Date	Hour	Summary of Events and Information	Remarks and references to Appendices
	1917			
REGNAUVILLE	12th May		Railhead BEAURAINVILLE. Supply column report breakage of another Daimler cylinder head. This makes 5 lorries off road through broken cylinder heads.	
REGNAUVILLE	13th May		Railhead BEAURAINVILLE. Temp. Capt. M.A.TOOMEY A.V.C. from 3rd Cavalry Supply Column to No 20 Ammunition Sub. Park. Division started move to PERONNE area. D.S.A.D.S. units moved as follows: H.Qrs. A.D.S. from REGNAUVILLE to HAVANS. Adv. H.T. Co. + No 3 Sect. 10th Reserve Park to BEAUVOIR RIVIERE - Supply Column remained at BEAURAINVILLE - Aux. Park remained at REGNAUVILLE.	
WAVANS	14th May		Railhead BOUQUEMAISON. H.Qrs. A.D.S., Aux. H.T.Co. +Adv. Reserve Park marched vers DOULLENS to TALMAS + billeted there.	
TALMAS	15th May		Railhead CORBIE. H.Qrs. A.D.S. Aux. H.T.Co. + Adv. 10th Reserve Park proceeded by	

Army Form C. 2118.

WAR DIARY
or
INTELLIGENCE SUMMARY.

(Erase heading not required.)

H.Qrs. 3rd Cavalry Divl. Adm.

Place	Date	Hour	Summary of Events and Information	Remarks and references to Appendices
	1917			
	16th May		March route from TALMAS to QUERRIEU. Supply Column located at LA MOTTE and Ammun. Park at REGNAUVILLE. SS/935 H.Q. 2.T. GRANT to England to join a Cadet Unit.	M.L.
QUERRIEU			Railhead CORBIE. Div. H.Qrs. remained in QUERRIEU, march to be continued tomorrow.	Jul.
	17th May		I/15/23 2/Lt F.W. ROBERTS to H.Qrs. 8 Cav. Bar. Railhead CORBIE. H.Qrs. A/6" Aus. HTCo. + Oct 10 Reserve marched from QUERRIEU to LA MOTTE-EN-SANTERRE. Received ruling in reference to diary entry 8th May. The Divisional Commander has decided that the O.C. A.A. share by responsible for the inspection of the limbers and teams of Machine Gun Squadrons. As regards R.H.A. Batteries, he will inspect all G.S. and S.A.A. limbered wagons and teams which actually carry stores and supplies but will not be responsible for ammunition wagons. (3rd Cav. Div. O.O. dt. 16-5-17).	Jul. H.W.

2353 Wt. W2544/1454 700,000 5/15 D.D.&L. A.D.S.S./Forms/C. 2118.

WAR DIARY
or
INTELLIGENCE SUMMARY.

HQ. 3rd Cavalry Div. A.6.

Army Form C. 2118.

Place	Date	Hour	Summary of Events and Information	Remarks and references to Appendices
	1917			
LA MOTTE-EN-SANTERRE	18th May		Railhead LA FLAQUE. Remained at LA MOTTE-EN-SANTERRE.	
" "	19th May		Railhead LA CHAPELETTE near PERONNE. HQu. A.B. proceeded with Div. HQu. to FLAMICOURT (PERONNE). Bus. A.T.C. to No 3 Sec., 10th Reserve Park to COURCELLE'S. Supply Column and Ammn. Park halted along road between VILLERS-CARBONNEL and PERONNE.	
FLAMICOURT	20th May		Railhead LA CHAPELETTE. Remained at FLAMICOURT. Location of other Units unchanged.	
FLAMICOURT	21st May		Railhead LA CHAPELETTE. Div. HQu. remained at FLAMICOURT. Received instructions that all motor lorries for extraneous duties are to be detailed by R.A.S.T. Cavalry Corps only and that requisitions for motor lorries for such duties are to be submitted to him.	
FLAMICOURT	22nd May		Railhead LA CHAPELETTE. Div. HQu. remained at FLAMICOURT. Ammunition Park now	

Army Form C. 2118.

WAR DIARY
or
INTELLIGENCE SUMMARY.
(Erase heading not required.)

H.Q. 3rd Cavalry Div. A/6.

Place	Date	Hour	Summary of Events and Information	Remarks and references to Appendices
			Located at J.16.c.2.5 (sheet 62C. 1/20,000). Reference diary entry of 21st:- Six lorries may now be taken over with the Divisional use. One motor car of H.Qrs. 3rd Cav. Div. A/6. is to be sent to Cavalry Corps Troops supply column on reduction of establishment. 3rd Cavalry Ammunition Parks & 59th Army Aux. Park to be amalgamated and will be known as "Cavalry Corps Ammunition Park". The C.O. A.S.C. will command (2nd Cav. Ammunition) but the Parks will continue to be administered by their respective Divisions. Received Cavalry Corps division that no personnel of Cav. Supply Column and Ammun Parks are to be detailed for extraneous duties without the sanction of Cavalry Corps Q.	M.L. M.L.
FLAVICOURT 25th May			Railhead AT CHAPELETTE.	M.L.

Army Form C. 2118.

WAR DIARY
or
INTELLIGENCE SUMMARY.
(Erase heading not required.)

W.D. 3rd Cavalry Div. A.b.

Place	Date	Hour	Summary of Events and Information	Remarks and references to Appendices
	2nd May		Div. H.Qrs. remained at FLAMICOURT. Advanced H.Qrs. will be formed tomorrow at VILLERS FAUCON. Received 8 M.T. Drivers, reinforcements from Base M.T. Depot. 3 M.T. S.S. to 5th Cav. Fld. Amb. and 3 to 7th B. of Ambulance. Temp. Lce. Serjt. T.E.W.D. SIMPSON, A.b. posted to 3rd Cav. Div. Clerk. H.Q. in place Temp. Lce. Serjt. C.H. SENDELL, A.b. (ordered to England on transfer to R.F.A.). Railhead LA CHAPELETTE.	M.1
FLAMICOURT			Advanced Divisional Head Quarters moved to VILLERS FAUCON in E.23.a.9.b.(Sheet 62c No.300). 3rd Cav. Div. Sig. remained at FLAMICOURT, together with portion of Divl. Staff. 25 P.B. men joined. 2/Lt. C.H. SENDELL, A.b. 3rd Cav. Aux. M.T.C. to England on transfer to R.H.A. 3rd Cavalry Division takes over 'D' sector of trenches now held by BELL SMYTH'S Bde. of 2nd Cav. Div. tonight.	M.1

2353 Wt. W2344/1454 700,000 5/15 D.D.&L. A.D.S.S./Forms/C.2118.

Army Form C. 2118.

WAR DIARY
or
INTELLIGENCE SUMMARY.
(Erase heading not required.)

A.D.Dn. 3rd Cavalry Divl. A.D.S.

Instructions regarding War Diaries and Intelligence Summaries are contained in F.S. Regs., Part II. and the Staff Manual respectively. Title pages will be prepared in manuscript.

Place	Date	Hour	Summary of Events and Information	Remarks and references to Appendices
	1917			
	25th May		3rd Cav. Dn. took over rationing of B/296, C/296 & D/296 Batteries R.F.A. so from conscription 30th inst. 2 V.J. arrived to 20th Mobile Veterinary Section.	Nil
FLAMICOURT	25th May		Railhead LA CHAPPALETTE. To change to TINCOURT tomorrow. Divisional troops supply, Detachment moves to TINCOURT. 10 R.B. men to DOINGT - 4 to VILLERS FAUCON - 2 to LONGAVESNES and 2 to EPEHY.	Nil
"	26th May		Railhead TINCOURT. All rations drawn from Railhead by horse transport. One R.B. man to each 6th, 7th, 8th Cav. Bde. HQrs. Notified O.C. No III sect. 10 Reserve Park, that the L.O.C. complains of My bad driving of the men of his section.	Nil
"	27th May		Railhead TINCOURT. One R.B. man to Divl. Gas School 28/5/17	Nil
"	28th May		Railhead TINCOURT.	Nil
"	29th May		Railhead TINCOURT.	Nil

Army Form C. 2118.

WAR DIARY
or
INTELLIGENCE SUMMARY.

(Erase heading not required.)

A.Q. 3rd Cavalry Divisional A.D.C.

Instructions regarding War Diaries and Intelligence Summaries are contained in F. S. Regs., Part II. and the Staff Manual respectively. Title pages will be prepared in manuscript.

Place	Date	Hour	Summary of Events and Information	Remarks and references to Appendices
FLAMICOURT	30th May		3rd Cav. Ammn. Park moves to BRAY-SUR-SOMME under orders of A.D.S.T. Cavalry Corps. V.B. Supply Col. intimates that he has three 400-gallon water tanks drawn from R.E. Dumps at FLIXECOURT which are to be fitted on 30 cwt lorries. These will be ready for use of the Division on 30th inst. Railhead TINCOURT.	A.1
	31st May		No. 2 Det. 3rd Cav. Div. Supply Column ordered by A.D.S.T. Cavalry Corps to CANDAS. Lorries not yet taken. Railhead TINCOURT.	A.1

Sgd Wyvern
Lt Colonel
A.D.S.S. 3rd Cavalry Div. A.D.C.
Commanding

Army Form C. 2118.

WAR DIARY
or
INTELLIGENCE SUMMARY.
(Erase heading not required.)

H.Qrs. 3rd Cavalry Div. A.C.

Vol 31

Place	Date	Hour	Summary of Events and Information	Remarks and references to Appendices
FLANICOURT	1917 1st June		Railhead TINCOURT. Ordered one water tank lorry to Div. Hdrs. and remaining two to 8th Cav. Bde. area.	
-"-	2nd June		Railhead TINCOURT.	W.O.
-"-	3rd June		Railhead TINCOURT.	W.O.
-"-	4th June		Railhead TINCOURT. Div. Hdrs. direct that units shall pay for all feeds entertained.	W.O.
-"-	5th June		Railhead TINCOURT. One water tank lorry placed at disposal of Fourth Army Well Boring Party. Sent 4 horses of Am. H.T. Co to VILLERS FAUCON to give assistance with farming. Court of Inquiry held at Supply Colm. to investigate the circumstances of death of No 78555 Pte. C. P. SHEPHERD, A.S.C. 5th Cav. Supply Column, who met his death by the explosion of a shell fuse which he was in possession	W.T.C.

Army Form C. 2118.

WAR DIARY
or
INTELLIGENCE SUMMARY.
(Erase heading not required.)

W.D.
3rd Cavalry Divisional A.V.

Instructions regarding War Diaries and Intelligence Summaries are contained in F. S. Regs., Part II. and the Staff Manual respectively. Title pages will be prepared in manuscript.

Place	Date	Hour	Summary of Events and Information	Remarks and references to Appendices
	1917			
FLAMICOURT	6th June		Q', contrary to orders, proceeded forward to 3rd Cav. Div. H.Q. with opinion of A.D. recorded thereon that Pte Hughes was to blame for the accident and that he was not on duty at the time.	Nil
			Railhead TINCOURT.	
	7 Jan		Lieut. A.J. WELLS assumed command of No. 3 Section, 10th Reserve Park, vice ¿ Capt. S.H. BOLTON, A.V.C, posted to 3rd Cavalry Reserve Park.	Nil
			Railhead TINCOURT.	Nil
	8 Jan		¿ Capt. S.H. BOLTON to 3rd Cavalry Reserve Park.	Nil
			Railhead TINCOURT.	Nil
	9 Jan		Capt. + Riding Master SADLER, A.V.C, joined for course of instruction in pack transport.	Nil
			Railhead TINCOURT.	Nil
	10 Jan		Railhead TINCOURT.	Nil
	11 Jan		Railhead TINCOURT.	Nil
	12th Jan		Railhead TINCOURT.	Nil

Army Form C. 2118.

WAR DIARY
or
INTELLIGENCE SUMMARY.
(Erase heading not required.)

War. 3rd Cavalry Divisional H.Q.

Instructions regarding War Diaries and Intelligence Summaries are contained in F.S. Regs., Part II. and the Staff Manual respectively. Title pages will be prepared in manuscript.

Place	Date	Hour	Summary of Events and Information	Remarks and references to Appendices
FLAMICOURT	1917 13 June		Railhead TINCOURT.	MEL
-"-	14 June		Railhead TINCOURT.	MEL
-"-	15 June		Railhead TINCOURT.	MEL
-"-	16 June		Railhead TINCOURT.	MEL
-"-	17 June		Railhead TINCOURT. Arrangements made to supply 18 horses to the Roads Officer to repair Roads round DOING T. Received Q.M.Gs decision reorganize Reserve Parks to provide each Cavalry Division with a Reserve Park comprising one light and one heavy section.	MEL MEL
-"-	18 June		Railhead TINCOURT.	MEL
-"-	19 June		Railhead TINCOURT. Corps Commander approves of cost of repairs (£5.0.0) to a lorry belonging to Supply Column which was run into by an engine at QUINCONCE Level Crossing being borne by the public.	MEL

Army Form C. 2118.

WAR DIARY
or
INTELLIGENCE SUMMARY.
(Erase heading not required.)

W.D.W. 3rd Cavalry Div. A.L.

Place	Date	Hour	Summary of Events and Information	Remarks and references to Appendices
	1917.			
FLAMICOURT	19.6.17 (cont.)		Received D.H.Q's proposal to effect a reduction in the establishment of officers with Cavalry Divisional A.L. Replied on this subject to the effect that one officer on each Echelon could combine duties of Requisitioning & Transport Officer, but otherwise no change could be effected.	Nil
"	20 June		Railhead TINCOURT.	Nil
"	21 June		Railhead TINCOURT. Captain Aldingraph H. SADLER A.L. left Unit on completion of this course of instruction in packsaddlery.	Nil
"	22 June		Railhead TINCOURT. No. 2 Section Supply Column, now moted from CANDAS to AMIENS.	Nil
"	23 June		Railhead TINCOURT. 96. A.L. visited 3rd Cav. Div. Reserve Park at MONTIGNY-L.S.- JONGLEUES to arrange details in connection with the reorganization of this Park. Arranged that No. 2 Section of the reorganized	Nil

Army Form C. 2118.

WAR DIARY
or
INTELLIGENCE SUMMARY.
(Erase heading not required.)

3rd Cavalry Divisional A.E.

Place	Date	Hour	Summary of Events and Information	Remarks and references to Appendices
	1917		Pain should be left completed at MONTIGNY and the remainder of the present Park be moved to VILLERS FAUCON, there to arrange final details in connection with the formation of H.Qrs & No 1 Section of the new Park. These will proceed on 29th inst.	nil
FLAMICOURT	23rd June		Railhead TINCOURT.	Nil
" "	24th June		Railhead TINCOURT. Reported on proposal of A.S.T. Cavalry Corps to throw on 2,3,3rd H.Q. Div. A.E. all personnel detached with Brigades and Divl troops — a system which, it was claimed, would result in bringing all detached personnel under the direct administration of the O.C. A.E. Replied that I could not see how the mere process of individing the personnel on the return would give more control but agreed present system is unsatisfactory.	Nil
" "	25th June		Railhead TINCOURT.	Nil
" "	26th June		Railhead TINCOURT.	Nil

T2134. Wt. W708—776. 500000. 4/15. Sir J. C. & S.

Army Form C. 2118.

WAR DIARY
or
INTELLIGENCE SUMMARY.
(Erase heading not required.)

H.Qrs. 3rd Cavalry Divisional A.S.C.

Place	Date	Hour	Summary of Events and Information	Remarks and references to Appendices
FLAMICOURT	1917 27 June		Railhead TINCOURT.	Nil
-,,-	28 June		Railhead TINCOURT. Can. H.Qrs. return to FLAMICOURT on 1st prox. During forthcoming move, 13 Cav. H.T. wagons to be allotted to each Brigade for carriage of horse supp. H.Q. Cav. Divl. Reserve Park reports their unit complete with the exception of five limbers & two triples.	Nil
-,,-	29 June		Railhead TINCOURT. Railhead at FAIQUE from 4 July.	Nil
-,,-	30 June		Railhead TINCOURT.	Nil

Sd/ W Wynne Lt Colonel
Comdg. H.Qrs. 3rd Cavalry Divisional A.S.C.

Army Form C. 2118.

WAR DIARY
OR
INTELLIGENCE SUMMARY.
(Erase heading not required.)

Headquarters.
3rd Cavalry Divisional A.S.C.

Place	Date	Hour	Summary of Events and Information	Remarks and references to Appendices
FLAMICOURT. (PERONNE)	1917. 1st July		Railhead TINCOURT. Advanced Divisional Headquarters returned to FLAMICOURT. Received D.H.Q's letter 3072/A/XIX/5 (O.A.1) of 22.6.17 :- that the Division will be accompanied on its move by (a) H.Q. + No. 1 Section, 3rd Can. Reserve Park and (b) No. 2 (S.A.A) Section of 3rd Can. Ammn. Park. No. 2 Section, Reserve Park, will remain in G.H.Q. Reserve and also one Section of Supply Column will be withdrawn into G.H.Q. Reserve as soon as the Division has completed its move.	Nil
- " -	2nd July		Railhead TINCOURT. 2nd Lieut. B.A. EMBY to be left behind as Supply Officer 2 Divisional Artillery and Dismounted Troops. Received copy of Cavalry Corps Q. Summary notifying move of No. 2 Section, 3rd Can. Div. Reserve Park (now in G.H.Q. Reserve) to GRIGNY (1½ m. N.E. of HESDIN). O.C. 3rd Can. Div. Reserve Park reports that he is a Captain Supplies and a Subalterns deficient owing to the promotion to Temp. captain of R.W.A. HEDGER. Eighteen lorries of 3rd Can. Div. Supply Column and 2 lorries of 59th Divisional Supply Column detached on command to O.C. A.S.C. 2nd Cavalry Division to the	Nil

Army Form C. 2118.

WAR DIARY
or
INTELLIGENCE SUMMARY.
(Erase heading not required.)

3rd Cavalry Divisional Art.

Place	Date	Hour	Summary of Events and Information	Remarks and references to Appendices
	1917			
FLAMICOURT	3rd July		Meeting of 3rd Cavalry Divl. Artillery 3rd Cavalry Divisional Battalion and 5q: Divisional Artillery (attached for rations 3rd Cav. Bn.) Railhead TINCOURT. Pte BRUCE, D. 1st Cameron Highlders, P.B. man, to rejoin cavalry units. 3rd Cavalry Divisional Auxiliary H.T.Co. moved to FLAMICOURT from vicinity of COURCELLES.	Kel
" "	4th July		Railhead LA FLAQUE. 3rd Cavalry Division moved by road to SUZANNE and HEILLY areas (10000 AMIENS sheet). Location of A.S.C. Units on night of 4th July — H.Qu. A.S.C. = TREUX — Supply Column = just S. of Mon. LEBLOND FARM on BOUQUEMAISON - FREVENT ROAD. Reserve Park = SUZANNE. Auxiliary H.T.Co. = TREUX. Annexe Park remained at LE MESNIL BRUNTEL (O.17.B.3.629). Divisional Headquarters at TREUX. Forwarded to Q. certificates of medical fitness of those officers whom it is proposed to attach to Infantry.	KU
TREUX	5th July		Railhead ROSEL (2 miles S. of BEAUVAL) Division moved to areas of AMPLIER and ETREE-WAMIN.	KU

Army Form C. 2118.

WAR DIARY
or
INTELLIGENCE SUMMARY.
(Erase heading not required.)

3rd Cavalry Divisional A.C.

Place	Date	Hour	Summary of Events and Information	Remarks and references to Appendices
	July 1917		Location of units on night of 5th July:— Div. H.Qrs and H.Qrs. A.S.C. at RUE DE LA SOUS-PRÉFECTURE, DOULLENS. Aux. H.T. Co. - MORT HORSE LINES, DOULLENS. Supply Column - on BOUQUEMAISON - FREVENT ROAD as yesterday. Reserve Park = HEILLY. Ammunition Park = LE MESNIL BRUNTEL as before.	Nil
DOULLENS	6 July		Railhead FREVENT. Division moved to area S. of ST POL. Div. H.Qr. - SAINS. H.Qr. A.C. FRAMECOURT. Aux H.T. Co. SAINS. Reserve Park with T. Co. Sec. Ammn. Park and Supply Column as yesterday.	Nil
FRAMECOURT.	7 July		Railhead BRUAY. Division moved to area round PERNES, AUCHEL and ACQ. Location of night of 7th July:— Div. H.Qrs and H.Qrs. A.S.C. - PERNES Ammunition Park remains at LE MESNIL BRUNTEL. Aux H.T.Co. - PERNES - Reserve Park TINCQUETTE-TINCQUES - Supply Column FOSSE 5 BRUAY.	Nil
PERNES	8 July		Railhead BRUAY. Reference entry in Diary to 24 June - Received instructions from A.D.S.T. Cavalry Corps, that the scheme to include all detached personnel on the Army Form B 2132	Nil

Army Form C. 2118.

WAR DIARY
or
INTELLIGENCE SUMMARY.
(Erase heading not required.)

3rd Cavalry Divisional H.Qrs. Vol. 6

Instructions regarding War Diaries and Intelligence Summaries are contained in F. S. Regs., Part II. and the Staff Manual respectively. Title pages will be prepared in manuscript.

Place	Date	Hour	Summary of Events and Information	Remarks and references to Appendices
	1917		of 3rd Cav. Divl. A.S.C. is to be carried out. Action taken accordingly. Following officers recommended for command of a Corps M.T. Unit (Lieut-Major):— Lieut. (S.R.) (T/Capt.) B.S. CUMBERLEGE, Temp. Capt. P.G.S. CLARK, both 3rd Cavalry Divn. Supply Column and Lieut. (T/Capt.) E.J.R. McWATTERS, 3rd Cavalry Divisional Ammunition Park.	Nil
PERNES	9th July		Railhead BRUAY. 3rd Cavalry Dismounted Battalion detrained at PERNES - CAMBLAIN from South Army Area. Strength 45 Officers, 1000 O.R., 4 horses. Arrangements made for rationing them as few conversation 11th instant. Received instructions from 3rd Cav. Divn. 'Q' to detail two lorries to postal work so that mails may be delivered to units the day of arrival at Railhead. These instructions were carried out but it was pointed out to O.C. Supply Column and Suffolks by me, that the supply of these two lorries could not be maintained during a move. In accordance with the direction of the D.H.Q., one section of the Supply Column will move tomorrow, 10th instant, to HESDIN to work	Nil

Army Form C. 2118.

WAR DIARY
or
INTELLIGENCE SUMMARY.
(Erase heading not required.)

H.Qu. 3rd Cavalry Div¹. Ad.

Instructions regarding War Diaries and Intelligence Summaries are contained in F. S. Regs., Part II. and the Staff Manual respectively. Title pages will be prepared in manuscript.

Place	Date	Hour	Summary of Events and Information	Remarks and references to Appendices
	1917			
PERNES	10 July		Under the Army Purchase Board – Applied to 'Q' to the opening of an Empress account by Lieut. Captain C.J. TINDELL-GREEN. Adc. as R.O. Divisional Staff. Railhead BRUAY.	Nil
			Received and distributed First Army Traffic notes. Received authentic copy of O.R.O. instructions that the section of Supply Column and the 2 section of Reserve Park are temporarily withdrawn to work under the Army Purchase Board in the area administered by OC GHQ Troops.	Nil
PERNES	11 July		Railhead BRUAY. Reported all Vauxhall Cars fitted with the Salata Belting Safety Device. Railhead BRUAY.	Nil
PERNES	12 July		Lt. GRAHAM K.6ᵗʰ Cavalry Field Ambulance. Acting M.P.M. H.V. ALEXANDER Ammunition Park recommended to Adc Boss. Records for promotion to temporary M.P.M. Railhead BRUAY.	Nil
PERNES	13 July		Railhead BRUAY.	Nil
PERNES	14 July		" "	Nil

Army Form C. 2118.

WAR DIARY
or
INTELLIGENCE SUMMARY.

(Erase heading not required.)

Hd.Qrs: 3rd Cavalry Divisional A/Q

Place	Date	Hour	Summary of Events and Information	Remarks and references to Appendices
			H.Qrs. and No. 1 Section of 3rd Cavalry Reserve Park inspected by A.D.C. 3rd Cavalry Division - June 10 am - Place of inspection - ST POL-ARRAS Road near TINCQUES. Forwarded to A.D.S.T., Cavalry Corps, the proceedings of a Court of Inquiry held at 3rd Cavalry Supply Column on 11th instant to investigate the circumstances under which Daimler lorry 7249, on charge of 3rd Cavalry Supply Column, became damaged. The lorry appears to have been damaged by skidding on a greasy road and then striking against a tree. Damage value £100. O.C. Supply Colm. considers no blame was due to driver and that cost should be borne by the Public. This was concurred in by O.C. A/Q. 3rd Cavalry Ammunition Column reports L.S. wagon E.9397s with axletree arm broken two wheels unserviceable, abandoned at SARTON in care of Town Major. Passed this report to A.D.S.T. Cavalry Corps. 3rd Cav. Div. Q. advises us that the authority for the new establishments and reorganization of Reserve Parks is W.O. letter 121/Cavalry/932 (S.D.2) dated 6th July, 1917.	W[?]

Army Form C. 2118.

WAR DIARY
or
INTELLIGENCE SUMMARY.
(Erase heading not required.)

HQrs. 3rd Cavalry Div. Ale

Place	Date	Hour	Summary of Events and Information	Remarks and references to Appendices
	1917			
PERNES	14 July (cont)		3rd Cavalry Ammunition Park moved to PERNES from South Army Area. Railhead BRUAY.	ALA
PERNES	15 July			
	16 July		Division moved to area between LILLERS and ST VENANT, with Div. HQ. at BUSNES. Location of A.L.b. Units :- HQrs. Div. Ale - BUSNES. Auxiliary H.T. Co - BUSNES. Reserve Park - MAREST. Ammn. Park remained at PERNES. Supply Column remained at Fosse 5, BRUAY.	
			Forwarded to 3rd Cav. Dv.Q. a report received from Supply Column of a unit sending remained clothing by supply lorry to Railhead. This resulted in the publication of a Div. Routine Order (№30) forbidding the sending of last worn clothing by lorry unless previously disinfected by the todew. A certificate that this has been done must in future be handed to the driver of the lorry collecting the clothing.	Nil
			Railhead AIRE.	
NOUVEAUMESH BUSNES	17th July		Ammunition Park moved from PERNES to HOLLANDERIE. P.20.c.9.5. (36ª 1/40,000). Reserve Park Supply Column to WIDDEBROUCQ. H.16. D.d.8. (36ª 1/40,000). to ST FLORIS in P.6.A.	ALA

Army Form C. 2118.

WAR DIARY
or
INTELLIGENCE SUMMARY.
(Erase heading not required.)

HQrs 3rd Cavalry Divl Ade

Instructions regarding War Diaries and Intelligence Summaries are contained in F. S. Regs., Part II. and the Staff Manual respectively. Title pages will be prepared in manuscript.

Place	Date	Hour	Summary of Events and Information	Remarks and references to Appendices
	1917			
BUSNES.	18 July		Railhead FIRE. Arrangements made for the Divisional Field Cashier to be attached to the Ammunition Park and for that unit to find a guard for his Treasure chests (3rd C.D. Hqrs A/17.7.17).— Interviewed Pte. H.W. COBBETT Ade. 3rd Cavalry Supply Column who made application for temporary commission in ASC. HT. Rejected — insufficient qualification.	Nil
BUSNES	19 July		D.A.D.O.S. 3rd Cav. Div. applied to have the Sie. 30 cwt. lorries allotted to him exchanged for 3 tonners.	Nil
BUSNES	20th July		Railhead FIRE. Recommended Temp. Lieut. C.B. PRICE and W.R. STEED for appointment to Acting Captain. Temp Lieut. J.N. ROBERTS, Ade. Joines 3rd Cavalry Divl. Reserve Park (authority DAQ.).	Nil
BUSNES	21st July		Railhead FIRE. Temp. Lieut. H.V. PEARCE, 3rd Cavalry Divl. Ade, admitted to No.	Nil

WAR DIARY
or
INTELLIGENCE SUMMARY.

Army Form C. 2118.

N Oro. 3rd Cavalry Divl. A.L.

57 Casualty Clearing Station, ST VENANT.

O.C Supply Colm. inspected his detached No 1 Section today and reported it in a satisfactory condition – The lorries of this section are located as follows :- 15 at DESVRES, 6 at DOULLENS, 1 at RUE, 6 at BOIS – JEAN and the remainder (30) at MARCONNE (HESDIN).

On the 2nd instant, we forwarded to 3Cav Dn Q. reports in connection with a motor collision between Surfer Car of 3rd Signal Sqn. and motor cycle 5791 of 3rd Cav. Ammn. Park. Accident appeared to be due to neither vehicle carrying lights and we recommended that driver of car (Pte Pratt A.S.C att. 7th Ausl) should pay 30/- and driver of cycle (Pte Cross) 7th H. today received decision of GOC Cavalry Corps that each man be put under a fortnight's stoppage of pay and that the balance (£12.13.4) be made a charge against the public. (CoV.W. Q/2657 d/ 17.7.17.) –

Letter received from 3rd C.D.Q (M/256) pointing out that vehicles of A.1. Echelon (limbers) had no brakes. We pointed out that some months ago a proposal to use the South African pattern brake

Army Form C. 2118.

WAR DIARY
or
INTELLIGENCE SUMMARY.
(Erase heading not required.)

HQrs 3rd Cavalry Divl. Ale.

Place	Date	Hour	Summary of Events and Information	Remarks and references to Appendices
	1917			
BUSNES	22nd July		was introduced but that the Saddle has not yet commenced. The majority of units prefer no trades but if they are required, ample opportunities exist for having trades fitted. Railhead FIRE.	
			Reference Diary entry of 14th July :- Corps Commander approves of lost of replacements to Divnl. lorry 7249 (Bk II.4) being borne by the Public (A.A.S.T. Cavalry lorries 7523/46) of 21-7-17. Lieut. (T/Capt) B.S. CUMBERLEGE Ade. S.R., reported returned to establishment of Supply Column in consequence of the issue of the revised establishment, Part VIII. There is one other officer surplus but this will be adjusted by the transfer of Sect. Lieut. R. DARBY, O.118, 2nd Echelon ordered to M.T. Inspection Branch.	W[?]
			Railhead FIRE.	
BUSNES	23rd July		O.C. Ade. appointed a Committee to inspect the wares of Divisional troops units and select them with a view to their being sent to the United Kingdom on demobilization for threshing purposes	W[?]

Army Form C. 2118.

WAR DIARY
or
INTELLIGENCE SUMMARY.
(Erase heading not required.)

H.Qrs. 3rd Cavalry Divisional Ad.

Place	Date	Hour	Summary of Events and Information	Remarks and references to Appendices
	1917		Court of Inquiry held at H.Q. Ad. to "investigate the circumstances under which Lieut. 2/Lieut. H.V. PEARCE, A.S.C. became a casualty." 2/Lieut. R. DARBY, A.S.C. (W) from 3rd Cavalry Supply Column to M.T. Inspection Branch, G.H.Q., 2nd Echelon. O/c. 3rd Cavalry Reserve Park today inspected his No 2 (Heavy) Section, Headquarters of which are at GRIGNY near HESDIN. There is a detachment of 10 wagons at LICQUES (a distance of 60 kilos) and 10 wagons at LUMBRES (45 kilometres away). He found the section in a satisfactory condition but complains that as the animals are only getting "I.of C. Ration" i.e. 3/4 of the field ration, they are likely to lose condition. Railhead AIRE.	Ad
BUSNES	2nd July		Temp. Capt. J.E. KOECHER, Ad. joined 3rd Cavalry Divisional Ad. He attached pending absorption. (Auth. Ad.Q. ---/16885 of 18.7.17). Received D. of T. instructions that all motor ambulances other than fords are to be fitted with the method of heating from the exhaust pipe. These instructions transmitted to the Subsid. Column.	Ad

T2134. Wt. W708—776. 500000. 4/15. Sir J. C. & S.

Army Form C. 2118.

WAR DIARY
or
INTELLIGENCE SUMMARY.
(Erase heading not required.)

N8ro.
3rd Cavalry Divl Ad

Instructions regarding War Diaries and Intelligence Summaries are contained in F.S. Regs., Part II. and the Staff Manual respectively. Title pages will be prepared in manuscript.

Place	Date	Hour	Summary of Events and Information	Remarks and references to Appendices
	1917			
BUSNES	25th July		Railhead AIRE.	Nil
"	26th July		Railhead AIRE. No. 1 section, 3rd Cavalry Divisional Supply Column joined up with column. Gap ration drawn from No. 40 Field Supply Depot, BETHUNE	Nil
"	27th July		Railhead AIRE.	Nil
"	28th July		Railhead AIRE. No. 2 Section, 5th Can. Div. Reserve Park joined up with the Park	Nil
"	29 July		Railhead AIRE. Directed 06 Supply Column to exchange at present 6 -joint lorries for Ordnance Supply for 3 ton lorries. Court of Enquiry assembled at N8ro Plan See on 4th Aug, to collect evidence as to the circumstances under which two unauthorized motor cycles came into possession of 3rd Carr Supply Column.	Nil
"	30th July		Railhead AIRE.	

Temp. Lieut. H.G. MORRISON. A.S.C. to No. 2 School, Eletos School.

Army Form C. 2118.

WAR DIARY
or
INTELLIGENCE SUMMARY.
(Erase heading not required.)

WDno 3rd Cavalry Divl Ob

Instructions regarding War Diaries and Intelligence Summaries are contained in F. S. Regs., Part II. and the Staff Manual respectively. Title pages will be prepared in manuscript.

Place	Date	Hour	Summary of Events and Information	Remarks and references to Appendices
	1917.			
BUSNES	31st July		BEDFORD. Authority Q.M.G. a66/16150 of 26.7.17. Railhead AIRE. 06 Supply Column complains of rabbit skins being sent to Railhead without being properly dried. This complaint passed to Q.	MC WR

St Munro. Colonel
Comdg. WDno 3rd Cavalry Divl Ab.

Army Form C. 2118

WAR DIARY
or
INTELLIGENCE SUMMARY
(Erase heading not required.)

HQrs. 3rd Cavalry Divisional A.C. 33

Place	Date	Hour	Summary of Events and Information	Remarks and references to Appendices
BUSNES	1st Aug. 1917		Railhead AIRE. Applied to I.G.C. in case of M/S 052996 Pte. R. SKELHORN. Ammn. Park.	Rd.
-"-	2nd Aug.		Railhead AIRE. Discussing the question of the provision of a Medical Officer for "B" Echelon, the A.D.M.S. suggested utilizing the services of the M.O.'s Supply Column — We agreed that this would meet the case.	Rd.
-"-	3rd Aug.		Railhead AIRE.	Rd.
-"-	4th Aug.		Railhead AIRE. Received approval for the issue of one motor cycle + side car and one 10 cwt Box Van to the Sanitary Section. Instructed O.C. Supply Column to indent for these.	Rd.
-"-	5th Aug		Railhead AIRE. Temp. Capt. S.H. BOLTON, A.I., 3rd Cav. Div. Reserve Park, ordered to No. 35 Reserve Park. Relief by 1st Lt. H.W. HARKE, A.I. Base Depot. Received from 3rd Cav. Div. Q. a proposal of 6th Cav. Bde. that each supply lorry carry a reserve of two boxes of Horse shoes. Passed this to O.C. Supply Coln. for remarks.	Rd.
-"-	6th Aug.		Railhead AIRE.	Rd.
-"-	7th Aug.		Railhead AIRE.	Rd.

Army Form C. 2118

WAR DIARY
or
INTELLIGENCE SUMMARY

(Erase heading not required.)

A.Q.M.G.
3rd Cavalry Divisional A.S.C.

Instructions regarding War Diaries and Intelligence Summaries are contained in F.S. Regs., Part II. and the Staff Manual respectively. Title Pages 3rd CAVALRY DIVISION will be prepared in manuscript.

Place	Date	Hour	Summary of Events and Information	Remarks and references to Appendices
BUSNES	1917 8th Aug.		Railhead AIRE. A.D.S.T. Cavalry Corps, called for remarks on a proposal to standardise the moves of motor ambulances with the Divisions - 3rd Cavalry Divn. there all Natives - Proposal agreed with.	MEL
-"-	9th Aug		Railhead AIRE.	MEL
-"-	10th Aug.		Railhead AIRE. Lieut. BATHGATE and party, detached for work under Central Purchase Board, to return to unit by 16th inst. Court of Enquiry reassembled to take evidence re two surplus motor cycles with Supply Column.	MEL
-"-	11th Aug		Railhead AIRE. Temp. Sec. Lieut. H.V. PEARCE evacuated to England 31-7-17.	MEL
-"-	12th Aug.		Railhead AIRE. Lieut. (T. Capt) B.S. CUMBERLEGE, O.B., S.R. ordered to join II.A. Hqs. Army Corps Mtr. for duty as Adjutant to S.M.T.O.	MEL
-"-	13th Aug		Railhead AIRE. Submitted to Q.Q. a claim for acting rank under G.R.O. 2507 on behalf	MEL

Submitted Temp. Lieut. R.C. LYLE
1875 Wt. W593/826 1,000,000 4/15 J.B.C. & A. A.D.S.S./Forms/C. 2118.

Army Form C. 2118

WAR DIARY
or
INTELLIGENCE SUMMARY
(Erase heading not required.)

H.Q.
3rd Cavalry Divisional Ad[mn]

Place	Date	Hour	Summary of Events and Information	Remarks and references to Appendices
BUSNES.	14th Aug 1917		Railhead AIRE. Lieut. (A/Capt) B.S. Cambridge Ado R.C. less 3rd Cavalry Supply Column for II. A. & N.Z. Army Corps.	Nil
-do-	15th Aug		Railhead AIRE.	Nil
-do-	16th Aug		Railhead AIRE.	Nil
-do-	17th Aug		Railhead AIRE.	Nil
-do-	18th Aug		Railhead AIRE. Recommended Lieut. Jas. R.E. Lyle for appointment to temporary Captain. Directed 96. Supply Column to indent for rifles for men with non authorized to the Sanitary Section.	Nil
-do-	19th Aug		Railhead AIRE.	Nil
-do-	20th Aug		Railhead AIRE. Ref. diary entry Aug 8th : A.D.S.T. decided to take no further action re standardisation of modes of ambulances.	Nil

Army Form C. 2118

WAR DIARY
or
INTELLIGENCE SUMMARY

(Erase heading not required.)

HQrs. 3rd Cav. Div. Alt.

Instructions regarding War Diaries and Intelligence Summaries are contained in F. S. Regs., Part II. and the Staff Manual respectively. Title Pages will be prepared in manuscript.

Place	Date	Hour	Summary of Events and Information	Remarks and references to Appendices
BUSNES	1917 21st Aug.		Railhead AIRE. O.C. alt. instructed transport of 6 Cav. Loe.	AEL
--	22nd Aug.		Railhead AIRE.	AEL
--	23rd Aug.		Railhead AIRE.	AEL
--	24th Aug.		Railhead AIRE.	AEL
--	25th Aug.		Railhead AIRE.	AEL
--	26th Aug.		Railhead AIRE.	AEL
--	27th Aug.		Railhead AIRE.	AEL AEL
--	28th Aug.		Railhead AIRE.	AEL
--	29th Aug.		Railhead AIRE.	AEL
--	30th Aug.		Railhead AIRE. Issued instructions to Supply Columns and Ammunition Park that lorries were not to be used to conveying canteen supplies from Base Ports. Lieut. W. R. STEED left 6 Cav. Sde. transport to No 1 Camp, BROCTON CAMP, STAFFS. Duties of S.O. taken over by Lieut. Calt. J. E. KOECHER.	
--	31st Aug.		Railhead AIRE. Instructed O.C. Ammn. Park to send 3 fitters to Cav. Cdn. 1. Lieut. on 3 Sect. St. Murray, Lt. Colonel	AEL

Vh 34

War Diary
for
September, 1917

H.Q., 3rd Cavalry Divisional Ak.

WAR DIARY or INTELLIGENCE SUMMARY

Army Form C. 2118

September, 1917
H.Q. 3rd Cavalry Division Sir A.H.

Place	Date	Hour	Summary of Events and Information	Remarks and references to Appendices
Busnes	1st Sept.		Railhead. AIRE	Nil
"	2nd Sept.		Railhead. AIRE	Nil
"	3rd Sept.		Railhead. AIRE. 6th Cav. Brigade proceeded to 6.15 Cav. Brigade to R.O. 6/5 Cav. Brigade as a temporary measure. T/2 Lt. T. Watson R.O. has over duties.	Nil
"	4th Sept		Railhead. AIRE	Nil
"	5th Sept		Railhead. AIRE	Nil
"	6th Sept		Railhead AIRE. Submitted to Div HQ. my remarks re War Office's suggested reorganisation of Div. A.S.C., which was to the effect that one Echelon Supply Column be disbanded and Reserve Park use as a Div. Supply Column. My report suggested four Reserve Park be disbanded and Second Echelon Supply Column retained.	Nil
"	7th Sept.		Railhead. AIRE. Inspected transport of 8th Cav. Brigade.	Nil Nil Nil Nil
"	8th Sept.		Railhead. AIRE.	Nil
"	9th Sept		Railhead. AIRE	
"	10th Sept		Railhead. AIRE. Reported to Div. H.Q. that crew supplied for L.G.S. & Reserve Park were ineffective. Received instruction that Mowing reduction went to the made in transport & Supply Column and Ammunition Park. One Motor Car and two Motor Cycles (each).	Nil

WAR DIARY or INTELLIGENCE SUMMARY

(Erase heading not required.)

3rd Cavalry Div. H.Q.

September, 1917. Army Form C. 2118

Place	Date	Hour	Summary of Events and Information	Remarks and references to Appendices
BUSNES	11 Sept.		R.H. AIRE	
"	12 Sept.		Railhead AIRE	
"	13 "		Railhead AIRE	
"	14 "		Railhead AIRE	
"	15 "		Railhead AIRE. Directed Supply Colm. to collect 100 Portuguese wire barrels from QUISTEDE and put on rail for Area Commandant, ABBEVILLE. a/s O.R.O. POOLE, J. a.h. from H.Qrs. 3rd Cav. Dn. to H.Q. XIX Corps.	
"	16 Sept.		Railhead AIRE.	
"	17 Sept.		Railhead AIRE.	
"	18 Sept.		Railhead AIRE. Director of Transport discovers a HARLEY-DAVIDSON moto cycle has been with 2nd Life Guards for some time past. Enquiries whether actual have been carried out and petrol & tyres issued made. enquiries of Supply Colm. & Corps Park	
"	19 Sept.		Railhead AIRE	
"	20 Sept.		Railhead AIRE. Have Reports the names of several N.C.O's submitted to A.h. Have Reports the names acting Rank by this Leavein in relation of appointment to acting Rank by this Leavein issue. Cav. Dn. A.h. reported to A.D.V.S. that no horse have been carried out on the mis to cycle shed by H.Q. L Guards	

WAR DIARY or INTELLIGENCE SUMMARY

September, 1917. Army Form C. 2118

H.Qrs. 3rd Cavalry Divisional Ads.

Place	Date	Hour	Summary of Events and Information	Remarks and references to Appendices
BUSNES	21st Sept.		Railhead AIRE. Received proposal from 3 Cav. Div. "Q" that Ads. personnel with Yeomanry Regts. now unauthorized, should be withdrawn and attached to the Div. A.T.C. in place of Cavalrymen, now authorized to be attached to that Company. Applied to D.A.G. Base for an A.S.C. Sergt. & 6 Cav. Field Ambulance to replace a R.A.M.C. N.C.O. as adverse reports on transport had been made. Reference Diary entry to 18th inst.— Enquiries show no repairs have been executed on the Harley-Davidson motor cycle with Life Guards, no spare tyres, spares etc. been issued. Reported these facts yesterday to A.D.S.T. Cavalry Corps.	App.
-"-	22nd Sept.		Railhead AIRE.	App.
-"-	23rd Sept.		Railhead AIRE.	App.
-"-	24th Sept.		Railhead AIRE.	App.
-"-	25th Sept.		Railhead AIRE.	App.
-"-	26th Sept.		Railhead AIRE. Lieut. Y.M. BATHGATE 3rd Cavalry Divisional Ads. left to report to No. 2 Infantry School, Luton School, BEDFORD, England. Authy.:- D.H.Q. A.dt/16/50/15 of 19.9.17.	App.
-"-	27th Sept.		Railhead AIRE.	App.

WAR DIARY or INTELLIGENCE SUMMARY

Army Form C. 2118.

September 1917

HQrs 3rd Cavalry Divl. Ale

Place	Date	Hour	Summary of Events and Information	Remarks and references to Appendices
BUSNES	28 Sep. 1917		Railhead AIRE. Directed O.C. Supply Column to place two lorries at disposal of the C.R.E. Cavalry Corps. Submitted to Qan. Dn. Q. a scheme for drawing supplies with a railhead at LILLERS, mainly by horse transport to effect a saving of M.T.	Nil
"	29 Sept.		Railhead AIRE. Received proposal of Q.M.G. to reorganize the Mechanical Transport of Cavalry Division - the reorganization to consist of the formation of a Cavalry Divisional M.T. Co. consisting of a H.Qrs. and 6 Sections.	Nil
"	30 Sept.		Railhead AIRE.	Nil

St. Vincent, Lt Colonel,
Commanding HQrs, 3 Cavalry Divl. Ale

A.S.C. HEADQUARTERS
3rd CAVALRY DIVISION

WM 35

War Diary of
 Headquarters,
  3rd Cavalry Divisional
   A.S.C. for
    October, 1917

Army Form C. 2118.

WAR DIARY of 1st Can. Cavalry Div. Ad.
or
INTELLIGENCE SUMMARY.

(Erase heading not required.)

October, 1917.

Instructions regarding War Diaries and Intelligence Summaries are contained in F. S. Regs., Part II. and the Staff Manual respectively. Title pages will be prepared in manuscript.

Place	Date	Hour	Summary of Events and Information	Remarks and references to Appendices
BUSNES	1917 1st October		Railhead AIRE. Notified A.S.T. that four gallons of glycerine per day required for use with Daimler lorries cars to prevent frost casualties.	R.C.L.
" "	2nd Oct.		Railhead AIRE. Reported Lieut. Capt. H.N. BUCKLEY O.C. Can. Div. Am. H.T.C. admitted to No. 1 Red Cross (Duchess of Westminster) Hospital on 28.9.17.	R.C.L.
" "	3rd Oct.		Railhead AIRE. Moseley car M15966 (H.Q. 3 Can. Div) came into collision with a Peerless motor lorry near THIENNES on 27.9.17, sustaining damage. Report of M.T.O. with a recommendation 16.16.10. Today forwarded reports to A.S.T. with a recommendation that cost should be borne by the Public.	R.C.L.
" "	4th Oct.		Railhead AIRE.	R.L.
" "	5th Oct.		Railhead AIRE.	R.L.
" "	6th Oct.		Railhead AIRE. Communicated to Ammn.Park. & Amn H.T.C. location of ammunition refilling point in forward area. Recommended to 3 Can. Div. A.9. that sentence of 1 yr. I.H.L. awarded 7443'15 N. F. McGAVIN A.d. 3 Can. Reserve Park, be now remitted.	R.C.L.
" "	7th Oct.		Railhead AIRE. Division to concentrate tomorrow, preparatory to work.	R.L.

A5834 Wt. W4973/M687 750,000 8/16 D.D. & L. Ltd. Forms/C.2118/13.

Army Form C. 2118.

WAR DIARY
or
INTELLIGENCE SUMMARY.

(Erase heading not required.)

HQrs. 3rd Cavalry Divl. A.b.

October, 1917

Place	Date	Hour	Summary of Events and Information	Remarks and references to Appendices
BUSNES	1917 8th Oct.		Railhead AIRE.	
			All Aux. H.T. Co. wagons concentrated at BUSNES. Reference Diary entry of 6th inst., the G.O.C. Cavalry Division remits sentence of one years I.H.L. inflicted on Belganu (reference 7220 of 7.10.17).	Rec.
"	9th Oct.		Railhead AIRE.	Rec.
"	10th "		Railhead AIRE.	Rec.
			7th Cavalry Brigade move to concentration area.	Rec.
"	11th "		Railhead AIRE.	Rec.
			8th Cavalry Brigade move to concentration area.	Rec.
"	12th "		Railhead AIRE.	Rec.
"	13th "		Railhead AIRE.	Rec.
"	14th "		Railhead AIRE.	Rec.
"	15th "		Railhead AIRE.	
			F.G.C.M. held at St FLORIS for trial of No. 7th/039992 Saddler Staff Sergt. A. HODGSON. A.b.C. 3rd Cavalry Reserve Park.	Rec.

Army Form C. 2118.

WAR DIARY
or
INTELLIGENCE SUMMARY.
(Erase heading not required.)

HQrs. 5 Cav. Div. Ad.
October, 1917.

Instructions regarding War Diaries and Intelligence Summaries are contained in F. S. Regs., Part II. and the Staff Manual respectively. Title pages will be prepared in manuscript.

Place	Date	Hour	Summary of Events and Information	Remarks and references to Appendices
BUSNES.	1917 16 Oct.		Railhead AIRE.	Ree.
— " —	17 Oct.		Railhead AIRE. The Division moved to an area round PERNES. Location of Divisional A.C. Units as follows:- HQrs. and Hrs. H.T.C. at PERNES. Supply Colm. remained at AIRE and Ammunition Park at HOLLANDERIE. H.Q. & No: 1 Section of Reserve Park at FIEFS and No: 2 Section at SAINS-LES-PERNES.	Ree.
PERNES	18 Oct.		Railhead AIRE. Temp. Sec. Lieut. W. TANNER Adc. reported for duty with 5th Cavalry Divisional Adc. to be attached pending absorption. Recd. to O.C. Supply Column the remarks of Divl. H.Qrs. on alleged extravagant demands for clothing &c. by that unit. & C. Cub on No/539992 Saddr. Sergt. H. Hodgson, Can. Div. Reserve Park promulgated. Sentenced to be reduced to the rank and stoppages of pay £5. Confirmed by GOC 17/10/17.	Ree.

Army Form C. 2118.

WAR DIARY
or
INTELLIGENCE SUMMARY

(Erase heading not required.)

H.Qrs. 3rd Canadry Div. A.L.

October 1917
Sheet IV

Place	Date	Hour	Summary of Events and Information	Remarks and references to Appendices
PERNES	1917 19th Oct.		Railhead AIRE. Corps Commander observes that, although march discipline is good, there is a tendency on the part of H.A.T.C. and Reserve Park whilst on the move, to allow their animals to stray across the road. (G. 369 of 19.10.17). Called the attention of O.C. concerned to this fault.	R.C.C.
-"-	20th Oct.		Railhead AIRE. Temp. Lieutenant B.A. EMBY, to No. 2 School, Elston School, BEDFORD for Infantry. Temp. Captain W.N. BUCKLEY, Can. Div. Am. A.T.C. discharged from Hospital and rejoined.	R.C.C.
-"-	21st Oct.		Railhead AIRE. Skeleton H.Qrs. of 3rd Cavalry Ammunition Park left the Division to report to Commandant, ABBEVILLE.	R.C.C.
-"-	22nd Oct.		Railhead FREVENT. The Division moved to the FREVENT area. Location of Units tonight :- H.Qrs. & Can. H.T.C. at HOUVIN-HOUVIGNEUL (4½ miles N.E. of FREVENT - LENS. Sheet 11 1/100,000); Supply Cols. BERNAVILLE, Amm. Park FREVENT. M.O. & No. 1 of Res. Park REBREUVIETTE. No. 2 at MONTRELET and FIEFFES.	R.C.C.

WAR DIARY
or
INTELLIGENCE SUMMARY.
(Erase heading not required.)

Army Form C. 2118.

No. 2 Cavalry Divl. Art.

October, 1917. Sheet V

Place	Date	Hour	Summary of Events and Information	Remarks and references to Appendices
HOUVIN-HOUVIGNEUL.	1917. 23rd Oct.		Railhead CANDAS. The Division moved to the CANAPLES area. Located as follows:- H.Qrs. r Amn. H.T.C. DOMART-EN-PONTHIEU. Supply column remained at BERNAVILLE. Ammunition Park joined up with the Supply Column at BERNAVILLE. M.O. Reserve Park at BUSSUS. 1000 men of the Division, forming a Pioneer Battalion, will proceed by lorry on 27th inst. to DOIGNT, rationed up to and to 29th.	Ref.
DOMART-EN-PONTHIEU	24th Oct.		Railhead CANDAS. Temp. 2nd Lieutenant E.M. KELSEY, A.V.C., joined 2nd Cavalry Divl. A.V.C. from A.V.C. Base Depot, to be attached pending absorption. Lieut. (Temp. Capt.) E.G. LAKE A.V.C., ordered to M.I. School of Instruction, but will not take place until further notice. Relief by Temp. 2nd Lieutenant E.J.B. LEVERSON.	Ref.
-"-	25th Oct.		Railhead CANDAS.	Ref.
-"-	26th Oct.		Railhead CANDAS. Informed O.C. Railw. Reserve Park that the G.O. does not consider horse rugs necessary for the mules of the Park provided they are under cover. Horse rugs for mules had not been indented for.	Ref.

Army Form C. 2118.

WAR DIARY of N.Bro. Car. Bri. Ad.
or
INTELLIGENCE SUMMARY. for October, 1917.

Sheet V/

(Erase heading not required.)

Instructions regarding War Diaries and Intelligence Summaries are contained in F. S. Regs., Part II. and the Staff Manual respectively. Title pages will be prepared in manuscript.

Place	Date	Hour	Summary of Events and Information	Remarks and references to Appendices
	1917			
DOMART-EN-PONTHIEU.	27th Oct.		Railhead CANDAS. Lieut. Second Lieut. E.M. KELSEY to 7th Cavalry Brigade for instruction. Arrangements made to form a Divisional Wheelers shop at DOMART-EN-PONTHIEU, to open on 1st November, for repair of all wagons in the Division. 3rd Cavalry Division Pioneer Battalion leaves for DOINGT. With them 50 lorries of the Supply Column, including a proportion of 3-ton, together with Workshops, under Lieutenant BAILLON	R.C.
— " —	28th Oct.		Railhead CANDAS.	R.C.
— " —	29th Oct.		Railhead CANDAS. Ordered 3 lettings from Ammunition Park to Cavalry Corps Troops Supply Column for temporary duty. 2/ Second Lieutenant E.J.B. LEVERSON, A.S.C. arrived from Base Depôt. Today commenced drawing supplies by horse transport. SCHEME :— 6th Car. Bae. Supply Column dumps in truck at LONG. Units draw by horse transport from their	R.C.

A 5834 Wt.W4973/M687 750,000 8/16 D. D. & L. Ltd. Forms/C.2118/13.

WAR DIARY or INTELLIGENCE SUMMARY

Army Form C. 2118.

H.Q. 3 Cav. Bde. A.E. for October 1917.

Place	Date	Hour	Summary of Events and Information	Remarks and references to Appendices
(cont)	1917. 29ᵗʰ Oct.		7ᵗʰ Cavalry Brigade. Also "K" Battery & 7ᵗʰ M.G.S. draw direct from Railhead. "K" Bat. & 7ᵗʰ M.G.S. draw by horse transport from Supply Column at BERNAVILLE. 8ᵗʰ Cav. Bde. Brigade, also 10 Hussars and Essex Yeomanry, rations drawn in bulk by supply column and dumped at VIGNACOURT. Units draw thence by horse transport. 10ᵗʰ Hussars and Essex Yeomanry draw direct from Railhead by horse transport. Divisional Troops. Rations drawn in bulk from Railhead by horse transport and delivered at DOMART-en-PONTHIEU, units draw thence by own transport. 10 L.S. Limber transports attached to H.Q. A.E. from Reserve Park for this purpose.	Rex
DOMART	30ᵗʰ Oct.		Railhead CANDAS.	Rex
" "	31ˢᵗ Oct.		Railhead CANDAS. Opening of Divisional Wheelers' Shop postponed owing to delay in obtaining material.	Rex

R L Y 7

for O.C. H.Dn. 3ʳᵈ Cavalry Div. A.E.
Capt. & Adjutant,

War Diary

H.Qrs. 3rd Cavalry Divl. A.D.C.

November, 1917.

Army Form C. 2118.

WAR DIARY
or
INTELLIGENCE SUMMARY.
(Erase heading not required.)

HQ, 3rd Cavalry Divl. Ad
for November 1917.

Place	Date	Hour	Summary of Events and Information	Remarks and references to Appendices
DOMART-EN-PONTHIEU	1917. Nov. 1st		Railhead CANDAS. Four men sent from Supply Column to DOIGNT to work Siebert driven pumps.	R.C.
" -	Nov. 2nd		Railhead CANDAS.	R.C.
" -	Nov. 3rd		Railhead CANDAS. Fifteen limbers (complete turnouts) from Reserve Park sent to report to 4th Cav. Div. Q at BRIE for work in the advanced area.	R.C.
" -	Nov. 4th		Railhead CANDAS. Following personnel and transport left their units to report for duty with Divisional School at DAOURS:- HQn. Adn. - 1 motor car and driver. Supply Column - 1 lorry and two drivers. Reserve Park - 1 limber, two mules and 2 drivers. Ave. H. to - 2 shoeing smiths and one Veterinary Sergeant.	R.C.
" -	Nov. 5th		Railhead CANDAS.	Aµl.
" -	Nov. 6th		Railhead CANDAS.	Aµl.
" -	Nov. 7th		Railhead CANDAS.	Aµl.
" -	Nov. 8th		Railhead CANDAS.	Aµl.

Army Form C. 2118.

WAR DIARY
of HQrs. 3 Cavalry Divl. Adm.

INTELLIGENCE SUMMARY.
November, 1917.

(Erase heading not required.)

Instructions regarding War Diaries and Intelligence Summaries are contained in F. S. Regs., Part II. and the Staff Manual respectively. Title pages will be prepared in manuscript.

Place	Date	Hour	Summary of Events and Information	Remarks and references to Appendices
DOMART-EN-PONTHIEU	1917 Nov. 9th		Railhead CANDAS. Royal Horse Guards came under administration of 3rd Cavalry Base and Leicestershire Yeomanry that of 8th Cavalry Brigade at midnight 7/8th November. Temp. Captain W.N. BUCKLEY, ADC. Aux. H.Co. admitted D.A. Military Hospital, Millbank, London S.W. on 2nd visit, whilst on leave.	Nil.
-,,-	Nov. 10th		Railhead CANDAS.	Nil.
-,,-	Nov. 11th		Railhead CANDAS.	Nil.
-,,-	Nov. 12th		Railhead CANDAS. Instructed O.C. Supply Column to send Dainite car M9942 to 1st Cavalry Division in exchange for an open Vaux hall. Reported to AQMG 1st Cavalry Corps and to Hav. Dr. 9 that the Reserve Park is now refilled with oats.	Nil.
-,,-	Nov. 13th		Railhead CANDAS.	Nil.
-,,-	Nov. 14th		Railhead CANDAS.	Nil.
-,,-	Nov. 15th		Railhead CANDAS.	Nil.

Army Form C. 2118.

WAR DIARY
or
INTELLIGENCE SUMMARY.

(Erase heading not required.)

M.O.S. Cavalry Div. A.C.
November 1917

Place	Date	Hour	Summary of Events and Information	Remarks and references to Appendices
DOMART-EN-PONTHIEU	Nov. 16.		Railhead CANDAS. Temp. Capt. H.N. BUCKLEY, 3rd Cavalry Div. A.T.Co. joined unit for duty for two months by Medical Board on 9th inst. and struck off the strength	
DOMART-EN-PONTHIEU	Nov. 17.		Railhead CANDAS. H.Qrs. and No. 1 Sect. of 3rd Cav. Reserve Park moved to CANAPLES	
DOMART-EN-PONTHIEU	Nov. 18.		Railhead LA FLAQUE. Cavalry Division moved to the SUZANNE area. Divisional A.T. Units located as follows:— H.Qrs. SUZANNE, Supply Column HARBONNIERES, Ammun. Park HARBONNIERES, Aux. H.T.Co. ETINEHAM, H.Qrs. & 1 Section Reserve Park at MERICOURT, No. 2 Section Reserve Park CHIPILLY.	
SUZANNE	Nov. 19.		Railhead LA FLAQUE. Temp. Captain E.W. BAKER, A.V.C. from Transport Officer 8th Cavalry Brigade, to command of 3rd Cavalry Divisional Auxiliary Horse Transport Company, vice temp. Capt. H.N. BUCKLEY.	

Army Form C. 2118.

WAR DIARY
or
INTELLIGENCE SUMMARY.
(Erase heading not required.)

Mrs. 3rd Cav. Div. Adm. Hdqrs. November, 1917. Sheet IV

Place	Date	Hour	Summary of Events and Information	Remarks and references to Appendices
	1917			
SUZANNE	Nov. 20th		Railhead LA FLAQUE.	Nil
SUZANNE	Nov. 21st		Railhead changed to ROCQUIGNY.	Nil
SUZANNE	Nov. 22nd		Railhead ROCQUIGNY.	Nil
			Lieut. E. BOLTON, Lancashire Hussars, attached A.S.C. pending transfer, joined 3rd Cavalry Divisional A.S.C. for duty.	
SUZANNE	Nov. 23rd		Railhead ROCQUIGNY.	Nil
			3rd Cavalry Division moved to the CONTAY Area. Divisional A.S.C. Units located as follows:- HQrs Adm (with Div. HQrs.) at BEAUQUESNES. Arrival M.T. at BEAUQUESNES. Reserve Park at RAINCHEVAL. Supply Column and Ammunition Park at ACHEUX.	
BEAUQUESNES	Nov. 24th		Railhead BELLE EGLISE.	Nil
BEAUQUESNES	Nov. 25th		Railhead BELLE EGLISE. Adm. 3rd Cavalry Divisional A.E. proceeded to 2nd Lieutenant S.H. COX. England to join No. 2 School, ELSTOW SCHOOL, BEDFORD, pending attachment to Infantry.	Nil
BEAUQUESNES	Nov. 26th		Railhead BELLE EGLISE.	Nil
			Instructed O.C. Supply Column that his lorries must fetch up unserviceable + ordnance stores when required to do so by units and dump them at Ordnance Dump, Div. HQrs.	

Army Form C. 2118.

WAR DIARY
or
INTELLIGENCE SUMMARY.

(Erase heading not required.)

Army Du Var On Ale November 1917

Place	Date	Hour	Summary of Events and Information	Remarks and references to Appendices
BEAUQUESNES	Nov. 27		Railhead BELLE EGLISE.	Ad
BEAUQUESNES	Nov. 27		Railhead BELLE EGLISE. Commenced drawing supplies by horse transport from Divisional hospo 2/Lieut. KNAGGS, R.F.A. (L.O.) joined 3rd Cavalry Division Ammunition Park for duty as Ammunition Officer.	Ad
BEAUQUESNES	Nov. 28		Railhead BELLE EGLISE. NOTES. Advanced Supply Dumps were formed at FINS on November 11th, 1917. Gap Ration Dump at BRAY was formed on November 12th, 1917. Gap Rations were issued on November 18th, 1917.	Ad
BEAUQUESNES	Nov. 29		Railhead BELLE EGLISE. Divisional Headquarters moved to CORBIE area. located at CORBIE. Am. H.T. Co. CORBIE. Amm Park moved from BEAUQUESNES to LACHAPELLETTE. Supply Column remained at ACHEUX and Reserve Park RAIN CHEVAL.	Ad
CORBIE	Nov. 30		Railhead BELLE EGLISE.	Ad

J.E. Turner L.Colonel
A. 3rd Cavalry Divisional Ad

WAR DIARY Hdqrs. 3rd Cavalry Divisional A.S.C.
or
INTELLIGENCE SUMMARY. for December, 1917.

Army Form C. 2118.

VKL 37/1

Place	Date	Hour	Summary of Events and Information	Remarks and references to Appendices
	1917			
CORBIE	1st Dec.		Railhead BELLE EGLISE. Lt. KNAGGS, R.A.F.(S.R.) from 3rd Cavalry Ammunition Park to H Brigade, R.H.A. for duty. A.A.-D.M.S. advises a case of Epizootic Lymphangitis in a mule of Amn. H.T.C. attached to 2nd Life Guards. Ammunition Park moves from LA CHAPELLETTE to TINCOURT. 3rd Cavalry Division Dismounted Brigade moves up to take over a portion of the line near HARGICOURT from 123rd Brigade, 24th Division.	M.E.
CORBIE	2nd Dec.		Railhead BELLE EGLISE.	M.E.
CORBIE	3rd Dec.		Railhead BELLE EGLISE.	M.E.
CORBIE	4th Dec		Railhead BELLE EGLISE. 105 Lr. H.C. Fallon A.S.C. tried at a.d. H.Q. by F.G.C.M. on charge of drunkeness & carelessly drawing a lorry and acquitted. Sergt. F. Follow? Lance Hussars attached a.d. O.S. dismissed to join 2nd Cavalry Divisional A.d. Relief by L/C P. Evan A.d. H.T.-O.M.G. notifies that an establishment of 1*28 riding horses for Reserve Park.	M.E.

WAR DIARY or INTELLIGENCE SUMMARY.

Army Form C. 2118.

HQ 1st Cavalry Div. A.A. December, 1915.

Place	Date	Hour	Summary of Events and Information	Remarks and references to Appendices
CORBIE (SOMME)	1915 5th Dec.		Railhead BELLE EGLISE.	Nil
" "	6th Dec.		Railhead changed to CORBIE. 3rd Cav. Supply Column moved from ACHEUX to LA NEUVILLE. Motor car M.805. on charge to Cav. Supply Column knocked down a French Civilian, J. ROCHE ZEPHIR of LOUVENCOURT, at ACHEUX today, resulting in death of J. ROCHE.	Nil
" "	7th Dec.		Railhead CORBIE.	Nil
" "	8th Dec.		Railhead CORBIE. 2nd Lieut. F. BOLTON. Northumberland Hussars Yeomanry attached A.S.C. proceeded to join 2nd Cavalry Divisional A.S.C. No. 2 (Cavalry) Station Reserve Park, from RAINCHEVAL to CORBIE.	Nil
" "	9th Dec.		Railhead CORBIE. 2nd Lieut. P. FAUX. S.S.B. joined 3rd Cavalry Divisional A.S.C. from 18th Divisional Train. 2nd Lieut. W.S. JONES. R.G.A. joined 3rd Cavalry Ammunition Park as Ammunition Officer from 110th Heavy Battery Royal Field Artillery.	Nil
" "	10th Dec.		Railhead CORBIE.	Nil

Army Form C. 2118.

WAR DIARY
or
INTELLIGENCE SUMMARY.

(Erase heading not required.)

3rd Cavalry Div. A.S.C.
December 1917.

Place	Date	Hour	Summary of Events and Information	Remarks and references to Appendices
	1917.			
CORBIE.	11th Dec.		Railhead CORBIE. Court of Enquiry held at ACHEUX to investigate the circumstances of the death of Mr. ROCHE, ZEPHIR of LOUVENCOURT who was killed by a motor car of 3rd Cavalry Supply Column on 6th instant (see entry for 6th). President - Major H.R.GARDNER A.S.C. Members - Capt. E.W. BAKER and Lieut. F.R. HODGSON A.S.C. The Court found that no blame was attributable to the driver.	Rec
CORBIE	12th Dec.		Railhead CORBIE.	Rec
CORBIE	13th Dec.		Railhead CORBIE. Divisional H.Qrs. informed, in response to their enquiry, that the number of revolvers held by the Reserve Park could, if necessary, be reduced to three but such reduction was not considered advisable.	Rec
CORBIE	14th Dec.		Railhead CORBIE.	Rec
CORBIE	15th Dec.		Railhead CORBIE.	Rec
CORBIE	16th Dec.		Railhead CORBIE. Informed A.A. & Q.M.G. in reply to his enquiry, that the number of rifles with the Reserve Park could well be reduced to 100.	Rec

Army Form C. 2118.

WAR DIARY
or
INTELLIGENCE SUMMARY.

(Erase heading not required.)

3rd Cavalry Divisional A.S.C.

December 1917.

Instructions regarding War Diaries and Intelligence Summaries are contained in F. S. Regs., Part II. and the Staff Manual respectively. Title pages will be prepared in manuscript.

Place	Date	Hour	Summary of Events and Information	Remarks and references to Appendices
	1917			
CORBIE.	17th Dec.		Railhead CORBIE.	
CORBIE.	18th Dec.		Railhead CORBIE.	
CORBIE.	19th Dec.		Railhead CORBIE. Temp. Lieut. T.E.W.D. SIMPSON, Div. H.Q. Co, admitted to hospital.	
CORBIE	20th Dec.		Railhead CORBIE. Temp. Lieut. B. SMALLWOOD, A.M.C. posted to 3rd Cav. Auxiliary H.T. Co.	
CORBIE.	21st Dec.		Railhead CORBIE. Advanced Divisional H.Qrs formed at BOUVINCOURT (due south of TINCOURT). Rear H.Qrs. moved to DOMART area. Following moves of M.T. Units took place:-- H.Qrs. M.T. from CORBIE to DOMART-EN-PONTHIEU. Div. M.T. Co. from CORBIE to DOMART-EN-PONTHIEU. Heavy Sect., Reserve Park from CORBIE to MONTRELET. M.T. Light Sect., Reserve Park from RAINCHEVAL to HENVILLERS.	
DOMART-EN-PONTHIEU	22nd Dec.		Railhead CANDAS. M.T. Light Section from LA NEUVILLE to CANDAS.	

Army Form C. 2118.

WAR DIARY
or
INTELLIGENCE SUMMARY.
(Erase heading not required.)

HQrs. 3rd Cavalry Div. F.S.C.
January, 1918.

WO 95 38

Instructions regarding War Diaries and Intelligence Summaries are contained in F. S. Regs., Part II. and the Staff Manual respectively. Title pages will be prepared in manuscript.

Place	Date	Hour	Summary of Events and Information	Remarks and references to Appendices
DOMART-EN-PONTHIEU	1918. 1st Jan.		Railhead CANDAS. No M.T. Post casualties to date.	Nil
" "	2nd Jan.		Railhead CANDAS.	Nil
" "	3rd Jan.		Railhead CANDAS. Ordered 8t 3rd Car. Reserve Park to send 2 M.T. wagons and teams to XVIII Corps at PROYART by 5th instant. M.T. Har. Supply Column reports first most casualties to M.T. Vehicles - one Daimler lorry with cracks in each set of cylinders - one Service lorry with several cracks in one cylinder. Instructions issued to Supply Officers and all others concerned as to delivery of ration when the thaw comes.	Nil
" "	4th Jan.		Railhead CANDAS.	Nil
" "	5th Jan.		Railhead CANDAS. Ref. entry of 16th Dec:- Received notification that Light Army convoys it impossible to take away rifles from any units which are in possession of them.	Nil
" "	6th Jan.		Railhead CANDAS.	Nil
" "	7th Jan.		Railhead CANDAS. Submitted to War Office, application of following officers for grant of 1914 Star:- 2nd Lieut. CASE, COPPAS and CLARK, Lieut QUICK, CODRINGTON and PRICE.	Nil

Army Form C. 2118.

WAR DIARY
or
INTELLIGENCE SUMMARY.

(Erase heading not required.)

Also 3º Cavalry Div. Ad. 11
January 1918.

Instructions regarding War Diaries and Intelligence Summaries are contained in F. S. Regs., Part II. and the Staff Manual respectively. Title pages will be prepared in manuscript.

Place	Date	Hour	Summary of Events and Information	Remarks and references to Appendices
DOMART-EN-PONTHIEU	1918 7th Jan.		Railhead CANDAS. Sup. Sec. Lieut. S.C.COW. A.C. joined 3rd Cavalry Divisional A.S.C. from 5th Cavalry Divisional Supply Column.	A/C
-"-	9th Jan.		Railhead CANDAS. Sup. Lieutenant P.FAUX. A.C. to Eng. class to No: 2 School Establishd. Bedford.	A/C
-"-	10th Jan.		Railhead CANDAS.	A/C
-"-	11th Jan.		Railhead CANDAS. Mass scheme comes into operation at 6 p.m. tonight.	A/C
-"-	12th Jan.		Railhead CANDAS.	A/C
-"-	13th Jan.		Railhead CANDAS. Instructed O.C. Supply Column to make every endeavour to get lorries out of Workshops as soon as possible owing to a possibility of a big case being made shortly. Mass scheme postponed.	M/C
-"-	14th Jan.		Railhead CANDAS. 7323 9/CO.W.SPRACKMAN, F. to 36th. Instructed O.C. Supply Column to send 35 lorries to VIGNACOURT at 4 p.m. tonight to convey 8th Dismounted Bde. and detachments of 5th, 7th & 8th M.Gun Sqd. to Willets. These detrain at 9 a.m. tomorrow. Also 49 lorries to be at LONGPRÉ then tomorrow for 6th & 7th Dismtd. Bdes. & H.Q. Dismtd. Bde.	A/C

Army Form C. 2118.

WAR DIARY
or
INTELLIGENCE SUMMARY.

(Erase heading not required.)

HQrs. 3rd Cavalry Divisional Ad
January 1918

Instructions regarding War Diaries and Intelligence Summaries are contained in F.S. Regs., Part II. and the Staff Manual respectively. Title pages will be prepared in manuscript.

Place	Date	Hour	Summary of Events and Information	Remarks and references to Appendices
DOMART EN PONTHIEU	1918 15th Jan.		Railhead CANDAS. Gas scheme came into operation at 6 p.m. tonight.	M1
— ,, —	16th Jan.		Railhead CANDAS. Dismounted Division returned from the trenches.	M2
— ,, —	17th Jan.		Railhead CANDAS.	M3
— ,, —	18th Jan.		Railhead CANDAS. Worked units against reaching personnel supplies to establishment. 7/20052 Sergt. W. BROCK absconded during 6.9 Qrs. ind. Corp from 10/1/18.	M4
— ,, —	19th Jan.		Railhead CANDAS. Forwarded H.Q. a full report on the fuel situation to recent considerable had been received regarding shortages.	M5
— ,, —	20th Jan.		Railhead CANDAS. 2nd Lieut. Capt. P.G.S. CLARK, Newby supply Column ordered to England. 2nd Lieut. J.L. COL — relief by Lt. (Temp) E.J.R. McWATTERS from Cavalry	M6
			Ammunition Park.	M7
— ,, —	21st Jan.		Railhead CANDAS. Gas scheme ceased at 6 p.m. and normal traffic increase Renault System of supplies	M8

Army Form C. 2118.

WAR DIARY
or
INTELLIGENCE SUMMARY.

(Erase heading not required.)

No. 9. 3rd Cavalry Divisional H.Q.
January 1916.

Instructions regarding War Diaries and Intelligence Summaries are contained in F. S. Regs., Part II. and the Staff Manual respectively. Title pages will be prepared in manuscript.

Place	Date	Hour	Summary of Events and Information	Remarks and references to Appendices
DOMART-EN-PONTHIEU	1916. 22nd Jan.		Railhead CANDAS.	
" "	23rd Jan.		Railhead CANDAS.	
" "	24th Jan.		Railhead CANDAS. Received warning order of impending move of Division.	
" "	25th Jan.		Railhead CANDAS.	
" "	26th Jan.		Railhead CANDAS. Recommended Capt. B. C. Bewley and Lt. (T.law) C.I.R. McAlister 3rd Cav. Supply Colm. for promotion to Major.	
" "	27th Jan.		Railhead CANDAS.	
" "	28th Jan.		Railhead CANDAS.	
" "	29th Jan.		Railhead CANDAS.	
" "	30th Jan.		Railhead LA CHAPPELETTE. The Division moved to forward area. Location :- Div. H.Q., A.D. & Reserve Park at MONCHY LAGACHE, Supply Column and 3rd Cav. H.T.C. at ESTRÉES-EN-CHAUSSEE.	
MONCHY LAGACHE	31st Jan.		Railhead - LA CHAPPELETTE	

Signed
O.C. H.Qrs. 3rd Cavalry Div.
L/Colonel

War Diary of

A.D. 3rd Infantry Div. A.I.F.

February, 1918.

Army Form C. 2118.

WAR DIARY
INTELLIGENCE SUMMARY.
(Erase heading not required.)

H.Qrs, 3rd Cavalry Div. All

February, 1918.

Instructions regarding War Diaries and Intelligence Summaries are contained in F.S. Regs., Part II. and the Staff Manual respectively. Title pages will be prepared in manuscript.

Place	Date	Hour	Summary of Events and Information	Remarks and references to Appendices
MONCHY LAGACHE	1918 1st Feb.		Railhead La Chapellette. Instructed R. Supply Column to send a Ston Halford lorry and one wheeler to the newly formed Fifth Army School of Cookery dining at ROSIERES.	Ref.
"	2nd Feb.		Railhead La Chapellette.	Ref.
"	3rd Feb.		Temp. Lieut. C.S. COW. RA.V.C. attached 3rd Cavalry Supply Column, admitted 9 Cavalry Field Ambulance and evacuated to 3rd Cavalry Clearing Station same day. 3rd Cavalry Supply Column comes under the direct control of Cavalry Corps at midnight 3/4 Feb. submitted to 3rd Cav. Dn. Q'a scheme for the evacuation of supplies in case of retreat.	Ref.
"	4th Feb.		Railhead La Chapellette. Cavalry Corps issued orders for the restriction of lorry traffic owing to bad state of roads in forward area.	Ref.

Army Form C. 2118.

WAR DIARY
or
INTELLIGENCE SUMMARY.
(Erase heading not required.)

Headquarters,
3rd Cavalry Div. A.C.
FEBRUARY 1918.

Instructions regarding War Diaries and Intelligence Summaries are contained in F. S. Regs, Part II. and the Staff Manual respectively. Title pages will be prepared in manuscript.

Place	Date	Hour	Summary of Events and Information	Remarks and references to Appendices
	1918 4th Feb. (continued)		A.D.S.T. Cav. Corps. notifies that vehicles of following units will be attached to 3rd Cavalry Supply Column for maintenance :- 48 H.Q. Workshops, 288 A.S.Co. and 258 Tunnelling Co. Temp. Capt. P.G.S. CLARK a.b. from 3rd Cavalry Supply Column to command of Cavalry Corps Troops Supply Column – Lieut. (A/Capt.) E.J.R. McWATTERS a.b. from 3rd Cavalry Ammunition Park to 3rd Cavalry Supply Column.	Nil.
MONCHY LAGACHE.	5th Feb.		Railhead La Chapelette. Instructed Supply Column to exercise greatest economy in use of oils and grease.	Nil
-"-	6th Feb.		Railhead La Chapelette. Cavalry Corps withdrew the use of six lorries which, when the Supply Column was previously under Corps control, were allowed the Division to general duties. The O.C. 3rd Cavalry Div. Auxiliary H.T. Co. reports the theft from his billet of a despatch box containing books and confidential papers of the Company. He has informed the A.P.M.	Nil

WAR DIARY or INTELLIGENCE SUMMARY

Army Form C. 2118.

5th Cavalry Divisional A.D.

FEBRUARY 1912.

Place	Date	Hour	Summary of Events and Information	Remarks and references to Appendices
	1918 6th Feb (cont)		Paras to Supply Column for action the approval of L.S.S.T. bombay orbs. for the evacuation of Wolseley car M799, beyond repair in Supply Column Workshop.	Nil
MONCHY LAGACHE	7th Feb		Maillard la Chapellette. Instructed O.C. Supply Column to send two cleaners to R.E. Dumps at ROISEL to relieve two men of 4th Can. Div. Cavalry Corps prohibit the running of lorries beyond ESTRÉES-EN-CHAUSSÉE. arrangements accordingly made to draw rations by horse transport from Tortille. Sent 4 carpenters from Supply Column to BR15 for duty in the tent making factory.	Nil
-"-	8th Feb		Maillard la Chapellette. Instructed O.C. Supply Column to detail a working party of 1 Officer and 60 other ranks to work on the protection of the aerodromes of 4th Squadron R.F.C. at FLEZ. Work to commence 9th inst. Authority received from Can. Corps to lease type lorries for the conveyance of this and a similar party (of 8th Bde. Cav.) to and from work. Authority L.A.Q.M.G. 4ou of Apr70 dispatched too.	Nil

Army Form C. 2118.

WAR DIARY
or
INTELLIGENCE SUMMARY.
(Erase heading not required.)

HQ 3rd Cavalry Divisional A.C.
February, 1918.

Instructions regarding War Diaries and Intelligence Summaries are contained in F. S. Regs., Part II. and the Staff Manual respectively. Title pages will be prepared in manuscript.

Place	Date	Hour	Summary of Events and Information.	Remarks and references to Appendices
MONCHY LAGACHE	1918 9th Feb.		Railhead la Chapelette. 3rd Cavalry Divisional Agricultural Organisation now in operation. Wagons of Aux H.T. used to cart, manure to general hangars.	166
"	10th Feb.		Railhead la Chapelette. All personnel withdrawn from Yeomanry Regts. Compliance to "Q" of the removal of a workshop of Supply Column by Ca. Corps without the cognizance of COLe.	M.E.
"	11th Feb.		Railhead la Chapelette. Circularized all units on the necessity of sending clean wagons to draw rations. Case has been reported of a limber sent to draw rations, which contained faeces of stable manure. O. Aux H.T.C. instructed to send four G.I. wagons to cover, to have them fitted with water tanks. Alt. Feste Sans transport employed on load construction, etc., to be released from duty from tomorrow inclusive, lorries being used for this purpose. Received approval of Q.a Br Q. to reduce straw December to 155,000 lbs. Oats and 186,000 lbs. Hay.	M.E.

Army Form C. 2118.

WAR DIARY
or
INTELLIGENCE SUMMARY.
(Erase heading not required.)

Army Headquarters
3rd Cavalry Div. H.Q.
February 1918

Instructions regarding War Diaries and Intelligence Summaries are contained in F.S. Regs., Part II. and the Staff Manual respectively. Title pages will be prepared in manuscript.

Place	Date	Hour	Summary of Events and Information	Remarks and references to Appendices
	1918			
MONCHY LAGACHE	12th Feb.		Railhead La Chapelette.	Nil
" - "	13th Feb.		Railhead La Chapelette. Two cheques from Supply Column to R.E. Dumps POISEUX. One lorries from Amm. H.T.E. to Essex Yeomanry for Agricultural Organization.	Nil
" - "	14th Feb.		Railhead La Chapelette.	Nil
" - "	15th Feb.		Railhead La Chapelette. Cyclist 3rd Cav. Div. in case of 703343 Pte. (2/91) Stevens, A. 7 Cavalry Amm. H.T.C. accused of theft.	Nil
" - "	16th Feb.		Railhead La Chapelette. Detailed 20 of the newly fitted water wagons, Aux. H.T.C., to proceed to Divnl. Train, VERMAND, today and also one to report to 3rd Cav. Pioneer Bn. VENDELLES. 3rd Cav. Div. Reserve Park moved to I. 33. c. 9. 1. (40,000.62.). 5th Cavalry Divn. Reserve Park moved to the cards at V. 13. c. 1. 3 vacated by 3rd Cav. Reserve Park. 3rd Cav. Res. Park (with destion) came under the administration of O.C. 3rd Cavalry Divn.	Nil

WAR DIARY or INTELLIGENCE SUMMARY

Army Form C. 2118.

HQrs. 3rd Can. Div. Am. Sub. Col.

February 1918.

Place	Date	Hour	Summary of Events and Information	Remarks and references to Appendices
MONCHY LAGACHE	17th Feb.		Railhead La Chapelette. Sent three ambulances to 5th Cavalry Division in exchange for one Daimler and 2 Holsley. Detailed five limbers from 5th Can Reserve Park for duty with 5th Field Squadron. Detailed 10 O.R. from 5th Can Reserve Park for duty under Cmdt Commandant.	A/1
— " —	18th Feb.		Railhead La Chapelette. Commenced drawing all supplies to the Division (except supply Colm. 3/3 R.C.Co. & Mob. Ord. Wkshp.) by horse transport. Temp. 2nd Lieut. R.H.F.P. SADLER Adt. posted to the Cavalry Amm. Park. Vice Lieut. (T.Capt.) W.J.R. McFATTERS.	A/2
— " —	19th Feb.		Railhead La Chapelette. Temp. 2nd Lieut. R.H.F.P. SADLER joined 3rd Cavalry Amm. Park. Re entry of 15th inst:- Under authority delegated by the G.O.C. 703rd N.(a.) St. STEVENS 1000 dealt with O.C. and released.	A/3

To No. 3 Dist, H.Q.'s, 1st Army Rxxxxx.

(A8001) Wt. W1771/M2031 750,000 5/17 D. D. & L., London, E.C. Sch. 52 Forms/C2118/14

Army Form C. 2118.

A.Dr. to Cavalry Div. HQ
September 1918. V/11

WAR DIARY
or
INTELLIGENCE SUMMARY.
(Erase heading not required.)

Instructions regarding War Diaries and Intelligence Summaries are contained in F. S. Regs., Part II. and the Staff Manual respectively. Title pages will be prepared in manuscript.

Place	Date	Hour	Summary of Events and Information	Remarks and references to Appendices
MORCHY LAGACHE	20th Feb.		Railhead to Chapelette. Divisional Commander orders a reduction of S/s on account of not too economic use of the division.	
"	21st Feb.		Railhead to Chapelette.	
"	22nd Feb.		Routine work.	
"	23rd Feb.		Routine work.	
"	24th Feb.		Routine work.	
"	25th Feb.		Railhead changed. Supplies were transferred at EPINICOURT (PERONNE) and conveyed by light railway to MONS-EN-CHAUSSEE. Drawn by Horse transport as usual from latter place.	
"	26th Feb.		Railway as for 25th. Lieut. Vinck 10th Huss. & 2/Lt. Carles detached to Cavalry Indian Base Depot to superintend musketry of Cavalry Corps.	
"	27th Feb.		Railhead FLAMICOURT.	

Army Form C. 2118.

WAR DIARY
or
INTELLIGENCE SUMMARY
(Erase heading not required.)

3rd Cavalry Divl. Ad. Feb 1918

Instructions regarding War Diaries and Intelligence Summaries are contained in F. S. Regs., Part II. and the Staff Manual respectively. Title pages will be prepared in manuscript.

Place	Date	Hour	Summary of Events and Information	Remarks and references to Appendices
MONCHY-LAGACHE	1918 28th Feb.		Reitheid FRANCOURT. 3rd Cavalry Reserve Park and right section, 5th Cavalry Field Am. ordered to move tomorrow to ESTRÉES-EN-CHAUSSÉE there they will encamp. Notification received that Lieut. 2/Lieut. C.S.COW Adj. the 3rd Cav. Div. Ad. was invalided to England on 17th instant. Ordered Cavalry Supply Column to send one officer and 60 other ranks now working on the FLEZ aerodrome on March 2nd to 258 Tunnelling Co. at JEANCOURT for duty.	

St Myers
Lt Colonel,
Commanding HQrs 3rd Cav. Divl. Ad.

Army Form C. 2118.

WAR DIARY
or
INTELLIGENCE SUMMARY.

HQrs 5th Cavalry Divnl Art.
March 1917

(Erase heading not required.)

40

Place	Date	Hour	Summary of Events and Information	Remarks and references to Appendices
MONCHY & LEGACHE	1918 1st March		Railhead Hamicourt.	Pel
" "	2nd March		Routine work.	Pel
" "	3rd March		Railhead Hamicourt.	Pel
			Lieut. W.O. Prescott Luboz Column admitted hospital	
" "	4th Mar		Railhead Hamicourt	Pel
" "	5th Mar		Railhead Hamicourt	Pel
" "	6th Mar		Railhead Hamicourt	Pel
			Household Cavalry & 7th Machine Gun Squadron continuing M.G. Edn. are to be relieved shortly by No. 5 & No. 6 Sqn M.G. Sqn.	
" "	7th Mar.	11 a.m.	Change of Regiments referred to above is to take place on 10th March. Military arrangements made accordingly.	Pel
" "	8th March		Cavalry Corps to hand over Corps front to XIX Corps 9-3-18. Cavalry Divn. comes under command of XIX Corps at 11am	Pel

Army Form C. 2118.

WAR DIARY
or
INTELLIGENCE SUMMARY.
(Erase heading not required.)

HQrs. 3rd Cavalry Divn. Ask.
March 1918

Place	Date	Hour	Summary of Events and Information	Remarks and references to Appendices
MONCHY LAGACHE	9th March	12½P	Railhead ELENCOURT. Divn. by light railway to MONS-en-CHAUSSEE. 2/Lieut J.H. MOORE, A.L., reported for duty with H.Qrs. 3rd Cav. Divn. A.L. from 2nd Can. Dn. A.L. vice T/Lieut C.S. COW (invalided).	Nil
" - "	10 March		Household Cavalry Regiments left the Division. Forwarded to Divl. H.Qrs. the case of No. 74933 Pte. Carr W. LEPPER A.L. who was reduced from the rank of Farr. H/Sgt. in connection by E.C. on a charge of assaulting base details N.C.O. which ment to be reduced on ground of previous character.	Nil
" - "	11 March		The working party of 1 Officer & 60 other ranks provided by the 3rd Can. M/Co. & 253 Remount Co. at JEANCOURT was withdrawn today.	Nil
" - "	12 March		10th Hussars to 6th Cavalry Brigade – North Somerset Yeomanry to 7th Cav. Bde. The D.M.T.O. XIX Corps, placed at the disposal of the Division one Divisional M.T. Co. 2 Lorries for postal service & to ordnance services, 2 lorry tipping purposes and H.Q. for general duties.	Nil
" - "	13 March		2nd Lieut Geo Lieut E.J.B. HAYERSON A.L. evacuated sick to No. 55 C.C.S. Divl. H.Qrs. and H.Qrs. Divl. A.L. moved from MONCHY LAGACHE to ATHIES. 3rd Cav. Reserve Park and 3rd Can. Divn. Sup. Col. H.Q. to MONS-en-CHAUSSEE. The Canadian Cavalry Brigade joined the Division. Instructed O.C. 3rd A.L.T.C. to evacuate to Ordnance Railhead the bodies of the Pte. Col. Lorries which have been fitted with water tanks.	Nil

Army Form C. 2118.

WAR DIARY
or
INTELLIGENCE SUMMARY.

(Erase heading not required.)

HQ. 3rd Cavalry Div. Sup. Col.
March 1917

Place	Date	Hour	Summary of Events and Information	Remarks and references to Appendices
ATHIES	1917 14th March		8th Cavalry Brigade moved to the LONGPRÉ area. 1 Sub. Lieut. R.T. CAMPBELL 2/Lt accompanied the Brigade as Brigade Supply Officer. Railhead changed to BRIE.	Nil.
- " -	15th March		O.O. A.S. inspected the transport of 6th Cavalry Brigade. Reference Reorganization of M.T. Units – 3rd Cav. Div. M.T.C. evacuated today to Fifth Army Vehicle Exchange Park at MARICOURT – 33 3-ton lorries, 1 workshop, 1 store lorry, 1 box car, and 10 motorcycles	Nil.
- " -	16 March		Railhead changed to LA CHAPELLETTE. Instructed O.C. Aux. M.T.Co. to return to Ordnance two of the three chauffeurs allotted to him. 3 are unnecessary and there is insufficient transport to carry them. 3rd Cav. Div. M.T.C. evacuated to Fifth Army Vehicle Exchange Park a further 33 3-ton lorries, 1 workshop, 1 store lorry, 1 box car and 5 motor cycles	Nil.
- " -	17 March		Instructed O.C. M.T.C. to return the H.Q.C.C attached lorries to 5th Cavalry Supply Column.	Nil.

Army Form C. 2118.

WAR DIARY
or
INTELLIGENCE SUMMARY.
(Erase heading not required.)

H.Q. 3rd Cavalry Div. A.A.
March 1918.

Instructions regarding War Diaries and Intelligence Summaries are contained in F.S. Regs., Part II. and the Staff Manual respectively. Title pages will be prepared in manuscript.

No. IV

Place	Date	Hour	Summary of Events and Information	Remarks and references to Appendices
	1918			
ATHIES	18th March		Reported to A.S.T. Cavalry Corps, the conduct of the A.S.O. AA CHAPELLETTE in dumping supplies off train without consulting R.O. or L.O. M.T.C.	Nil
"	19th March		Applied for the use of Fokr extra lorries to carry on with present purpose. It was found impossible to carry on with present allowance of transport. Instructed M.T.C. that demands to motor cycles should be sent under further orders to A.S.T. Car Corps and not to Advanced M.T. Depot. Forwarded to Col. Q. proceedings of a Court of Enquiry regarding the loss of a Triumph motor cycle (frame no. 1000 ??) from Railhead - Div. M.T.C. were held to blame.	Nil
"	20th March		10 G.S. wagon turnouts received from 8 Cavalry Brigade and despatched to their unit (See Car Aux. H.S.E.)	Nil
"	21st March		Division placed at two hours notice to move.	Nil
"	22nd March			Nil
VARESNES	23rd March		The Division moved from ATHIES & VARESNES (3 m. S.E of NOYON)	Nil
CARLEPONT	24th March		The Division moved from VARESNES to CARLEPONT (5 m. E. of NOYON).	Nil
"	25th March		Remained at CARLEPONT. Moved to OLLEN PONT.	Nil

WAR DIARY
or
INTELLIGENCE SUMMARY.

Army Form C. 2118.

1st Cavalry Divl. Art.

March 1918

(Erase heading not required.)

Instructions regarding War Diaries and Intelligence Summaries are contained in F.S. Regs., Part II. and the Staff Manual respectively. Title pages will be prepared in manuscript.

Place	Date	Hour	Summary of Events and Information	Remarks and references to Appendices
OLLEINPONT	26 March	1918	Divisional Head quarters moved to CHOISY-au-BAC. "B" Echelon demoralized and under the command of Colonel CUMING, O.C.A. marched to CHOISY-au-BAC near COMPIEGNE. Thence to COMPIEGNE FOREST where it parked with the head of the column at level crossing 3 m. N. of first E in COMPIEGNE (707,000 – 2L BEAUVAIS). Lieut. A.V. CAMPBELL detailed as Supply Officer to PORTAL'S column which goes out today.	Nil
COMPIEGNE FOREST	27 March		Remained in COMPIEGNE FOREST. Railhead for today COMPIEGNE.	Nil
"	28 March		Position of Div. H.Q., "B" Echelon remained unchanged. Supplies were drawn today from ESTREES-ST DENIS.	Nil
"	29 March		"B" Echelon, including the Reserve Park and Am. H.T.C. marched to LES CARIGNONS 5½ m. N. of CLERMONT. Divl. H.Qrs. at LE MESNIL-SUR-BULLES.	Nil
LES CARIGNONS	30 March		"B" Echelon to WAILLY (1 m. SSE of AMIENS). Rear Divl. H.Qrs. also at WAILLY. Railhead LOEUILLY (1 m. N.E. of AMILLY).	Nil
WAILLY	31 March		Position of the Echelon remained unchanged.	Nil

J.R. McCumming Colonel
O.C. 1st 1st Cavalry Division

Army Form C. 2118.

WAR DIARY or INTELLIGENCE SUMMARY.

(Erase heading not required.)

Headquarters, 3rd Cavalry Divisional H.Q.

April, 1918.

Instructions regarding War Diaries and Intelligence Summaries are contained in F. S. Regs., Part II. and the Staff Manual respectively. Title pages will be prepared in manuscript.

Place	Date	Hour	Summary of Events and Information	Remarks and references to Appendices
WAILLY	1st April		Railhead AMIENS. Supplys moved to AMIENS-POIX Rd 1½ m. W. AMIENS. "B" Echelon including Reserve Park and Div. M.T.Co. marched to PONT-DE-METZ (3 m. S.W. AMIENS). Rear D.H.Q. at SAHURS.	
PONT-DE-METZ	2nd April		Position of units and railhead remained unchanged.	
"	3rd April		1st & 2nd Lifeguards evacuated to England 22/3/18. Details off strength. "B" Echelon Canadian Cavalry Brigade rejoined the Division from 2nd Cavalry Division and was accommodated at PONT-DE-METZ.	
"	4th April		Following exchange of officers took place on 1st instant:- 2nd Lieut. J.H.MOORS from 10th. (D.) Cavalry Divl. A.Co. to 3rd Cavalry Div. M.T.C. 2nd. Lieut. R.W.F. MALLIDAY from 3rd Cav. Div. M.T.C. to 10th. (D.) Cavalry Div. A.C. Casualties:- Tpr. No. 5311 J. Bridge L.G. (1st C.P.A.) missing 26/3/18. Lieutenant C. (?Capt) Monxxxxx 4th H.D. 75/769. Lt. Cook U.S. 16th (Can.) wounded 14/4/18. No.107473. Sgr. Russell 4th H. wounded 14/4/18. No.1531959 A/L Lyons 4th H. killed in action 14/4/18. 75690 L/C Wilson R. wounded (lately) 2/4/18.	

Army Form C. 2118.

WAR DIARY
or
INTELLIGENCE SUMMARY.

(Erase heading not required.)

H.Q. 3rd Cavalry Div. A.L.

Place	Date	Hour	Summary of Events and Information	Remarks and references to Appendices
PONT DE METZ	1918 5th April		Division relieved in the line by 5th Australian Division and troops placed under orders to move.	
" "	6th April		Division concentrated in the CAMON area. "B" Echelon (less Horse Brigade) in the CAMON area. HQrs 3rd moved to RIVERY (N.E. of Amiens) and had accommodated with 1st at L'HOSPICE ST VICTOR.	
RIVERY	7th April		Received orders to move to AILLY - SUR - SOMME.	
" "	8th April		Cavalry today - Epsom at BVT FG (Lt/A) killed, Sgts & Bircher Q. & CPL wounded.	
" "	9th April		Nothing to report.	
" "	10th April		— " —	
" "	11th April		"B" Echelon again discovered and moved across communs. J 66 A to LONG (9 miles S.E. of ABBEVILLE)	
LONG	12th April		"B" Echelon moved from LONG to VAULX (3m. NNE of AUXI-LE-CHATEAU)	
VAULX	13th April		Nothing to report. Remained at VAULX awaiting orders.	
" "	14th April			

Army Form C. 2118.

WAR DIARY
or
INTELLIGENCE SUMMARY.
(Erase heading not required.)

HQrs. 3rd Cavalry Bde. A.D.

April 1918

Place	Date	Hour	Summary of Events and Information	Remarks and references to Appendices
	1918			
VAULX	15th April		"B" Echelon remained at VAULX.	MS
" "	16th April		Nothing to report.	MS
" "	17th April		"B" Echelon 3rd Cav. Div. marched to the PERNES area and rejoined respective regiments. 3rd M.G. and Heavy Section Reserve Parks remained at VAULX. Locations of 3rd Cav. Div. units now as follows:- H.Qrs. at PERNES. M.G. Co. at SAINS-LES-PERNES. H.Qrs. & Light Section Reserve Park at SAINS-LES-PERNES. Ambulance H.T. Co. at VAULX. Heavy Section Reserve Park at VAULX.	MS
PERNES	18th April		Nothing to report.	MS MS
" "	19th April		Railhead PERNES. Position of units remained unchanged.	MS MS
" "	20th April		Ford car B24 returned from roadside by 3rd Signal Squadron, sent to M.G. Co. to be held pending instructions as to disposal. Reported to A.D.S.T. that Lieut. Cpl. Brice A.S.C. is surplus to establishment of 3rd Cavalry Div. A.S.C.	MS
" "	21st April		In response to an enquiry, informed 3rd Cav. Dn. D. that H5 3 ton lorries would be required to carry 2nd Echelon of supplies	MS

Army Form C. 2118.

WAR DIARY
or
INTELLIGENCE SUMMARY.
(Erase heading not required.)

H.Qrs. 3rd Cavalry Divl Art
April, 1918

Instructions regarding War Diaries and Intelligence Summaries are contained in F. S. Regs., Part II. and the Staff Manual respectively. Title pages will be prepared in manuscript.

Place	Date	Hour	Summary of Events and Information	Remarks and references to Appendices
	1918			
PERNES	22nd April		Lieut. J.H. Mooer, A.S.C. from 3rd Cavalry Div. Co. to 2 D.S.T. First Army, on duty as supernumerary Railhead Supply Officer.	Nil
-"-	23rd April		H.O.T. Cav. Corps wired that heavy section Reserve Park must be completed to its full complement of 7500 cwt rations. 1 To Cav. Div. S of S instructions as it is authorised to do this unless 7 wagons detached (light det.) 5. Can. Corps 2. Can. Div. Depot detach 1) are returned. Instructed 1st Can. H.T. Co. that ammunition lorries are not to be used for any purpose other than supply of ammunition without reference to Div. "Q". Instructed O.C. 3rd Cav. Div. Co. that every effort is to be made to conserve mob. ambulances owing to the shortage of reserve vehicles. Small box respirators of H.Qrs. Brit. A.A. states in Qrs.	Nil
-"-	24th April		Routine work.	Nil
-"-	25th April		Reference entry of 23rd inst. - App. Q.S.O. sanctions the drawing of 3 bars of S.A.A. as a temporary measure. Authorities of A.S.T. application to strike of charge five mob. cycles Motorettes which were lost during recent operations.	Nil

Army Form C. 2118.

WAR DIARY
or
INTELLIGENCE SUMMARY.

(Erase heading not required.)

HQrs. 5th Cavalry Bde. A.C.
April 1918.

Place	Date	Hour	Summary of Events and Information	Remarks and references to Appendices
PERNES	1918 26th April		Railhead changed to BRYAS.	
" "	27th April		Railhead BRYAS.	
" "	28th April		Railhead BRYAS.	
" "	29th April		Railhead changed to PERNES. 1st Lieut. N.R. COCKSHUTT, 3rd Can. R.T.C. to 179th Army Field Artillery Brigade for duty.	
" "	30th April		Railhead PERNES. R.A.S.T. approved of issue of hard wood in lieu of coal. Authority received in the evacuation of Daimler car No. 65. worn by Y.O.B. 5th Cav. Bde.	

S.A. Mummery
Colonel
Comdg. HQrs. 5th Cavalry Divisional A.C.

Army Form C. 2118.

WAR DIARY
or
INTELLIGENCE SUMMARY.
(Erase heading not required.)

WO2 Lt. Evelyn Cecil OBE
April 1916

Instructions regarding War Diaries and Intelligence Summaries are contained in F. S. Regs., Part II. and the Staff Manual respectively. Title pages will be prepared in manuscript.

Place	Date	Hour	Summary of Events and Information	Remarks and references to Appendices
PERONNE	1st May 1916		Railhead DIEVAL	
" "	2nd May		Railhead PERNES.	
" "	3rd May		Both Divisions advising of the new areas to be taken over. Operations much shelled off.	
			Visited 2 Div G. "Q" 1st Division of London Bombay District. Went up to the standard of the back of the Army for a review are being made for a detailed inspection.	
			Lieut. G. Henrici's instructions that each body of M.T. of traffic in hours of 1000 hours, are in a week. No advance received.	
			[illegible continuation] ...joined a Medical Board with a view to transportation. He has been recommended for Major to Can. In command unit to remain at the front.	
			Capt. (A/Maj) R.P.C. Palmer from Bn. HQrs 6th Bde C.M.R. to O.C. 5 Can. M.T.Co	
			A/Lt. (A/Capt) S.S. Chaplin from 6 2 C.H.Q Res. M.T. to 1 Can. M.T.Co.	

Army Form C. 2118.

WAR DIARY
or
INTELLIGENCE SUMMARY.
(Erase heading not required.)

HQ. 3rd Cavalry Divl Art
May 1916.

Place	Date	Hour	Summary of Events and Information	Remarks and references to Appendices
PERNES	1916 4th May		Railhead PERNES. The Division moved to an area N.E. of HESDIN. HQ Divl Art located with Divl HQ at HAIX. HQrs & 1st 2nd Bde Hy Bde moved from SAINS-LES-PERNES to GUINÉCOURT.	Nil
HAIX	5th May		Railhead remained at PERNES. The Division moved to an area N.W. of PUKHIEN [?] CRÉCY. HQ Divl Art located at YVRENCH. Mt Co moved from SAINS-LES-PERNES to standing [?] at western end of DOMART-EN-PONTHIEU.	Nil
YVRENCH	6th May		Railhead changes to ST LEGER-LES-DOMART. The Division moved to its final area around CONTAY (pr. N.E. ALBERT). HQ Divl Art at CONTAY. Div H.T. Co and Heavy Section Reserve Park from VAUX to BEAUCOURT. 1st & 2nd Brde Reserve Park from GUINÉCOURT to BEAUCOURT.	Nil
CONTAY	7th May		Railhead ST LEGER-LES-DOMART. Followed moves of Divisional Art units took place. Div H.T. Co (Heavy Section Reserve Park - BEAUCOURT to SURCAMPS (2 miles W. of DOMART-EN-PONTHIEU). H.Q. 1st Bde Reserve Park from BEAUCOURT	Nil

Army Form C. 2118.

WAR DIARY
or
INTELLIGENCE SUMMARY.

(Erase heading not required.)

N.Q. 1st Cavalry Div. 24
May 1917.

Instructions regarding War Diaries and Intelligence Summaries are contained in F. S. Regs., Part II. and the Staff Manual respectively. Title pages will be prepared in manuscript.

Place	Date	Hour	Summary of Events and Information	Remarks and references to Appendices
	1917			
CONTAY	8th May		BEHENCOURT (S.A. CONTAY). Railhead remained at ST LEGER des DOMART. Position of units unaltered.	Nil
"	9th May.		The five walk out wagons with Gen. H.T. Co are to be exchanged for G.S. wagons. Fourth Army approves with a view to the instructors Lieut. E.M. KELSEY to report to O.C. 4th H.T. Co. 1st instant with a view to undergoing a course of instruction in railhead supply duties	Nil
"	10th May		No. 9 instructs that W.R. to L/Cpl. wagons of Army Motor Reserve Park, are to be placed at disposal of 3rd Field Squadron 51/072,087 Sgt. WRIGLEY F., and (?) 10039 R. KENDRICK S. Adjt. art. H.Q. PPCLI are awarded the Military Medal. Issues & all consumers a programme of dates on which divisional motor cars should be sent into Workshops in rotation.	Nil
"	11th May		Exchange of G.S. wagons with H.T. carried out under G.R.O. 3858.	Nil
"	12th May		Nothing to report.	
"	13th May		Lieut. C.E. Price ordered to S.Q. Divisional Train. Horse recce panted in. Programme of inspection of M.T. & ambulances issued to all concerned.	Nil

Army Form C. 2118.

WAR DIARY
or
INTELLIGENCE SUMMARY.
(Erase heading not required.)

HQrs. 3rd Cavalry Brigade. May 1918

Place	Date	Hour	Summary of Events and Information	Remarks and references to Appendices
CONTAY	14th May	1916	Fourth Army direct that 39 lorries of M.T.Co. and the Heavy Section, 3rd Cavalry Reserve Park, shall be held at the disposal of the Army.	Nil
-	15 May		Orders received for the move of the Divn. to the YZEUX area. (X.H. M12.a.8.1) on 17th instant. Sergt. T. MATSON. A.D. att. 1st Can. Div. awarded the MILITARY CROSS. Issued TRACER Ammunition to A.D. Companies to use with the Hotchkiss Rifles which has been issued for Anti-aircraft work.	Nil Nil
-	16 May		Railhead ST LEGER LES DOMART. (New Brigade)	
-	17 May		The Division moved to an area around YZEUX. HDrs. Divl. A.D. located at YZEUX. Following moves of A.D. units took place:- HQrs and No.1 Section from BETHENCOURT to BETHENCOURT STOLEN. Amm.Pk.Co. and Heavy Section Reserve Park, SURCAMPS to BETHENCOURT STOLEN.	Nil

Army Form C. 2118.

WAR DIARY
or
INTELLIGENCE SUMMARY.
(Erase heading not required.)

WD 3rd Cavalry Div. A.T.
Maj. D.C.

Instructions regarding War Diaries and Intelligence Summaries are contained in F. S. Regs., Part II. and the Staff Manual respectively. Title pages will be prepared in manuscript.

Place	Date	Hour	Summary of Events and Information	Remarks and references to Appendices
YZEUX.	1918 18th May		Railhead remained at ST LEGER LES DOMART. 2/Lieut. J.F.A. BECK. A.D. posted to 3rd Cav. Div. A.T. vice 2/Lieut. H. TANNER.	In
" —	19th May		Complained to Comdt. 8/9/4th Res. for condition of Ammn. H.T.O. horses returning from H.B. 7th Can. Bde. Royal Dragoons to 8th K.R.I. Divisional Troops at BETHANCOURT SOUTH and FARABIL before transportation from Railhead by horse transport commencing tomorrow. 2/Lieut. J.N. ROBERTS. Res. Reserve Park passed to this Depôt with a view to appearing before a Medical Board.	2n
" —	20th May		2/Lieut. C.B. PRICE, A.D. to 59th Divl. Train. (17th instant).	3n
" —	21st May		2/Lieut. J.N. ROBERTS, 3rd Can. Reserve Park, to Base Depot. 2/Lieut. J.F.A. BECK, A.D. joins 6 Cavalry Brigade as Bde. Transport Officer, from A.T.C. Base Depôt.	4n
" —	22nd May		2 lbs. of oats to be deducted daily from ration of each mule of Amm H.T.C. & Reserve Park transferred to Echo.	5n

Army Form C. 2118.

WAR DIARY
or
INTELLIGENCE SUMMARY.
(Erase heading not required.)

Headquarters 3rd Cavalry Brig. Ade.

May 1918.

Place	Date	Hour	Summary of Events and Information	Remarks and references to Appendices
YZEUX	1918 23rd May		Orders Aus. H.Q. to provide 6 horses for temporary work on Third Army Farm at VAN DENANSON.	
-"-	24th May		Lieut. H.L. WHITEHEAD and Jeune S. R. J. MOTLEY attached to 3rd Can. Div. M.T. Co. from No: 16 L/H.Q. Reserve M.T. Co. 17.5.18.	
-"-	25th May		Routine work.	
-"-	26th May		Routine work.	
-"-	27th May		A class of instruction in the use of the Hotchkiss Rifle to M.T.Co. Reserve Park & Aux. H.T.Co. starts on 29th instant at the lines of Lord Strathcona's Horse, ST OUEN.	
-"-	28th May		Routine work	
-"-	29th May		Routine work.	
-"-	30th May		The Brig. Commander inspects Reserve Park Aux. H.T.Co. en 1st scheme.	
-"-	31st May		Routine work	

E. Nunn
Major
For O.C. H.Q. 3rd Can. Div. Alt.

War Diary of
H.Q. 3rd Cav. Div. A.S.C.
June 1918.

Army Form C. 2118.

WAR DIARY
or
INTELLIGENCE SUMMARY.
(Erase heading not required.)

Hqrs. 3rd Cavalry Divisional A.T. / I
June 1918.

Instructions regarding War Diaries and Intelligence Summaries are contained in F.S. Regs., Part II. and the Staff Manual respectively. Title pages will be prepared in manuscript.

Place	Date	Hour	Summary of Events and Information	Remarks and references to Appendices
	1918			
YZEUX	1st June		Railhead ST LEGER LES DOMART. Distributed Fourth Army Routine Orders on scale of one per 145 a/s Brown in the Division.	Ref.
"	2nd June		Routine work.	Ref.
"	3rd June		Routine work.	Ref.
"	4th June		Routine work.	Ref.
"	5th June		Routine work.	Ref.
"	6th June		Routine work.	Ref.
"	7th June		O.C. Amm. S.A.A. reports the receipt of 3 G.S. wagons which are to replace the water tank wagons now on charge.	Ref.
"	8th June		Temp. Serjeant. B.F.A.G. SMALLWOOD, Reserve Park, ordered to join the 4 Cavalry Reserve Park. Arrangements made and instructions issued to the N.T.O. to send a three ton lorry to No. 12 Sanitary Station in temporary exchange for a Ford Box Car. This arrangement to form to be necessary pending receipt of the Box Cars authorized by W.T.O. establishment.	Ref.

Army Form C. 2118.

WAR DIARY
or
INTELLIGENCE SUMMARY.
(Erase heading not required.)

H.Qrs.
3rd Cavalry Div. A.C. [?] June 1918

Place	Date	Hour	Summary of Events and Information	Remarks and references to Appendices
YZEUX	1918 9th June		Received from Div. Q. proposed allotment of Aux. H.T. wagons transport ammunition, tools, kits, and water supply appliances in the Division.	
"	10th June		1 N.C.O. and 5 men of M.G. Dvl. Adj. commenced a course of instruction in the use of the Hotchkiss Rifle, held by 3rd Hotchkiss Rifle Wing, the course is to last 7 days.	
"	11th June		E.9923 Nr [?]. R. Lawton, N.Bro. M.Bro. Dvl. Adj. tried by F.G.C.M. on charges under Section 9(2) & 40 A.A. He was acquitted.	
"	12th June		Routine work.	
"	13th June		Routine work	
"	14th June		G.O.C. Division orders that drivers of vehicles should carry their rifles in the bucket clips on the wagons and not in rifle buckets on the horses.	
"	15th June		A Divisional organization for Salvage comes into force. Instructed Hussars [?] Rsr and Aux H.T. to have all wagons and limber covers catches as a protection against aircraft.	

Army Form C. 2118.

WAR DIARY or INTELLIGENCE SUMMARY.
(Erase heading not required.)

WAR DIARY 3rd Cavalry Div. Arty.
June 1917

Instructions regarding War Diaries and Intelligence Summaries are contained in F. S. Regs., Part II. and the Staff Manual respectively. Title pages will be prepared in manuscript.

Place	Date	Hour	Summary of Events and Information	Remarks and references to Appendices
	1917			III
	15th June (cont)		The Divisional Commander inspected the 3rd Cav. Div. Reserve Park and Auxiliary H.T. Company.	AC1
YZEUX	16th June		Forwarded to A.D.S.T. Cavalry Corps through the 3rd Cav. Div. "Q". the proceedings of a Court of Enquiry held to investigate the circumstances of an accident to Thornycroft lorry No: 40225, resulting in damage to the value of £110.5.0. The accident was attributable to the inexperience of the driver and it was recommended that the cost should be borne by the public and that O.C. units should have an opportunity of seeing their men-drivers drivers to school of instruction. Nearly all the drivers received now as reinforcements are practically untrained.	AC1
— —	17th June		Routine work.	AC1
— —	18th June		2nd Lieut. R.H. COURTENAY posted to 3rd Cav H.T.Co. from No.12 C.H.D. Reserve M.T.C. The move of Temp. Sec. Lieut. B.F.A.C. SMALLWOOD A.R. from 3rd to 4th Cavalry Reserve Park, referred to in 5th inst, has been cancelled.	AC1
— —	19th June		Routine work. Lieut. H. TAYLOR, Can. reported yesterday for duty with Canadian Cavalry Brigade.	AC1

D. D. & L., London, E.C.
(A8004) Wt W1771/M2931 750,000 5/17 Sch. 52 Forms/C2115/14

Army Form C. 2118.

WAR DIARY
or
INTELLIGENCE SUMMARY.
(Erase heading not required.)

M.Gun Sqn Cav Bn Cdn
June 1918

Instructions regarding War Diaries and Intelligence Summaries are contained in F. S. Regs., Part II. and the Staff Manual respectively. Title pages will be prepared in manuscript.

Place	Date	Hour	Summary of Events and Information	Remarks and references to Appendices IV
YZEUX	20 June 1918		Routine work.	App
-"-	21st June		Forwarded to Lieut. Col. "S" O/C M.G. report on his inspection of Canadian Cav. Bde. His transport is in poor condition	App
-"-	22nd June		Routine work.	App
-"-	23rd June		Captain T.F.A. HALL, C.B.E, ordered to join 2nd Canadian Res. to duty.	App
-"-	24th June		Received same orders to send out 8 limbers for Brigade to carry "A 2" rations in lieu of limbers from Machine Gun Squadron.	App
-"-	25th June		Routine work. Divisional Commander's inspects the M.G. tomorrow.	App
-"-	26th June		Routine work.	App
-"-	27th June		Captain T.F.A. HALL and Lieut. H.P. BONNICK, C.A.L., admitted Hospital 24/6/18.	App
-"-	28th June		Routine work.	App

Army Form C. 2118.

WAR DIARY
or
INTELLIGENCE SUMMARY.
(Erase heading not required.)

H.Q. 5th Cavalry Div. A.b.
June 1918.

Place	Date	Hour	Summary of Events and Information	Remarks and references to Appendices
YZEUX	29th June		Owing to Ambulance being unable to cope with the numbers of P.U.O. patients discharged to their units from hospital, made arrangements to receive patients at 6th C.F.A. daily for this unit.	
-do-	30 June		Atkins A. CDST. to 3 Base off charge Isnewals no sick cycl. from no. 273045, expires January #5505, on charge of Canadian Service Troops, which became different during recent operations.	

E.W. [signature]
Lt Colonel
Comdg H.Qrs. 5th Cavalry Dn. A.b.

Army Form C. 2118.

WAR DIARY
or
INTELLIGENCE SUMMARY.

(Erase heading not required.)

1st(?) Can. Div. Div.
July 1918

Instructions regarding War Diaries and Intelligence Summaries are contained in F. S. Regs., Part II. and the Staff Manual respectively. Title pages will be prepared in manuscript.

Place	Date	Hour	Summary of Events and Information	Remarks and references to Appendices
YZEUX (AMIENS-ABBEVILLE Road)	1918 1st July		Advise K.S.N.S. the round of distribution of Cavalry Establishment traversed by date on 29th June. There is a mistake which amounts to first evolution	App
"	2nd July		Lieut. M. MORGAN, F. BRENER, and R. COLLIS joined the Div.	App
"	3rd July		Routine work.	App
"	4th July		Temp. Lieut. J.P. JONES, Adj., joined 3rd Can. Div. M.T.Co.	App
"	"		Lieutenant H. P. BONNICK, C.A.S.C., discharged hospital & resumed duty	App
"	5th July		Routine work.	App
"	6th July		Routine work.	App
"	7th July		An additional G.S. limbered wagon, with 4 horses and 2 drivers, authorized for each Cavalry Regt. by W.O. letter France/2399/J.S.2. dated 27th June 1918	App
"	8th July		Routine work.	App
"	9th July		Routine work.	App
"	10th July		Routine work.	App

Army Form C. 2118.

WAR DIARY
or
INTELLIGENCE SUMMARY

(Erase heading not required.)

Army. 3rd Cavalry Bde. A.L.
July 1918.

Instructions regarding War Diaries and Intelligence Summaries are contained in F. S. Regs., Part II. and the Staff Manual respectively. Title pages will be prepared in manuscript.

Place	Date	Hour	Summary of Events and Information	Remarks and references to Appendices
YZEUX	1918 11th July		Drew the attention of O.C. Reserve Park and Am. H.T.Co. to the fact that no economies in labour were being effected by their units.	
"	12th July		"Routine work. Nothing to report.	
"	13th July		Routine work.	
"	14th July		Routine work.	
"	15th July		Routine work.	
"	16th July		Received approval to write off the following motor cycles :- 1. Triumph Frame No. 293045, Engine No. 45503 - collided with French lorry and had to be abandoned - (Auth: Car Cpo 91/4254 5.7.18). 2. Triumph Frame No. 272931, Engine No. 45076 - destroyed by hostile shell fire. (Auth: Car Cpo 91/4585d. 13.7.18). Both these machines were on charge to Canadian Cavalry Brigade Signal Troop.	

Army Form C. 2118.

WAR DIARY
or
INTELLIGENCE SUMMARY.
(Erase heading not required.)

M₂o.
6th Cav. Bde Ade. July 1918

Instructions regarding War Diaries and Intelligence Summaries are contained in F. S. Regs., Part II and the Staff Manual respectively. Title pages will be prepared in manuscript.

Place	Date	Hour	Summary of Events and Information	Remarks and references to Appendices
	1918			
YZEUX	17th July		G O C inspected the transport of the 6 Cavalry Brigade.	Nil
"	18th July		Applied for G C. in case of No. H/256 Pte L.G. Munnie, 3rd Cavalry Amn. H/T Co. on a charge under Section 40. A.A.	Nil
"	19th July		Hay ration reduced by 1lb. from 21st instant. Substitutes not allowed to be purchased in lieu of amount cut. Lieut. J.N. ROBERTS struck off and Temp. Lieut. B.F.A.G. SMALLWOOD brought on the strength of 3rd Cavalry Reserve Park as from 30/5/18.	Nil
"	20th July		Nothing to report. Routine work.	Nil
"	21st July		G O C. inspected the transport of 6th Cavalry Field Ambulance. Railhead changed from St LEGER LES DOMARTS to HANGEST. First drawing today. All units drew rations by Horse transport, except M.T. Co. and Field Squadron who drew by lorry.	Nil
"	22nd July		Routine work.	Nil

Army Form C. 2118.

WAR DIARY
or
INTELLIGENCE SUMMARY.

(Erase heading not required.)

MBn. 3rd Cavalry Brigade a/c IV
July 1918.

Place	Date	Hour	Summary of Events and Information	Remarks and references to Appendices
YZEUX	23rd July	1918	Three remaining motor tank wagons with Auxiliary H.T.Co. were exchanged for G.S. wagons to-day at Advd. H.T. Depot, ABBEVILLE.	WD
-"-	24th July		Routine work.	WD
-"-	25th July		Routine work.	WD
-"-	26th July		Routine work.	WD
-"-	27th July		Routine work.	WD
-"-	28th July		Routine work.	WD
-"-	29th July		All reserve horse shoes now carried by the M.T.Co. are being replaced by hand made shoes turned out by the School of Farriery, ABBEVILLE.	WD
-"-	30th July		Routine work.	WD
-"-	31st July		G.O.C. approved of 10 lorries being sent to LE TREPORT in M.T. pros to give the men of M.T.Co. a day's leave.	WD

S.E. Tunney
Lieutenant
Comdg. MBn. 3rd Cavalry Brigade, A.S.C.

Army Form C. 2118.

WAR DIARY
or
INTELLIGENCE SUMMARY.
(Erase heading not required.)

Instructions regarding War Diaries and Intelligence Summaries are contained in F.S. Regs., Part II. and the Staff Manual respectively. Title pages will be prepared in manuscript.

Army: HQrs.
3rd Canadian Divl. A.R.C.

Place	Date	Hour	Summary of Events and Information	Remarks and references to Appendices
YZEUX	1918 1st Aug.		Routine work.	Nil
"	2nd Aug.		Routine work.	Nil
"	3rd Aug.		Routine work.	Nil
"	4th Aug.		Routine work.	Nil
"	5th Aug.		Lieut. R.B.A. Orr, Canadian A.D.C. joined the Canadian Cavalry Brigade, in duty as understudy to Capt. N.P. Ronnick. Railhead at HANGEST as usual.	Nil
"	6 Aug.		Railhead changed to VILLE DE MARCLET. The Division moved to a concentration area around PONT DE METZ (S.W. of AMIENS) Preparatory to operations. 1 Officer & 10 O.R. of H.Q. Adv. with 5 horses, moved with "B" Echelon to SOUES, the remainder with "A" Echelon to PONT DE METZ, arriving there at 3 am 7 Aug. Supply arrangements:— Rations loaded in detail and descurbed in the PONT DE METZ area. Rendezvous 12 noon at P in PONT DE METZ (AMIENS 100,000). The Adm. H.Qo. loaded with ammunition and forming an extra	A.I.

Army Form C. 2118.

WAR DIARY
or
INTELLIGENCE SUMMARY.

(Erase heading not required.)

A.Pro. Havsey Div. Ade

August 1918

Place	Date	Hour	Summary of Events and Information	Remarks and references to Appendices
	1918		section of the Div.l. Ammun. Column, moved up and parked near the Railway Arcks on the SALOUEL – PONT DE METZ Road. The M.T. Co. after dumping rations, parked on the SALEUX road. Reserve Pepo. Remained at BETHENCOURT S'OUEN (light holding tomorrow).	
PONT DE METZ	7 Aug		Railhead SALEUX	
			O.C. Adj. and officers moved to T. 3. B. 3. 3. (62 D) the Company remaining at PONT DE METZ.	
PONT DE METZ	8 Aug		Railhead Remained at SALEUX. Company moved in the afternoon to beyond DOMART SUR LUCE and encamped near the ROYE road between the British German trenches evacuated that morning.	
Near DOMART SUR-LUCE	9 Aug		Railhead changed to LONGUEAU. O.C. Adj and other officers moved up to Rear N.H.Q. Company remaining at previous nights encampment.	
-ʺ-	10 Aug		Railhead remained at LONGUEAU. Moved to CAYEUX.	

Army Form C. 2118.

WAR DIARY
INTELLIGENCE SUMMARY.
(Erase heading not required.)

No. 3rd Can. Tu Ple
August 1918

Instructions regarding War Diaries and Intelligence Summaries are contained in F.S. Regs., Part II. and the Staff Manual respectively. Title pages will be prepared in manuscript.

Place	Date	Hour	Summary of Events and Information	Remarks and references to Appendices
	1918			
CAYEUX	11 Aug		Railhead Longueau. Moved to Railway crossing on CAIX–WARVILLERS road and later in the day to BOVES WOOD.	Wel
BOVES WOOD	12 Aug		Railhead Longueau. Remained in Boves Wood.	Wel
BOVES WOOD	13 Aug		Railhead Longueau. Moved from BOVES WOOD to SAINS-EN-AMIENOIS. Remained at Sains-en-Amienois	Wel
SAINS-EN-AMIENOIS	14 Aug		Railhead AMIENS.	Wel
– " –	15 Aug		Returned from SAINS-EN-AMIENOIS to YZEUX.	Wel
YZEUX	16 Aug		Railhead AMIENS. M.T. Co. returned to DOMART-EN-PONTHIEU. Reserve Park and Am. M.T.Co. to BETHENCOURT ST OUEN.	Wel
YZEUX	17 Aug		Railhead changed to ST LEGER LES DOMART.	Wel

Army Form C. 2118.

WAR DIARY
or
INTELLIGENCE SUMMARY.
(Erase heading not required.)

HQrs 3s Cav Bde
Aug 1916

Place	Date	Hour	Summary of Events and Information	Remarks and references to Appendices
	1916			
YZEUX	18 Aug		Railhead ST LEGER	Nil
"	19 Aug		Railhead changed to HANGEST.	Nil
"	20 Aug		Railhead HANGEST. All units less M.G. Co. drew rations from Railhead by Horse Transport.	Nil
			All don rations in the Bivs. examined yesterday and today on their condition rendered today on Form Q.	Nil
"	21 Aug		Routine work.	Nil
"	22 Aug		Routine work.	Nil
"	23 Aug		Routine work.	Nil
"	24 Aug		Routine work.	Nil
"	25 Aug		1/c Division moved to an area around FONTAINE L'ETALON (6 miles N.W. of AUXI-LE-CHATEAU). HQrs Bde located at CHERIENNE. Reserve Regt CAUMONT. Railhead remained at HANGEST.	Nil
CHERRIENNE	26 Aug		Division moved to an area between FREVENT and WAIL. Location tonight - HQrs. Regt. 6 - WAIL (4 miles S.E. HESDIN). Reserve Regt. GALAMETZ. M.G.Co. - TOLLENT.	Nil
			Railhead AUXI-LE-CHATEAU.	

Army Form C. 2118.

WAR DIARY
or
INTELLIGENCE SUMMARY.
(Erase heading not required.)

HQrs. 3rd Cavalry Divl. Arty.
August, 1918.

Place	Date	Hour	Summary of Events and Information	Remarks and references to Appendices
	1918			
WAIL	27th Aug.		Railhead FREVENT. Tonights location – HQrs. Arty. WAIL. Div. Park. EPLAMETZ. Amn. H.T.Co. WILLENCOURT. M.T.Co. VACQUERIE with 43rd Bde. R.F.A. AVERDOIGT.	AA1
WAIL	28th Aug.		Railhead changed to TINCQUES. Applied to D.A. Cav. Corps in case of 2nd Lt. Foggo's & Lt. W.C. Hunter, 7" R.H.G. Reserve Bde. att. 3rd Cav. Divl. Arty. charged with moving insubordinate language when electd tried. Case subsequently tried by O.C. A.A.	AA2
WAIL	29th Aug.		Nothing to report.	AA6
WAIL	30th Aug.		Nothing to report.	AA6
WAIL	31st Aug.		"B" Echelon rejoined the Division.	AA6

S.C. Murray, Lt.Colonel
Commanding HQrs. 3rd Cavalry Divl. Arty.

Army Form C. 2118.

WAR DIARY
or
INTELLIGENCE SUMMARY.
(Erase heading not required.)

HQrs. 3rd Cavalry Div. A.S.C.
September 1918.

Place	Date	Hour	Summary of Events and Information	Remarks and references to Appendices
WAIL	1st Sept. 1918		Remained at WAIL standing to	Nil
WAIL	2nd Sept.		Nothing to report	Nil
-"-	3rd Sept.		-"- -"-	Nil
-"-	4th Sept.		-"- -"-	Nil
-"-	5th Sept.		-"- -"-	Nil
-"-	6th Sept.		Divisional Headqrs moved back to the FONTAINE L'ETALON area, HQrs. A.D.S. being located at CHERIENNE as before. 3rd Cavalry M.T. Coy moved to VACQUERIE-LE-BOURCQ. Following moves of officers took place :- 1/Capt. R.W.F. HEDGER, 3rd Cavalry Reserve Park to 29th Divisional Train - 1/Capt. E.W. BAKER, 3rd Cavalry Aux. H.T. Coy. to 37th Divisional Train.	Nil
CHERIENNE	7th Sept.		Railhead changed to FREVENT.	Nil
-"-	8th Sept.		Capt. W.E. RIDER A.S.C. joined from 37th Divisional Train and took over command of 3rd Cavalry Aux. H.T. Company	Nil
-"-	9th Sept.		Complained to Divisional "Q" of unsuitable worn clothing being despatched by units in lorries to Railhead	Nil

Army Form C. 2118.

WAR DIARY
or
INTELLIGENCE SUMMARY.

(Erase heading not required.)

HQrs. 2nd Cavalry 2nd A.Bde.
September, 1918.

Instructions regarding War Diaries and Intelligence Summaries are contained in F. S. Regs., Part II. and the Staff Manual respectively. Title pages will be prepared in manuscript.

Place	Date	Hour	Summary of Events and Information	Remarks and references to Appendices
	9 Sept. cont.		Canadian Cavalry Brigade commence drawing rations from Railhead by Horse transport. 7 Cav.Bde. also draw their B.M.C.	Nil
CHERIENNE	10 Sept.		Received notification of reduction in horse establishment of HQrs. Divl. A.C. by two riders. HQrs. Light Section of Reserve Park moved from GALAMETZ to TOLLENT. Positions now as follows:- Divl. HQrs. FONTAINE L'ETALON. HQrs. A.C. CHERIENNE. M.T. Coy. VACQUERIE-LE-BOURCQ. Res. Park (H.D.) TOLLENT Res. Park (H.S.) WILLENCOURT. Aux. H.T. Coy WILLENCOURT.	Nil
"	11 Sept.		7 Cavalry Brigade rations delivered by M.T. Canadian Brigade only draw by horse transport. Captain H.P. BONNICK, Canadian A.S.C., to 3rd Canadian Divisional Train for duty.	Nil

Army Form C. 2118.

WAR DIARY
or
INTELLIGENCE SUMMARY.

(Erase heading not required.)

H.Qrs. 3rd Cavalry Sve. Ave. III
September 1918.

Place	Date	Hour	Summary of Events and Information	Remarks and references to Appendices
CHERIENNE	1918 12th Sept		Routine work.	Nil
"	13th Sept		Forwarded to Divisional "Q" a protest against the reduction of riding horses with HQrs. A.V.C. Divisional "Q" ruled that these horses must be sent to D.R.O.M.C. Cavalry Corps in the event of operations, in addition to the one lorry now lent to each C.F.A. for the carriage of walking wounded, i.e. no horses detached on medical duties alone.	Nil
"	14th Sept		Great difficulty and inconvenience being caused by the failure of units to report casualties to detached R.S.C. personnel. Requested Div. Q. to publish an order directing that casualties be immediately reported to the unit concerned.	Nil
"	15th Sept		Routine work.	Nil
"	16th Sept		Routine work.	Nil
"	17th Sept		Routine work.	Nil
"	18th Sept		Routine work.	Nil
"	19th Sept		Routine work.	Nil

Army Form C. 2118.

WAR DIARY
or
INTELLIGENCE SUMMARY.
(Erase heading not required.)

Instructions regarding War Diaries and Intelligence Summaries are contained in F. S. Regs., Part II. and the Staff Manual respectively. Title pages will be prepared in manuscript.

Army Troops Coy RE ....
September 1918 ....

Place	Date	Hour	Summary of Events and Information	Remarks and references to Appendices
	1918			
CHERIENNE	20 Sept.		Reconnoitred to N.E. of "Q". The view of future operations. Field C.E.E.M.R.T.O.'s 1.2.	Nil
" "	21 Sept.		Toured up to front.	Nil
" "	22 Sept.		Sub. C.E. I. M.F.R. & I. joined Reserve Park.	Nil
" "	23 Sept.		D.f.C. to inspect Reserve Park & A.A.I. Co. this week.	Nil
" "	24 Sept.		Routine work.	
" "	25 Sept.		Division moved up to take part in operations on South Army front. Chis. O.E. motors to MARIEUX near ALBERT. Brigades instructed to return to Coy. all Store Appurtenances less H. per Brigade for water appliances and surplus medical equipment.	Nil
MARIEUX	26 Sept.		Remained at MARIEUX. Lieutenant R.E.S. CARR, to H.Q. tip the Brivers to join the Canadian Divisional Train.	Nil

Army Form C. 2118.

WAR DIARY
or
INTELLIGENCE SUMMARY
(Erase heading not required.)

14th Div. Sig. Cdn. Hd. Qrs. September 1918.

Place	Date	Hour	Summary of Events and Information	Remarks and references to Appendices
	1918			
MARIEUX	27 Sept		Railhead changed to MOISLAINS. Moved from MARIEUX to CLERY-SUR-SOMME. (Vicinity of)	Nil
Near CLERY	28 Sept		Railhead changed to PLATEAU near MARICOURT. Locations of units tonight :— Reference 1/40,000 62c. H.Q. Offs. M.T.a. A. 5. Sec. C. near PLATEAU ATT E. H. S. C. Return A. 30. 3.	Nil
Near CLERY Near H.Q.S. 62C	29 Sept		Moved from Clery to POEUILLY. Locations as follows :— Ref. Offs. S. 28. a. 2. 4. Sec. B. HEM. Sec. P. M.T.A. (diff large) Sec. A. HEM STATION (small size) T.M. HEM STATION	Nil
POEUILLY	30 Sept		Stood by awaiting orders	Nil

S.A. Cumming Lieut Colonel
Comdg. 14th Div. Sig. Cdn.

Army Form C. 2118.

WAR DIARY
or
INTELLIGENCE SUMMARY.
(Erase heading not required.)

Army: 3rd Cavalry Brigade H.Q.
October 1918

Place	Date	Hour	Summary of Events and Information	Remarks and references to Appendices
POEUILLY Bde Hd Qrs	1918 1st Oct.		Railhead PLANICOURT. Remained at POEUILLY.	Nil
"	2nd Oct.		Division moved up to PONTRU preparatory to the Cavalry attack but returned later to POEUILLY area. Revd. Pain A.Mr. School of Instruction from Bd. W&HQrs.	Nil
"	3rd Oct.		Three numbers of 3rd Bde Adv moved up with troops to 1st Bn H.Q. and remained there. Bd. Adv. returned to POEUILLY with Bd. H.Qrs.	Nil
"	4th Oct.		Position as yesterday.	Nil
"	5th Oct.		All troops of H.Qrs. Bd. returned to POEUILLY. Complaines 1-8 of 4th Dragoon Gds. having on 28/9/18. 2750 lb Oats & 1500 lb of Hay from our 2nd Echelon Dump.	Nil
"	6th Oct.		Remained at POEUILLY.	Nil
"	7th Oct.		3Bde Adv (Brig/a) moved up to JONCOURT. OC. All remained at POEUILLY.	Nil
"	8th Oct.		16 Adv with Hd Bde Adv moved out to MAISSY-LE-FOSSE. Rear Hd Qrs. Adv. remaining Hdq at POEUILLY. The Division advanced with objective Railway Junction at BUSSIGNY and	Nil

Army Form C. 2118.

WAR DIARY
or
INTELLIGENCE SUMMARY.
(Erase heading not required.)

H.Qrs. 3rd Canadian Div. Arty.

October, 1918. II.

Place	Date	Hour	Summary of Events and Information	Remarks and references to Appendices
	1918			
NAISSY-ET-FOSSE	9ᵗʰ Oct.		LE CATEAU thence turning north in the direction of VALENCIENNES. Advd. H.Qrs. Arty. to U.26.b.8.0.	NIL
U.26.b.8.0.	10ᵗʰ Oct.		Rear H.Qrs. Arty. moved to MARETZ. Advd. H.Qrs. Arty. to O.11.D.5.W (near MONTIGNY).	NIL
O.11.b.5.W.	11ᵗʰ Oct.		Rear H.Qrs. Arty. moved and joined up with Advcd. H.Qrs. at O.11.D.5.W.	NIL
O.11.b.5.W	12ᵗʰ Oct.		H.Qrs. Arty. moved with 3rd. Cdn. Div. to BERTRY but owing to severe shelling of that place, the whole moved later in the day to ELINCOURT.	NIL
ELINCOURT	13ᵗʰ Oct.		Division moved to the HENNOIS WOOD area & units located as follows:— Divl. H.Qrs.} HENNOIS WOOD (10.M.N.N.E. PERONNE). H.Qrs. Arty. } M.T. Coy. — BARASTRE. PERONNE (Waterluies) Res. Pare. } MESNIL - AN - ARROUISE. A.H. Coy.	NIL
HENNOIS WOOD	14ᵗʰ Oct.		General clearing up proceeded with.	NIL
"	15ᵗʰ Oct.		Railhead changed to RE TRANSLOY. Major E.T. CARVER, S.L.O., to hospital	NIL

Army Form C. 2118.

WAR DIARY
or
INTELLIGENCE SUMMARY.
(Erase heading not required.)

Hdqrs. 3rd Cavalry Bde. R.J.B.

October 1918

Instructions regarding War Diaries and Intelligence Summaries are contained in F. S. Regs., Part II. and the Staff Manual respectively. Title pages will be prepared in manuscript.

Place	Date	Hour	Summary of Events and Information	Remarks and references to Appendices
HENNOIS WOOD.	1918 16th Oct.		Nothing to report.	Nil
"	17th Oct.		— " —	Nil
"	18th Oct.		O.C. A.S.C. made an inspection of the transport of 6 Cavalry Brigade.	Nil
"	19th Oct.		Major Carter rejoined from Hospital. Motor cycle certificates issued to Units.	Nil
"	20th Oct.		Routine work.	Nil
"	21st Oct.		Routine work.	Nil
"	22nd Oct.		Routine work.	Nil
"	23rd Oct.		Detailed four N.C.O.s (H.T.Co. A.S.C. + Mr. Lewis) for course of instruction in the Hotchkiss Rifle at St Jacques 26th October to 11th November.	Nil

Army Form C. 2118.

WAR DIARY
or
INTELLIGENCE SUMMARY.
(Erase heading not required.)

Head Qtrs 8th Essex Devl A.S.C.

October 1918

Instructions regarding War Diaries and Intelligence Summaries are contained in F. S. Regs., Part II and the Staff Manual respectively. Title pages will be prepared in manuscript.

Place	Date	Hour	Summary of Events and Information	Remarks and references to Appendices
HERRIN'S WOOD	24th Oct		Routine Work. Dembury H.Q. by group moved from Le MESNIL to ROUQUIGNY	Oct
"	25th Oct		Routine Work	Oct
"	26th Oct		Routine Work	Oct
"	27th Oct		Nothing to Report	Oct
"	28th Oct		Routine work. G.O.C. inspected Coys H.T.& G.S. full morning dress	Oct
"	29th Oct		Nothing to Report	Oct
"	30th Oct		Routine Work	Oct
"	31st Oct		Routine Work	Oct

R.W.
Capt & Adjt

Lt Col Commanding Head Qtrs 8th Essex Divl A.S.C.

Army Form C. 2118.

HQrs 1st Cavalry Div. Art.

November 1918

WAR DIARY
or
INTELLIGENCE SUMMARY.
(Erase heading not required.)

Instructions regarding War Diaries and Intelligence Summaries are contained in F. S. Regs., Part II. and the Staff Manual respectively. Title pages will be prepared in manuscript.

Place	Date	Hour	Summary of Events and Information	Remarks and references to Appendices
HENNOIS WOOD	1st Nov. 1918		Routine work. Nothing of interest to report.	
"	2nd Nov.		"	
"	3rd Nov.		"	
"	4th Nov.		"	
"	5th Nov.		Warning orders received for the Division to take part in operations. Brigades & Div. troops to be ready to move at 2½ hours notice all wagons to be packed.	
"	6th Nov.		HQrs of unit remained with Div. HQrs at Hennois Wood but the transport moved to INCHY-EN-ARTOIS. Railhead today at St Tranaloy	
"	7th Nov.		HQrs remained at Hennois Wood. Railhead Marcoing.	
"	8th Nov.		Railhead changed to Don. HQrs A.S.C. with D.H.Q., proceeded by march route to Sainghin 5 miles S.E. of Lille.	

Army Form C. 2118.

WAR DIARY
or
INTELLIGENCE SUMMARY.
(Erase heading not required.)

Headqrs. 3rd Cavalry Divl. Ade.
December 1918

Place	Date	Hour	Summary of Events and Information	Remarks and references to Appendices
	1918			
Dauphin	9th Nov.		Proceeded by march route to Antoing, near Tournai. Railhead remained at Don. 7th Cavalry Brigade left the Division for temporary attachment to the Second Army, taking with it section of the M.G. Coy and Reserve Park. S.A.A. Co. filled up with ammunition after dumping loads.	Nil Ref Ref
Antoing	10th Nov.		Location Antoing – Railhead Don.	Ref
"	11th Nov.		Railhead changed to Stroke near Lille. Hostilities ceased at 11 a.m.	Ref
"	12th Nov.		Nothing to report.	Ref
"	13th Nov.		— " —	Ref
"	14th Nov.		— " —	Ref
"	15th Nov.		Railhead changed to Ascq.	Ref
"	16th Nov.		Nothing to report.	Ref

Army Form C. 2118.

WAR DIARY
or
INTELLIGENCE SUMMARY.
(Erase heading not required.)

Hdrs. 3rd Cav. Div. A.S.C.
November, 1918.

Instructions regarding War Diaries and Intelligence Summaries are contained in F. S. Regs., Part II. and the Staff Manual respectively. Title pages will be prepared in manuscript.

Place	Date	Hour	Summary of Events and Information	Remarks and references to Appendices
	1918			
Antoing	16 Nov.		Nothing to report.	
—	17 Nov.		3rd Cavalry Division, with the 1st Cavalry Division, having been allotted position of Advance Guard to the Second Army on its move to Germany to form the Army of Occupation, commenced its move to the Frontier. Following moves took place:— Hdrs. Adv. ANTOINE to BASSILLY. Res. Park. VEZON to STOUQUOI. A.H.T. Coy. BARRY to BASSILLY.	
Bassilly	18 Nov.		Continued march. Following positions reached:— Hdrs. A.S.C. ENGHIEN Reserve Park — PETIT ENGHIEN A.H.T. Coy. — ENGHIEN	

Army Form C. 2118.

WAR DIARY
or
INTELLIGENCE SUMMARY.
(Erase heading not required.)

HQ. 3rd Cav. Div. Ade
November, 1918.

Place	Date	Hour	Summary of Events and Information	Remarks and references to Appendices
	1918			
Enghien	19 Nov.		Remained at Enghien and vicinity. Heavy Section, Reserve Park, left the Division and proceeded to LONTE for work under Fifth Army.	RC
"	20 Nov.		M.T. Company moved to Enghien.	RC
"	21st Nov.		Continued march to WATERLOO. A.H.T. Co. also at Waterloo. Reserve Park at Mont St Jean.	RC
Waterloo	22nd Nov.		HDrs A.T.C. and A.H.T.Co. to PERWEZ. Reserve Park to Jauchelette.	RC
Perwez	23rd Nov.		Nothing to report.	RC
"	24 Nov.		HDrs changed to Balasez - St. Paris - Waelhes (H.K. from Perwez)	RC
Balasez - St Paris - Waelhes	25 Nov.		Nothing to report	RC

Army Form C. 2118.

WAR DIARY
or
INTELLIGENCE SUMMARY.
(Erase heading not required.)

HQrs. 5th Cavalry Divl. Ade.

November, 1918.

Instructions regarding War Diaries and Intelligence Summaries are contained in F.S. Regs., Part II. and the Staff Manual respectively. Title pages will be prepared in manuscript.

Place	Date	Hour	Summary of Events and Information	Remarks and references to Appendices
MALEVES- STE MARIE-WASTINES	1918 26 Nov.		6 limbers from Reserve Park sent out to each Brigade with iron rations and oats for use in the event of the supply train failing.	
" "	27 Nov.		Railhead changed to AUDENARDE. O.C. D.T. Coy. notifies that he has formed a Rest House at Enghien for the use of the Officers passing through the unit	
" "	28 Nov.		Notification received that Railhead changed to AVELAIS near NAMUR, but supplies continued to be drawn at AUDENARDE owing to the failure of the supply train to get through. Reserve section of R.P. sent out to Brigade	
" "	29 Nov.		Nothing to report.	
" "	30 Nov.		Nothing to report.	

R.M.C.
Capt. r Ady.
for O.C. H.Q. Cavalry Divl. Ade.

Army Form C. 2118.

WAR DIARY
or
INTELLIGENCE SUMMARY.
(Erase heading not required.)

H.Qrs. 3rd Cavalry Div. A.S.C.

December, 1918.

Instructions regarding War Diaries and Intelligence Summaries are contained in F. S. Regs., Part II. and the Staff Manual respectively. Title pages will be prepared in manuscript.

Place	Date	Hour	Summary of Events and Information	Remarks and references to Appendices
MALEVES-STE MARIE-WASTINES (ODENGE)	1918 Dec 1st		Nothing to report.	
"	Dec 2nd		"	
"	Dec 3rd		"	
"	Dec 4th		Reference map BRUSSELS (I.J.5). Complained to Divl. "Q" of the late arrival of supply train. The train is arriving as much as 48 hours late on occasion and is causing much inconvenience and overwork to all concerned.	
"	Dec 5th		Nothing to report.	
"	Dec 6th		Received a message of appreciation from Corps Commander on the work performed by the A.S.C. during the advance through Belgium.	
"	Dec 7th		Nothing to report.	
"	Dec 8th		"	
"	Dec 9th		"	

WAR DIARY
or
INTELLIGENCE SUMMARY.

(Erase heading not required.)

Army Form C. 2118.

H.Q. 1st Cav. Div. R.A.

December, 1918.

Place	Date	Hour	Summary of Events and Information	Remarks and references to Appendices
ODENGE	1918 Dec 10th		Nothing to report.	Nil
"	11th		" " "	Nil
"	12th		" " "	
"	13th		" " "	Nil
"	14th		" " "	
"	15th		" " "	Nil
"	16th		Moved from ODENGE to TINLOT Chateau (MARCHE E.1).	Nil
TINLOT	17th		Nothing to report.	
"	18th		" " "	
"	19th		One G.S. wagon, 2 drivers & 4 mules sent to Cavalry Corps Concentration Camp (formed today at SERAING) from H.Q. R.A.S.C. for temporary attachment.	Nil
"	20th		Nothing to report.	Nil
"	21st		" " "	
"	22nd		" " "	
"	23rd		" " "	Nil

WAR DIARY
or
INTELLIGENCE SUMMARY.

(Erase heading not required.)

Army Form C. 2118.

HQ. Xxx Xx. Xxxx
Dec. 1918

Instructions regarding War Diaries and Intelligence Summaries are contained in F.S. Regs., Part II. and the Staff Manual respectively. Title pages will be prepared in manuscript.

Place	Date	Hour	Summary of Events and Information	Remarks and references to Appendices
	1918			
TIN LOT	Dec 24th		Nothing to report.	nil
"	25th		"	nil
"	26th		"	nil
"	27th		"	nil
"	28th		"	nil
"	29th		"	nil
"	30th		"	nil
"	31st		"	nil

FH Mummery, Colonel
Comdg. HQ. Xxx Xx. RAFC

Headquarters, 3rd Cavalry Divisional R. A. S. C.

War Diary, January, 1919.

WAR DIARY
or
INTELLIGENCE SUMMARY

(Erase heading not required.)

Army Form C. 2118.

HQtrs. 3rd Cavalry Bde R.A.S.C.

January 1919.

WO 30

Place	Date	Hour	Summary of Events and Information	Remarks and references to Appendices
TINLOT	1919 1st Jan		Nothing to report	Ner
"	2nd "		" "	Ner
"	3rd "		" "	Ner
"	4th "		" "	Ner
"	5th "		" "	Ner
"	6th "		" "	Ner
"	7th "		Lieut. H.N. ROBERTS joined 3rd Cav. Reserve Park.	Ner
"	8th "		Nothing to report	Ner
"	9th "		" "	Ner
"	10th "		" "	Ner
"	11th "		" "	Ner
"	12th "		" "	Ner
"	13th "		" "	Ner
"	14th "		" "	Ner
"	15th "		" "	Ner
"	16th "		" "	Ner
"	17th "		" "	Ner

WAR DIARY
or
INTELLIGENCE SUMMARY.
(Erase heading not required.)

Army Form C. 2118.

W.O. to Car for CAJC
January 1919

Place	Date	Hour	Summary of Events and Information	Remarks and references to Appendices
TINCOS	1919 18 Jan		Capt. C.C. THOMAS Canadian ASC struck off strength from this date on reposting to CASC Depot.	RIC
"	19 Jan		Nothing to report	MEL
"	20 Jan		— " —	MEL
"	21 Jan		Embargo placed upon the demobilization of R.A.S.C. personnel and arrangements made to send divisional parties to Corps Concentration Camps which has been formed at SORAING.	MEL
"	22 Jan		Parsed all Supply Officers to help a very careful check upon ration demands during period of demobilization.	MEL
"	23 Jan		Nothing to report	MEL
"	24 "		— " —	MEL
"	25 Jan		" Concentration Camps today — 3 Aux. D.S. M.T.C.	MEL
"	26 "		— " —	MEL
"	27 "		— " — 4 Aux. D.S. A.J.T.C.	MEL
"	28 "		3 Aux. D.S. M.T.C. & 2 Aux. D.S. & 2 Supply M.T.C.	MEL

Army Form C. 2118.

WAR DIARY
or
INTELLIGENCE SUMMARY.

(Erase heading not required.)

HQ 5th Cav Bde MGS

January 1919

Instructions regarding War Diaries and Intelligence Summaries are contained in F. S. Regs., Part II. and the Staff Manual respectively. Title pages will be prepared in manuscript.

Place	Date	Hour	Summary of Events and Information	Remarks and references to Appendices
TIRLOT	1919 29 Jan		1. Current Camp Estab:- 1 HQ St + 1 MG Artillery Reserve Sect.	Nil
" "	30 Jan		Nothing to report.	Nil
" "	31st "		Ditto.	Nil
			1. Large quantities of war material abandoned by the enemy were collected during the month, viz stated to them various kinds of FNGS including guns wagons and motor vehicles.	
			2. During the month South Army started a scheme in employing men/officers periodicals & Koran, but owing to the time taken and the failure of the work carried and material being available fewer than 5,000 copies [illegible] the scheme is not considered a success so far as may be known.	
			3. Difficulty is being experienced by the large numbers of available labour - due to almost total absence of numbers not retained from large own units. Nothing being done however by about 140 men. The usual work has been carried on with a reduced establishment by all Cable sections being kept on keeping strength.	

S.E. Murray Ross
Lieut Colonel
Comdg HQ 5th Cav Bde MG Bde

WD 51

War Diary for February, 1919.

A.D. 3rd Cavalry Div. A.H.S.C.

WAR DIARY
or
INTELLIGENCE SUMMARY.

(Erase heading not required.)

Army Form C. 2118.

HQrs. 3rd Can. Div. Staff
February, 1919

Instructions regarding War Diaries and Intelligence Summaries are contained in F. S. Regs., Part II. and the Staff Manual respectively. Title pages will be prepared in manuscript.

Place	Date	Hour	Summary of Events and Information	Remarks and references to Appendices
SOHEIT TINLOT, LIEGE, BELGIUM	1919 1st Feb.		Railhead ENGIS. Locations — HQ. Staff, Sig. Coy, Sig. Park, A.H.J. Cy. SOHEIT TINLOT, ENGIS, TERWAGNE, MODAVE	Md
-"-	2nd "		Nothing to report.	Md
-"-	3rd "		-"-	Md
-"-	4th "		-"-	Md
-"-	5th "		-"-	Md
-"-	6th "		-"-	Md
-"-	7th "		-"-	Md
-"-	8th "		Ordered Court of Inquiry to be held tomorrow 9th at H.Q. to enquire into death of No. 1336.34 Pte Brown, M. M.T.Co.	Md
-"-	9th "		Nothing to report.	Md
-"-	10th "		-"-	Md
-"-	11th "		-"-	Md
-"-	12th "		-"-	Md

Army Form C. 2118.

WAR DIARY
or
INTELLIGENCE SUMMARY.

(Erase heading not required.)

419 Squadron Sqd.
February 1917

Instructions regarding War Diaries and Intelligence Summaries are contained in F. S. Regs., Part II. and the Staff Manual respectively. Title pages will be prepared in manuscript.

Place	Date	Hour	Summary of Events and Information	Remarks and references to Appendices
Shera Ombi	Feb. 1919	13th	Made application for services of photo and staff at Eng. Boulham	nil
		14th	Nothing to report	nil
		15th	—	nil
		16th	—	nil
		17th	—	nil
		18th	—	nil
		19th	Captain J.H.D. Faithfull joined from 11 Sqd. taken on duty as Adjutant vice Capt. R. Lyle RFC demobilised	nil
		20th	Nothing to report	nil
		21st	—	nil
		22nd	—	nil
		23rd	—	nil
		24th	—	nil
		25th	—	nil
		26th	—	nil

Army Form C. 2118.

WAR DIARY
or
INTELLIGENCE SUMMARY.

(Erase heading not required.)

H.Q. Hav. Div. Sob. February 1919

Place	Date	Hour	Summary of Events and Information	Remarks and references to Appendices
Sihr Caire	1919 Feb. 27"		Nothing to report.	Md
	28"		—	Md
			During the month a gradual process of demobilisation was carried on, otherwise there was not much of interest	MM

A.W. Murray
Colonel
Comdg. HQ 3rd Cav. Div. Sob.

WAR DIARY
or
INTELLIGENCE SUMMARY.

Army Form C. 2118.

HQrs 3rd Cav. Div. Raff.

March 1919

(Erase heading not required.)

Afrique MARCHE + LIÉGE

Place	Date	Hour	Summary of Events and Information	Remarks and references to Appendices
TINLOT	1919 Mar.	1st	Nothing to report.	
"		2nd	Forwarded to "B" proceedings of a Court of Inquiry held to investigate loss by theft of a Maclaine stove with cover & table, on charge of 7th Cav Field Ambulance. Court considered no one to blame and recommends cost to come on public.	
"		3rd	Nothing to report.	
"		4th	" " "	
"		5th	Got dispersal today - 4 M.T. 2 H.T. 3 Supply.	
"		6th	Nothing to report.	
"		7th	" " "	
"		8th	En dispersal today. 3 M.T. 4 H.T. 3 Supply. Snow shows arranged to be withdrawn from events to form a Lutsche Flags at EYNATTEN (S/of Aix la CHAPELLE) for troops passing through area 'B'.	
"		9th	Nothing to report.	
"		10th	Forwarded to "B" proceedings of a Court of Inquiry held to investigate the loss by theft of Triumph motor cycle Frame No. 282908. Court found that no one could be held to blame and that cost should be borne by the public.	

Army Form C. 2118.

WAR DIARY
or
INTELLIGENCE SUMMARY.
(Erase heading not required.)

HQtrs. 3rd Cavalry Bde. Staff

Adj: Major MARCHE y LIEGE

March 1919

Instructions regarding War Diaries and Intelligence Summaries are contained in F. S. Regs., Part II. and the Staff Manual respectively. Title pages will be prepared in manuscript.

Place	Date	Hour	Summary of Events and Information	Remarks and references to Appendices
	1919			
TINLOT	March 11th		Nothing to report	
"	"	12th	— " —	
"	"	13th	— " —	
"	"	14th	— " —	
"	"	15th	Demobilisation today – 2 Nos.T., 12 N.T.s, 5 Supply.	
"	"	16th	Nothing to report	
"	"	17th	— " —	
"	"	18th	— " —	
"	"	19th	Capt. J.M.D. FAITHFULL, S.A.E. Joined for duty as Adjutant (on probation) vice Lieut. Capt. R.C. LYLE, M.C. (demobilised).	
"	"	20th	Nothing to report	
"	"	21st	— " —	
"	"	22nd	— " —	
"	"	23rd	All Reserve Parks of Cav. Corps come under administration of 3rd Cavalry Bde. HQrs. Whilst are concentrating in the neighbourhood of REMAGNE & EUKASNY preparatory to entraining for Army H.T. Vehicle Reserve Parks.	

Army Form C. 2118.

WAR DIARY
or
INTELLIGENCE SUMMARY.
(Erase heading not required.)

H.Q. 3rd Cavalry Div. M.T.

March 1919.

Place	Date	Hour	Summary of Events and Information	Remarks and references to Appendices
	1919			
TINLOT	March 24th		Acting Major P.L. Shafford, 3rd Cav. M.T. Coy. to command of M.T. Company. Unit handed over to Temp. Capt. H.C. Beveley. Lieut. J.J. Bride joined 3 Cav. Div. vice 2 Lieut. J.A. Beck (demobilised)	
"	25		Nothing to report.	
"	26th		Recommended 2 Lieut. H.B. Davis (M.R) for appointment to Acting Captain with pay, as he will be in command of M.T. Coy in case of T. Capt. B.C. Beveley which has been ordered.	
"	27th		H.Q. had ordered to replace to cadre. They will move on 1st from 4 neighbour hood of retaining party for this purpose. All remaining units of Division, less do.T. R.H.T. Corps ordered to cadre.	
"	28th		T. Capt. B.C. Beveley to England. 2 Lieut. H.B. Davis takes over command of the M.T. Coy.	
"	29th		Nothing to report.	

WAR DIARY
or
INTELLIGENCE SUMMARY.
(Erase heading not required.)

Army Form C. 2118.

HQrs. 3rd Cavalry Div. Reile

March, 1919

Place	Date	Hour	Summary of Events and Information	Remarks and references to Appendices
	1919			
TINLOT	March 30th		Received authority of D.A.G. Base to include following releasable Clerks in Cadres:— S/2790+ W/Sgt. C.C. Ferrier. S/107025 Sgt. G. Read. SS/622 Corpl. H.W. Palmer. S/31456 1/Sergt. R. Gaurport. SS/25 2/Sergt. J. Steele. Authority A.926 of 30.3.16.	
" "	" 31st		Lieut-Colonel A.E. Numming departed for England to report E. War Office. Command taken over by Major F.T. Carrier. Capt. J.E. Keeler, on leave to UK, written report on return to OC 1st Cavalry Divisional Rail to duty.	

F.T. Carrier Major.
Commdg. HQ. 3rd Cavalry Div. Reile

April, 1919. War Diary

H.Qrs., 3rd Cav. Div. Rade.

WAR DIARY
or
INTELLIGENCE SUMMARY.

Army Form C. 2118.

(Erase heading not required.)

HQrs. 1st Can. Div. Sub. WC 53
April 1919

Hurl Marche Liège

Place	Date	Hour	Summary of Events and Information	Remarks and references to Appendices
TINLOT	1st April		HQrs. 1st Canadian Div. Sub. Bde. moved to AUX HOUX to be relieved to leave strength and two guns T.J. BRIDE to 1st Can Div.	
AUX HOUX	2nd		Nothing to report.	
"	3rd		A.H.Q. disposal of all animals, wagons and equipment with a view to statement of future personnel will be disposed of under orders of D.O.S.T.	
"	4th		Do. Do. Area.	
"	5th		" — "	
"	6th		" — "	
"	7th		Nothing to report.	
"	8th		1st Canadian Reserve Park entrained at FLEMALLE HAUTE to join Army H. Vehicle Reception at RAISMES where the unit will be disbanded.	
"	9th		HQrs. 1st Can. D. Sub. Bde. to WARFUSÉE and A.H.Q. and details of H.Q. to FLEMALLE HAUTE (W. of LIEGE)	

WAR DIARY
or
INTELLIGENCE SUMMARY.
(Erase heading not required.)

Army Form C. 2118.

HQ 2nd Cav. Div. MT. Lottie.

April 1919.

Place	Date	Hour	Summary of Events and Information	Remarks and references to Appendices
MAUX WARFUSÉE	1919 10 April		Lieut. (a/Capt.) H. Williams R.A.F. (I.O.) joined and assumed command of the Cavalry M.T. Coy.	
			Cavalry Corps Troops Motor Reserve Park and the Heavy Section of 2nd Cavalry Reserve Park entrained at FLESSELLES for the Second Army HQ. White Neuston Park at ST. ANDRÉ LILLE	
			Offr. of M.T.S.P.T. Car Cpo. ceases to function from midnight and we pass to the control of A.D.S.T., No.4 Area.	
WARFUSÉE	11"		Nothing to report.	
-"-	12"		2nd Cavalry Reserve Park entrain 1st at FLESMAINE HAUTE today for Eighth Army M.T. Vehicle Reception Park at St André Lille	
-"-	13"		Two further section of lorries dispatched today to duty with 2nd Cav. Hrs Cpo. troops M.T. Detachment now numbers 48 lorries. Nothing to report.	

Army Form C. 2118.

WAR DIARY
or
INTELLIGENCE SUMMARY
(Erase heading not required.)

Instructions regarding War Diaries and Intelligence Summaries are contained in F. S. Regs., Part II. and the Staff Manual respectively. Title pages will be prepared in manuscript.

M.Dis. Info. Sn. Rail
April 1919

Place	Date	Hour	Summary of Events and Information	Remarks and references to Appendices
WAREGEM	14 Apr.		The Bo Car abv Reuve Sale entrained at FLEMALLE HAUTE for third Army. Khaki Reception Parr at PONT REMY. All Combat Reserve have now left our censentials.	
			Received a letter from OC R.I. Cay. regarding a certain Frestenango amongst the men of his unit who Friday see themselves the late Tsar of Russia. Gave instruction to GOC of Carra See personally & Ht C. who is to examine them that these men however he agreed with any complicate game up as far a foreign.	
	15"		Sent 25 men of Rant. Late into Comerada Camp this chains NO have held at 2 extra strength plus two officers	
			One offices & 75 men became of A.H.T.F. that have arrived 20 compulsedly action reservists in them leaving 55 OR & the numbers & O.S.T. No & Come	
	16"		Nothing without	

Army Form C. 2118.

Instructions regarding War Diaries and Intelligence Summaries are contained in F. S. Regs., Part II. and the Staff Manual respectively. Title pages will be prepared in manuscript.

WAR DIARY
or
INTELLIGENCE SUMMARY.
(Erase heading not required.)

40. Soler Su. Rate   April 1917

Place	Date	Hour	Summary of Events and Information	Remarks and references to Appendices
MARFUSCE	1917 16 Apr 17		We have received 50 vacancies of demobilisation to this Co. for the following week. These will eventually complete the position by W.O. regarding demobilisation. A further 50 vacancies have been asked for. Arrangements are being made to eat these men demobilised by men of late categories.	
"	18	"	"	
"	19	"	"	
"	20	"	"	
"	21	"	"	
"	22	"	"	
"	23	"	"	
"	24	"	Nothing to report.	
"	25	"		

Army Form C. 2118.

H.Q. 3rd Cav. Bde. Rale

April 1919.

WAR DIARY
or
INTELLIGENCE SUMMARY.
(Erase heading not required.)

Place	Date	Hour	Summary of Events and Information	Remarks and references to Appendices
WARFUSÉE	April 26th	9.9	Arrangements made with A.S.C. M.T. Coy to deal direct with him re all motive connected with demobilisation &c. of the M.T. Company.	
"	27th		Nothing to report.	
"	28th		—	
"	29th		—	
"	30th		No. 1 Company 3rd Cav. Bde., moved to SPA.	

S. Mercer Major
Comdg. H.Q. 3rd Cav. Bde. Rale

Army Form C. 2118.

WAR DIARY
or
INTELLIGENCE SUMMARY.
(Erase heading not required.)

Instructions regarding War Diaries and Intelligence Summaries are contained in F. S. Regs., Part II. and the Staff Manual respectively. Title pages will be prepared in manuscript.

Place	Date	Hour	Summary of Events and Information	Remarks and references to Appendices
	1919			
		1		
		2		
		3		
		4		
		5		
		6		
		7		
		8		
		9		
		10		
		11		
		12		
		13		
		14		
		15		
		16		
		17		
		18		
		19		
		20		

Army Form C. 2118.

WAR DIARY
or
INTELLIGENCE SUMMARY.

(Erase heading not required.)

Instructions regarding War Diaries and Intelligence Summaries are contained in F. S. Regs., Part II. and the Staff Manual respectively. Title pages will be prepared in manuscript.

Place	Date	Hour	Summary of Events and Information	Remarks and references to Appendices

www.ingramcontent.com/pod-product-compliance
Lightning Source LLC
Chambersburg PA
CBHW081422300426
44108CB00016BA/2279